Sports Video: Recording, Analysis and Live Streaming

Your All-in-One Guide for Coaches, Analysts, Educators and AV Integrators in Sports

Paul W. Richards

ISBN: 9798345957318

Sports Video

DEDICATION

To the school broadcast clubs and the dedicated coaches, teachers and mentors who inspire young minds to see beyond the game. Thank you for mentoring the next generation, for believing in their potential and for proving that every story is worth sharing.

ONLINE COURSE ON UDEMY

Looking to take your sports video production skills to the next level? The *Sports Video* course on Udemy is the perfect resource. This course dives deep into advanced techniques and tools, with video tutorials that bring concepts to life in ways that text alone can't fully demonstrate.

While Udemy offers the added benefit of a certificate upon completion, you can also access the same video tutorials for free on YouTube. Start learning today at Udemy.com/Sports-Video.

CONTENTS

Acknowledgments   i

SECTION 1: For Coaches, Athletic Directors, Volunteers and Sports Video Pros.

1   Introduction   1

2   The Power of Sports Video: Why It Matters   Pg 7

3   Recording Sports Video   Pg 14

4   Improving Your Team with Sports Analytics   Pg 34

5   Capturing the Bigger Picture: Tactical Camera Use in Sports   Pg 47

6   Elevating Player Profiles: Creating Content That Attracts Scouts   Pg 61

SECTION 2: For Coaches, Athletic Directors and Sports Video Pros.

7   Sports Video Essentials - Level 1   Pg 78

8   Portable Video Systems   Pg 90

9   Sports Video Essentials - Level 2 - Sports Analytics Systems   Pg 108

10   Fundamentals of Live Streaming   Pg 116

SECTION 3: Sports Video Pros, Advanced Students and Media Teams.

11   Sports Video Essentials - Level 3 - Multi-Camera Productions   Pg 125

12	Setting Up Cameras for Different Types of Sports	Pg 127
13	Camera Operation Best Practices for Sports	Pg 173
14	Building a Sports Production Team	Pg 182
15	Choosing the Right Equipment	Pg 189
16	Audio for Sports Productions	Pg 201
17	Working with Commentators	Pg 205
18	Graphics for Sports	Pg 211
19	Instant Replay	Pg 227
20	Sports Video Essentials - Level 4	Pg 237
21	Remote Sports Production	Pg 241
23	Handling Technical Challenges	Pg 252
24	Engaging Your Audience	Pg 257
25	Live Streaming Platforms and Distribution	Pg 261
26	Pre, Post and Watch-Along Live Streams	Pg 266
27	Case Studies and Examples	Pg 274
28	Future Trends in Sports Video	Pg 279

ACKNOWLEDGMENTS

This book wouldn't have been possible without the incredible support and inspiration from the sports and broadcasting communities. To the athletes, coaches and production teams who shared their stories and insights, especially those who invited our team to record video on site—thank you for your passion and dedication, which bring the magic of sports to life for fans everywhere.

Why Read This Book?

Sports Video is an exciting, fast-paced endeavor — but it comes with plenty of challenges. From buying the right gear to setting up bulletproof workflows, this book will guide you through the process step by step. Avoid the common mistakes and fast-track your way to professional-grade sports video without the frustration.

Book Organization

Section 1: Unlocking the Power of Sports Video

Who It's For: Coaches, Athletic Directors, Volunteers and Aspiring Sports Video Pros.
What It Covers: This section introduces the transformative potential of sports video for teams, athletes and fans. It lays the foundation for understanding how sports video can improve team performance, expand fan engagement and elevate overall game experiences.

Section 2: Building the Foundation for Sports Video Success

Who It's For: Coaches, Athletic Directors and Sports Video Enthusiasts
What It Covers: This section provides a comprehensive guide to essential sports video systems, including setup options for beginners and scalable solutions for more advanced teams.

Section 3: Mastering the Art and Science of Sports Production

Who It's For: Sports Video Professionals, Advanced Students and Media Teams
What It Covers: This section dives deep into technical skills, team roles, production workflows and advanced tools needed for professional-level sports video coverage.

There is, intentionally, some duplication of certain content within this book. This is because we believe that this book won't necessarily be read cover-to-cover but instead be used as more of a reference book. So, if certain content has a natural fit within more than one chapter, I may have chosen to reprise it.

Similarly, there are a huge number of recommendations here - far too many for any one person to implement at any given time. So, I hope that you'll also consider this "an idea book," from which you can draw inspiration and best practices. Take from it what you will now, refer back to the book as needed and implement more as you can.

1 INTRODUCTION

Everyday sports are being played all around the world. Each year it's becoming more popular for coaches, athletes and team managers to use video as a resource to improve their game. In this book, you'll learn how to make sports video accessible to coaches, fans and athletes. You will learn how to record video, live stream, deliver sideline instant replay and create highlight reels.

Sports video professionals young and old are working together to set up, test and prove that video can enhance the game in more ways than one. Live streaming has opened up a new world of accessibility and fan engagement, enabling viewers to experience games from anywhere, at any time. Recorded video is easier than ever to share online, allowing athletes better access and teams new communication routes that were once only available to professional teams. And Sideline Instant Replay systems provide coaches with video to review with players and referees to help teams improve in real-time.

For schools, local clubs and smaller leagues, modern sports video tools have improved team communication, analysis, scorekeeping and fan engagement. Sports video makes it easier to capture and share game footage for coaching, recruitment and community outreach. Parents who can't make it to the game or a fan from across the country can still catch every moment in real time. Statistics and graphics on live broadcasts are getting easier to use. Graphics allow fans to understand the game more thoroughly and connect with athletes and coaches in deeper and more meaningful ways. This accessibility has changed sports for the better, leveling the playing field between large organizations and smaller sports teams who now have the power of digital scorekeeping, live streaming and sports analytics in the palm of their hands.

Many of these exciting advancements are made possible by production teams small and large, putting their heads together and using live video production tools to produce sports video. During the writing of this book, I spent many hours setting up and breaking down sports video systems sometimes in the same venues as the official NBC Sports broadcasters. While I often used a video system that costs less than a single camera used for professional sports, the same fundamentals of sports video apply.

Team Schedule   Team Roster   Score Keeping

GameChanger makes it easy to manage a team roster, schedule and scorekeeping.

One of the amazing things about technology is the great democratization and accessibility advancements allowing so many people to contribute with varying skill levels. Using online tools, a coach can now easily help build out the team roster and input the team schedule to connect not just the athletes and parents, but volunteers and assistant coaches too. Parents can help in new meaningful ways to keep score and RSVP for upcoming games. Similarly, video production teams have unique roles, from video switching, to camera operation and audio production. In this book, you'll learn how everything fits together and how the people on your team can work together productively to increase team spirit and ultimately the overall success of your sports productions.

GameChanger has a live streaming feature which can be integrated into the scorekeeping allowing users to collaborate.

Whether it's a coach organizing logistics, parents contributing to the game-day experience or a video production team capturing the action, everyone has a role to play. When everything comes together, technology and collaboration can make amazing things happen. With so many new roles and opportunities to contribute, take advantage of your team's emerging video needs and aspirations by promoting volunteerism and video team membership.

GameChanger is a perfect example of an app that combines a team roster, schedule and scorekeeping. I have spent many games on the sidelines scorekeeping for my son's soccer games. The app allows you to easily attribute goals to specific individuals which in turn can enable powerful statistics and post-game reports. Similarly, when you combine real-time scorekeeping with live streamed video, GameChanger knows exactly when the keyplays have happened. This allows the app to automatically make highlight reels from the live streamed video.

Each person's role in a sports production team is valuable. Coaches can go the extra mile by providing team rosters and schedules to keep everyone on the same page about the team's future. Parents and volunteers contribute by keeping score, helping with logistics or even assisting with equipment setup. Meanwhile, video production teams collaborate on tasks like camera operation, video switching and audio management. By integrating tools like GameChanger, real-time scorekeeping can be synced with live video, allowing for automatic highlight reels and detailed player statistics. When everyone works together, technology empowers the team to capture the excitement of the game and share it in innovative ways.

Roles in a Sports Video

Coach/Organizer   Technical Director   Camera Operator   Scorekeeper

Content Creator   Commentator   Video Editor   Marketing

While you may be able to do many of these tasks yourself, here's a list of roles and responsibilities in sports video.

Pre-Production Roles

- **Coach/Organizer**
  - Provides team rosters and game schedules.
  - Coordinates logistics such as player arrival times and venue setup.
  - Works with the production team to highlight key plays or moments to capture.

Pro Tip: As a coach, you can use apps like GameChanger or Team Snap to organize your team roster and game schedules. Ask athletes and parents to join and upload player pictures before the first practice/game. This makes it much easier for your team to match names to faces and helps build a sense of community and familiarity within the team from the start. Plus, having all the information in one place streamlines communication and ensures everyone stays on the same page.

- **Parents/Volunteers**
  - Help set up equipment (tripods, cameras, etc.).
  - Manage pre-game activities and support logistics (snacks, uniforms, etc.).
  - Act as liaisons between the production team and the sports team.
  - Use apps like GameChanger or Team Snap to RSVP athlete attendance.
  - Ideal Volunteer Opportunities: Scorekeeper, Camera Operator, Commentator, Data Analyst, Video Editor.
- **Technical Director**
  - **Collaborates with the Video Director**: Works together to plan camera angles, placements and overall production workflow.
  - **Ensures Equipment Readiness**: Oversees the operation of all equipment, including cameras, audio systems, physical scoreboards or data feeds integrated into software.
  - **Handles Connections**: Sets up and manages electrical, Ethernet and WiFi connections for live streaming and recording.
  - **Manages Key Roles**: Takes on both pre-production and production responsibilities, often acting as a switcher or instant replay operator while executing directions from a

dedicated director.

Production Roles

- **Camera Operator**
  - Captures live game footage with a focus on players, action and audience.
  - Adjusts cameras to follow the action dynamically.
- **Scorekeeper**
  - Uses applications like GameChanger to record goals, points and statistics.
  - Syncs real-time scorekeeping with live video feeds.
- **Director**
  - Oversees the video production process, including camera switching and overlays.
  - Ensures the production aligns with the narrative (e.g., highlight key players or moments).
  - Communicates with camera operators and technical staff.
- **Commentator**
  - Provides live commentary, giving context and excitement to the video.
  - Engages viewers by sharing player stats and backstories.
  - Talks with field reporters who themselves may be interviewing players or coaches during time-outs and other breaks in the action
  - Operates Telestrator to hand draw over video to explain plays.

Post-Production Roles

- **Editor**
  - Creates highlight reels using applications like GameChanger, Premier or Final Cut Pro.
  - Synchronizes live-streamed footage with key plays and statistics.
  - Adds graphics, music and transitions to enhance the video.
- **Data Analyst**
  - Analyzes the recorded footage and synced statistics for performance insights.
  - Generates reports for coaches and players to review.
- **Marketing/Media Coordinator**
  - Publishes highlights and game footage on social media or team websites.

○   Promotes the team and players for scouts or recruitment.

In this book, you'll discover how to harness the power of technology and teamwork to create high-quality productions that not only showcase the game but also bring the community closer together. Congratulations for taking it upon yourself to enhance your sports streaming skills. In this next chapter, we'll explore the motivations behind live streaming sports, the benefits it brings to different audiences and why now is the perfect time to dive into the world of sports streaming.

2 THE POWER OF SPORTS VIDEO: WHY IT MATTERS

The rise of sports video isn't just a trend—it's a new standard for sports coverage. Over the past decade, we've seen major sports leagues embrace streaming platforms via new apps and campaigns on social media. From entire organizations to individual players, sports is being experienced on a new frontier. Smaller organizations, such as high schools and community leagues, are able to record and live stream games with the dual benefit of connecting fans and providing coaches with valuable replay footage to review after the game.

Reviewing the high school sports video system at Salesianum School.

We are seeing the rise of DIY sport commentary shows made by super fans who are using free software such as Open Broadcaster Software (OBS) to create video and live streams that engage live audiences. Coaches, assistants and volunteers are using sports video management solutions and video editing software to make video accessible to players, parents, fans and even scouts. Streaming services and dedicated sports platforms are emerging, allowing sports enthusiasts to follow niche sports and local teams they wouldn't have been able to watch otherwise. As a result, players and fans are more excited and engaged than ever before.

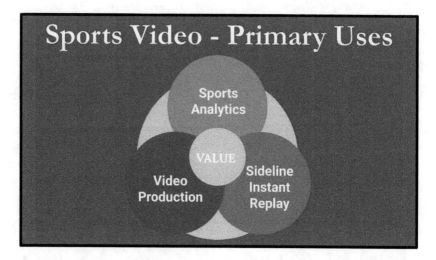

Sports video gives you the power to fine-tune your team's strategy in the heat of the moment and confidently confirm critical calls. After the game you can connect with your community using highlight reels that bring every exciting play to fans of your team. This isn't a dream—it's the new reality of modern coaching. With the rise of tools that blend sports analytics, sideline instant replay and innovative video production, you have more resources than ever before to sharpen your coaching vision and elevate the athlete's experience.

As a coach, you've no doubt seen the transformative power of data firsthand. Now, thanks to accessible video tools and cutting-edge analytics software, you can break down game video at a level of detail that was once reserved only for the pros. Every play, positioning error or successful tactic can be captured and analyzed, enabling you to develop strategies with greater precision. Instead of waiting until after the game to digest what happened, you can share clips and insights with your team in real time— whether it's at halftime, a quick sideline huddle or even between sets or innings. You can even enlist comments from others who are watching a live stream of the game - from anywhere in the world. Your athletes can then make immediate adjustments, improving their performance before the final whistle.

And it's not just about what happens on the field. It's also about strengthening the bond with your players, parents and fans off the field. Using intuitive editing tools and broadcasting software, you can produce engaging highlight reels, player spotlights and behind-the-scenes footage that celebrates your team's journey. These videos aren't just about flaunting success; they're about inspiring your players, boosting their confidence and showing that their hard work is recognized and appreciated. In doing so, you'll foster a culture of growth, excitement and community pride that motivates everyone to give their best.

SAR High School Broadcast Club works on editing sports video footage.

After a year of broadcasting SAR High School's sports teams, Josh Lewis, the school's IT Director, noticed the growing impact of recorded games. Coaches began reaching out, asking where they could access the footage and it became clear that on-demand replays were just as valuable as live broadcasts.

"Even if only 5 or 10 people watch live, our videos usually get a couple hundred views on YouTube the next day," Lewis explained. "Coaches and student-athletes use the footage to break down games, spot areas for improvement and even analyze opposing players for a competitive edge."

I understand that this may seem like a lot of additional work and in some cases, it is. However, advancements in AI tools are making the process increasingly manageable. Today, AI-powered cameras can automatically record and live stream game footage with minimal setup. Automated highlight reel clipping tools significantly reduce the time spent on post-game editing. Additionally, near real-time sports analytics and game breakdown services are now available, enabling coaches to concentrate on their athletes rather than the technology. These innovations streamline the sports video, making all of these advantages easier to access than ever before.

Ultimately, the integration of sports analytics, instant replay and video production empowers you to coach smarter, faster and more creatively. You'll be guiding your players with insights rooted in solid evidence rather than athlete memories and verbal cues. You'll be leading them through a season with a level of clarity and engagement that they can experience on and off the field. It's time to embrace these tools and open the door to more dynamic practices, sharper in-game adjustments and a truly enriched sports experience for all involved.

Sports video's surge in popularity is driven by several factors:

- **Accessibility**: Sports video is available on any device—whether it's a phone, tablet or computer.
- **Excitement**: The popularity of highlight reels, reducing hours of footage into bite-sized moments of action-packed excitement, capturing the most thrilling plays and key turning points that keep fans engaged and coming back for more.
- **Interactivity**: Sports team management platforms allow for player and coach interaction through real-time feedback, statistics and engagement features, making the experience more immersive.
- **Team Work**: New apps and technology are making it easier for coaches, assistants, parents and even players to work together to build out interactive experiences for entire leagues; complete with statistics, videos, live streams and more.
- **Detailed Analysis**: With sports analysis software, coaches are able to connect with their players using impactful visuals on wireless tablets on the sidelines and in the locker room. Additionally, post-game analysis that was once only available for the pros, is now easier to use and more accessible than ever before.

By the end of this book, you'll understand how to enjoy these trends and the growth of sports video.

Who Should Use Sports Video?

The beauty of sports video is that it's not limited to professional leagues. It can benefit a wide range of sports organizations, offering opportunities for engagement, visibility and even revenue generation:

- **Local and Amateur Leagues**: Smaller teams and leagues can attract attention and build a fan base without the need for traditional TV deals. Adding on-screen sponsorships to live streams can help generate revenue and support these organizations.

- **Schools and Universities**: Parents, students and alumni can tune in to support their school's sports teams. Schools can also showcase student talent and generate income through sponsor logos or advertisements integrated into the broadcast. It's quite common to use large LED screens to feature instant replays, sponsorship loops and engaging content for fans.
- **Clubs and Associations**: From community soccer leagues to martial arts tournaments, live streaming elevates the visibility of smaller events. On-screen sponsorships and branded content loops can turn these streams into valuable promotional tools.
- **School Broadcast Clubs**: Schools with broadcast clubs can leverage student enthusiasm for video production to record and stream sports events. This not only provides students with hands-on experience but also offers opportunities to attract sponsors for the streams.
- **Esports**: Competitive gaming has become a major segment of sports streaming, with tournaments and leagues attracting millions of viewers. These broadcasts provide an ideal platform for sponsorships and branded content, contributing to the growing revenue potential in esports.

2019 Major League Pickleball New York City live stream on YouTube.

Even sports that have niche audiences can build a dedicated following through live streaming. Whether it's pickleball, fencing or ultimate frisbee, there's an audience ready to watch, engage and support these events.

| Youth Sports | High School Sports | Professional Sports |

My Research Process

Throughout the development of this book, I conducted hands-on research by recording, live streaming and analyzing sports at youth, high school and professional levels. This process covered both indoor and outdoor environments, spanning individual sports like tennis and team sports such as soccer and lacrosse. I worked extensively with a variety of recording and live streaming systems, coaching and sideline instant replay tools and sports analysis software from multiple vendors. These real-world experiences allowed me to gain practical insights and share valuable knowledge to help others enhance their sports video production capabilities.

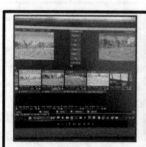  

| Recording and Live Streaming Systems | Coaching / Sideline Instant Replay Tools | Sports Analysis Software |

A Look Ahead

In the following chapters, we'll dive deeper into the nuts and bolts of sports video. From choosing the right equipment and setting up cameras to mastering production techniques and distributing your stream, this book will provide you with everything you need to know. By the time you finish, you'll be ready to define what your team needs out of sports analytics, the setup required to capture high-quality video and how to effectively leverage your footage and data to enhance team performance and engage your audience. Whether you are a coach, producer or sports enthusiast, this book will equip you with the knowledge and skills to elevate your sports video production and streaming capabilities to the next level.

3 RECORDING SPORTS VIDEO

Capturing sports on video is essential not only for coaches and athletes, but also for athletics directors, volunteers and dedicated media professionals. By recording practices, games and competitions, you create a resource that allows a chain of new value to be created. Video allows coaches to pinpoint areas for improvement, gives players visual feedback on their performance and provides fans with enriched content and deeper engagement. Once recorded, sports video can be shared and viewed online through modern, cloud-based platforms, providing athletes, coaches, scouts and fans with convenient, on-demand access to the sports they love and player performances they may need to see.

Why Recording Matters
At its core, sports video recording serves several critical functions. For coaches and athletes, having access to recorded material means no longer relying solely on memory or subjective impressions. Instead, footage can be reviewed methodically, frame by frame, to analyze tactics, player positioning and technical execution. This visual feedback loop leads to more targeted training, strategic adjustments and ultimately, improved performance on the field.

Common Challenges in Recording Sports
Sports differ from many other types of video production because the subjects are constantly in motion and the action can shift unpredictably. This is why Chapter 11, is dedicated to setting up cameras for different types of sports. A single key play may unfold in seconds, requiring the camera operator to anticipate movement and quickly adjust framing.

Basketball sports video system at the SAR High School.

Increasingly, coaches are relying on AI-enabled cameras that can follow the play from a single angle and record the game automatically. These cameras, such as Pixellot, Veo and Hudl Focus, use advanced computer vision (and stationary multi-lens, non-motorized cameras) to track the ball and players without a dedicated camera operator. Not only do they free up staff time and resources, but they also integrate with analytics platforms to help coaches break down game footage for strategic insights. As a result, even smaller teams and amateur clubs can access professional-level video production and performance analysis.

While AI-cameras are convenient they often only offer one camera angle. Balancing wide coverage with close-up detail for sports analysis is often a priority as coaches grow their sports video programs. A long shot from a high vantage point might capture the entire field of play, allowing viewers to see strategies develop. But and this is an important 'but"it may not clearly show individual player actions or subtle details. As of this writing, none of the cameras in this category are capturing 4K 60 fps video and don't have optical zoom lenses, vs. PTZ cameras that provide both; offering much clearer, higher-resolution video with significantly greater close-up capabilities. Conversely, zooming in too much risks missing the broader context of how players move and interact. A key skill in sports videography is learning to dynamically shift between these perspectives, ensuring you never lose track of the essential story playing out on the field, court or rink.While AI-enabled cameras offer remarkable convenience and help streamline the recording process, there's still tremendous value in having real camera operators on hand. With a dedicated operator—whether a member of a school's broadcast club, a student-athlete currently sidelined by injury or a group of trained volunteers—it's nice to have someone dynamically adjust framing, zoom levels and focus to capture the exact angles that yield the most useful insights.

For example, in American Football, you might see video zoomed into the kicker or the player holding the ball. In Lacrosse, there are key plays like faceoffs which have critical details that need to be zoomed -n on. By involving people who understand both the sport and the storytelling aspect of videography, you create more engaging, context-rich footage. As your sports video program evolves, consider recruiting dedicated team members who can master the nuances of PTZ (Pan-Tilt-Zoom) camera control, coordinate with coaches and respond in real time to the ebb and flow of the game. Over time, this human touch not only enhances your production values but also ensures that you're always getting the angles and details needed to support meaningful sports analysis.

Understanding the Basics of Composition and Framing

Recording sports is about more than just pointing a camera at the action—it's about capturing the essence of the game in a way that is visually clear, engaging and informative. Good composition and framing give the audience a front-row seat to the athletes' effort and skill, while also revealing the strategies unfolding on the field or court. Mastering these basics ensures that your footage is both watchable and useful, whether for post-game analysis, highlights or live broadcasts.

Choosing Angles and Perspectives

One of the first decisions in sports videography is selecting where and how to position your camera. Different sports and playing surfaces present unique challenges and opportunities. An elevated angle from the stands can offer a broad, tactical view—useful for coaches wanting to analyze team shape or player positioning. In contrast, a lower, field-level vantage point might highlight the intensity of one-on-one battles or showcase the skillful footwork of a forward breaking past a defender.

Get the PTZ Camera Operators Handbook

Certain sports have long traditions of "ideal" camera locations that will be explored in the upcoming chapters of this book. For instance, a central, elevated position near the half-line in soccer or basketball often provides the best overall perspective on the match. In basketball, a position at midcourt but slightly elevated captures full-court transitions while still allowing viewers to see details like foot placement during a three-point attempt. A camera like this is often 20-30' above the court and can be captured from a tall vantage point or with a PTZ camera on a 20' tripod. By understanding these conventions and experimenting with different viewpoints, you can find the sweet spot that best suits your team's needs and your audience's expectations.

Elevated PTZ cameras on balcony area for tennis match.

Following the Action

Sports move fast. Players sprint, balls fly through the air and the play can shift direction on a dime. Chapter 14 is dedicated to sports video camera operations, to give detailed instructions to your team. The camera operator's goal is to keep the subject of interest—usually the ball or the leading players—in frame and in focus. Anticipating the flow of the game becomes second nature with experience: operators learn to track the ball's trajectory, predict where a player might run next and be ready to pan the camera smoothly as the action shifts from one end of the field to the other.

Depending on your team's goals, you'll want to discuss the nuances of what your team values with sports video. Over time, your team will develop an intuitive feel for when to start your movements so that the action flows naturally through your frame.

If your team is using PTZ cameras, I highly recommend having them read the PTZ Camera Operators Handbook.

Basic Camera Settings

While composition involves "where" and "what" you point at, camera settings influence "how" the scene looks. The right frame rate can mean the difference between crisp, fluid action and choppy, hard-to-follow video. Many videographers choose higher frame rates (like 60 frames per second) for sports because it better captures fast motion.

Sports look clearer with high resolutions and frame rates. This is especially true if you plan to use slow motion in your videos.

Consider exposure settings carefully: a fast shutter speed can reduce motion blur, making it easier to see a baseball's spin or a basketball player's footwork. However, if you're filming at dusk or under poor lighting conditions, you may need to adjust ISO, gain or aperture (aka "iris") to ensure a bright, clear image. Be careful though, the more you open the aperture (the numbers get smaller), the shallower your depth-of-field will be. That's the area in focus in front of and behind your selected focus point. So, while a shallow depth of field is great for blurring backgrounds in portraits, it leaves no room for error in focus point selection. Conversely, a wider depth of field will tend to keep more in focus. White balance is another key factor—lighting can vary dramatically between indoor arenas and sunny outdoor fields and proper color calibration ensures that uniforms, equipment and the playing surface all look as intended. Matching camera *settings* across all cameras (in order to match cameras) is equally important in order to avoid distraction and provide a professional-looking product. This works best if all the cameras are the same make and model. You often get pretty close to matching different cameras by spending some time "tweaking" the settings.

Taken together, thoughtful composition and well-chosen settings bring your footage to life. By starting with a strategic vantage point, following the flow of the game and fine-tuning your camera's parameters, you ensure that the result is both beautiful and functional. Viewers, coaches and players alike will benefit from footage that's easy to follow, accurately exposed and color matched and framed to reveal exactly what's happening in every crucial moment.

Pre-Game Preparation and Planning

Great sports video production doesn't happen by chance. Before the whistle blows, the lights come on or the athletes take the field, careful planning sets the stage for successful recording. From scouting the venue to ensuring everyone on your team understands their role, preparation is the key to capturing crisp, meaningful footage without scrambling at the last minute.

Scouting the Venue

Before any camera is set up or tripod extended, take a walk around the field, court or gymnasium. Assess the layout, take pictures and identify potential vantage points. Is there a press box or elevated platform you can use to get a wide-angle view of the field? If you're recording outdoors, note the position of the sun (at the time-of-day you'll be shooting)—filming directly into harsh sunlight can wash out details, so you may want to set up on the opposite side. Indoors, look for the best lighting conditions and avoid obstructed views caused by pillars, bleachers or support beams. Is there a power outlet nearby? Where are the ideal cable pathways?

Also consider the practicality of your position. Ensure that there's enough space for your equipment, that you won't be blocking spectators' views and that you can easily pivot to follow the action. In some cases, establishing a primary camera location near midfield and a secondary angle at one end zone or baseline can give you flexibility. By thinking ahead and scouting thoroughly, you'll save yourself from scrambling to adjust once the game has already begun.

Communication and Coordination

Even if you're working solo, chances are you'll need to coordinate with someone—be it a coach, event staff or a colleague helping with commentary or analytics. If you have a production team, outline each person's responsibilities before the event. The camera operator might focus exclusively on tracking the action, while another team member handles switching angles or updating score graphics. When available, I like to have one camera operator dedicated to the wide 2/3rds shot and another dedicated to a closer up 1/3rds shot who also gets closeups when available. Salesianum High School's broadcast program likes to have one dedicated PTZ camera operator "hunting" for the best close up moments during the game. They might not have the perfect shot all the time, but when they get the perfect shot of a kick off or a touchdown the video switcher can take advantage of that viewpoint.

Clear communication also extends to understanding the event's schedule. Know when warm-ups begin, when player introductions occur and when the game officially starts. This knowledge helps you capture important pre-game moments, such as coaches' pep talks or player warm-ups, which can be valuable in highlight reels and analysis sessions later.

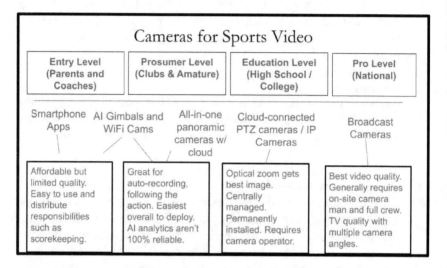

Choosing the Right Camera and Recording Tools

Selecting the right camera setup is a critical step in your sports videography journey. Your choice will depend on your goals, budget and the level of production quality you hope to achieve. Whether you're a parent filming your child's weekend game, a coach wanting to improve team strategy or a professional broadcaster delivering content to thousands of fans, there's a camera solution suited to your needs.

Entry Level (Parents & Coaches): Smartphones and Affordable Apps
For many people, the most accessible camera is the one already in their pocket. Modern smartphones offer surprisingly good video quality and, with the help of dedicated sports-recording apps, such as SportsCam (available for iOS and Android) you can provide on-screen score overlays on all your video. This low barrier to entry makes them ideal for parents and volunteer coaches who need a quick, convenient way to capture key moments.

The trade-offs at this level are limited zoom, potentially shakier footage and challenges in low-light conditions. Many parents who start to consistently film sports, decide to buy a dedicated camera such as a GoPro or Mevo so they can keep their smartphone and stop worrying about battery life during games. Still, with a simple tripod or a small smartphone gimbal, you can stabilize the shot enough to produce watchable video. For those just starting out, this is a practical and cost-effective way to begin recording and analyzing gameplay.

Prosumer Level (Clubs & Amateur): AI All-In-One Cameras and Gimbals

As you move beyond the basics, consider all-in-one cameras that leverage artificial intelligence to track the action automatically. These devices are designed with sports in mind: once positioned, they can follow the ball or key players without requiring constant manual adjustments. This is especially beneficial for clubs and amateur teams looking to elevate their production quality without hiring a dedicated camera operator. Many of these AI-driven cameras come integrated with AI analytics tools, easy cloud storage options and electronic pan-tilt-zoom (EPTZ) capabilities.

Education Level (High School / College): Panoramic Cameras and Cloud-Connected PTZ/IP Cameras

High schools, colleges and other institutions often seek solutions that combine convenience with higher-quality production values. All-in-one panoramic cameras can capture the entire playing field at once, enabling coaches and analysts to zoom in on any segment of the action after the fact. This top-down view of the game lends itself to strategic analysis—coaches can easily review player formations, spacing and tactical decisions from a single wide-angle recording.

Cloud-connected PTZ (Pan-Tilt-Zoom) like PTZOptics Move SE and Move 4K cameras offer even greater control. Managed remotely, these cameras can be adjusted in real-time for close-ups, follow individual players or seamlessly switch between different parts of the field. This flexibility comes closer to broadcast quality, but it also demands a bit more technical know-how. A small team or a dedicated staff member might be needed to operate and maintain these systems. Still, for those who want a truly professional feel and comprehensive tactical insight, this level of investment is a game-changer.

Pro Level (National): Broadcast Cameras

At the highest level of sports production—think major college athletics or national broadcast networks—professional broadcast cameras set the standard for quality and versatility. These cameras feature top-tier lenses, large sensors for low-light performance and customizable settings to achieve perfect exposure, color balance and focus under any conditions.

Using broadcast cameras typically involves a full crew: camera operators who know how to anticipate and frame the action, directors calling the shots from a production truck and technicians ensuring the image is pristine. The cost and complexity are significantly higher, but so is the production value. This level of equipment transforms a simple recording into a polished, television-quality broadcast that can be distributed to large audiences, either via traditional TV networks or professional streaming platforms.

By understanding your production goals and constraints, you can choose the camera solution that fits best. Entry-level options enable individuals to start recording right away with minimal setup, while prosumer and education-level systems offer more sophisticated features without breaking the bank. At the pro level, you're stepping into a world that rivals the best broadcasts on air, complete with dedicated crews and cutting-edge gear. Whether you're filming for player development, coaching strategy, fan engagement or major league television, the right camera choice empowers you to tell the story of the game with clarity, insight and excitement.

Matching Your Goals and Budget with the Right Tools

Once you understand the broad spectrum of camera and recording options—ranging from smartphone setups to professional broadcast rigs—it's time to decide which level best suits your specific situation. This decision often hinges on two key factors: what you want to achieve and how much you're willing or able to invest.

UTILIZING RECORDING TOOLS

Record Video	→ Create Highlight Reels
Use for Coaching	→ Email out to Team
Create Stats/Analysis	→ Set Goals for Player
After Game Stats Review	→ Compare Games

Determining Your Purpose

Begin by clarifying your main reason for recording. Are you a coach looking to give players more concrete feedback, reviewing footage to highlight mistakes and successes? Or is your priority building engagement with fans, streaming matches live to viewers who can't attend in person? Perhaps you're creating highlight reels for recruitment purposes or aiming to produce content that can be monetized through sponsorships or ticketed streams.

Your goals will guide you toward the appropriate technology. For basic player review and tactical breakdowns, an entry-level or prosumer solution might meet all your needs. However, if you're looking to produce polished, near-broadcast-quality content, you'll need to consider more advanced options.

Budget Considerations

Budget plays a significant role in shaping your choices. For many amateur clubs, youth teams or volunteer-run organizations, starting simple might be best. Investing in a few key accessories for a smartphone or a consumer camcorder can stretch your dollar and still produce watchable footage. These lower-cost solutions can be surprisingly effective, helping you gain experience, refine your technique and learn what features matter most before investing more heavily.

If you're working within a school system or club with access to modest funds, you might look into a mid-tier PTZ setup that offers better control, cloud integration and improved quality. For those at the top of the sports pyramid, where viewership and commercial stakes are high, professional broadcast equipment will likely be a necessity—justified by the potential revenue and credibility it brings.

Choosing the Right Recording Solution

Selecting the appropriate recording solution depends on several factors, including your team's budget, the level of production quality desired, available technical expertise and the specific needs of your sports video program. Here's a quick comparison to help guide your decision:

- **AI All-In-One (Panoramic) Cameras**
  - **Pros:** Easy to use, automated tracking, integrates with analytics.
  - **Cons:** Limited to one angle, hardware and subscription costs, dependent on AI accuracy.
- **Camcorders and GoPros**
  - **Pros:** Flexible angles, no ongoing costs, high portability.
  - **Cons:** Requires manual operation, potential for shaky footage, less automation. GoPros only provide wide-angle

coverage rather than close-ups (from a distance).
- **Recording Systems (Magewell Director Mini, YoloBox)**
  - **Pros:** Multi-camera support, professional production features, live streaming.
  - **Cons:** More cables, higher initial cost, space and power needs.
- **IP Cameras**
  - **Pros:** Ideal for permanent installations, scalable, remote control. They can live stream and record in the cloud. They can be remotely controlled in the cloud.
  - **Cons:** Requires network setup, dependence on network stability, higher cost for quality.
- **PTZ Cameras**
  - **Pros:** Dynamic and versatile coverage, high zoom capability, remote operation. They can live stream and record in the cloud. They can be remotely controlled in the cloud.
  - **Cons:** Can be expensive, requires trained operators, may or may not have on-board recording.

By understanding the various practical recording solutions available, you can tailor your sports video program to meet your specific needs and resources. Whether you opt for the simplicity of AI all-in-one cameras, the flexibility of camcorders and GoPros, the advanced capabilities of recording systems, the strategic placement of IP cameras or the dynamic coverage of PTZ cameras, each option offers unique benefits and challenges. Evaluate your team's goals, budget and technical capacity to choose the best combination of tools that will help you capture, analyze and share compelling sports footage.

Balancing Quality and Complexity
Another crucial aspect is the complexity you're ready to handle. A single parent or volunteer coach may not have time to operate multiple camera angles, manage advanced analytics software or troubleshoot complex network connections. Simplicity can be a virtue, ensuring you actually get the shots you need rather than getting bogged down in technical details.

On the other hand, if you're building a small production team—perhaps tech-savvy students, an assistant coach with an eye for detail or a dedicated media volunteer—you can afford more complexity. With extra hands, you can manage higher-end cameras, integrate performance analysis tools or experiment with live streaming for fans and family at home.

Choosing the right camera and gear setup is about finding the balance that lets you achieve your goals without overburdening your resources. Start where you are comfortable, both financially and technically and scale up as your needs grow. Over time, you may discover that adding a single PTZ camera or upgrading from a smartphone setup to an AI-driven camera system is all it takes to elevate the quality and usefulness of your footage. Ultimately, your best path forward is the one that helps you improve the way you capture, analyze and share the game—making the most of every minute of recorded action.

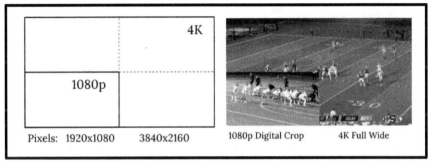

4K video has four times more pixels than 1080p video allowing for lossless digital cropping (to a 1080p image) ideal for highlight reels.

1080p vs. 4K: Pros and Cons for Recording Sports Video

At some point, you may need to make a decision about whether to record your sports video in 1080p (Full HD) or 4K (Ultra HD). 1080p video offers a more affordable and manageable option with smaller file sizes, making it easier to store, share and upload content. For this reason 1080p video is beneficial for live broadcasts and instant replays, where high frame rates like 60fps are crucial and budget constraints are a consideration. 720p and 1080p video workflows tend to be more accessible and popular in youth and K12 sports.

On the other hand, 4K video provides superior image quality with greater detail and clarity, enhancing the overall viewing experience. 4K cameras have larger sensors and offer better color accuracy and performance which make a clear difference when viewed on a 4K television or LCD monitor. However, the higher resolution comes with significantly larger file sizes and increased bandwidth for streaming. Also, the initial investment for 4K cameras and compatible recording and streaming equipment is considerably higher. Despite these challenges, 4K future-proofs your content and most 4K video equipment can be set up to be used in 1080p mode while you transition your video workflow over time. For sports, the 4K quality difference is real and it offers greater flexibility in post-production, allowing for detailed edits and "punch in" crops without compromising image quality. When recording or live streaming 1080p, YoloBox, Vmix and other live switching systems allow you to crop-in on a 4K image which effectively gives you a longer focal length lens that's double the length of the one you're using - with no loss of image quality.

1080p (Full HD) vs. 4K (Ultra HD)

1080p (Full HD)

Pros:

- Smaller File Sizes:
  - Easier to store and manage your footage. Faster uploading and sharing online.
- Cost-Effective Equipment:
  - More affordable cameras, recording devices and switching equipment.
  - Lower costs for implementing instant replay systems, especially at high frame rates like 60fps.
- Lower Bandwidth Requirements:
  - Streams smoothly with less demand on internet bandwidth.
- Post-Production Flexibility:
  - Faster editing and rendering times due to smaller file sizes.

Cons:

- Lower Image Resolution:
  - Less detail and clarity compared to 4K, which may be noticeable on larger screens.
- Less Future-Proof:
  - As higher resolutions become standard, 1080p may become outdated.
- Limited Detail for High-End Productions:
  - May not meet the quality demands of premium broadcasts or high-end promotional materials.

Adobe Premier, pictured above, is a video editing software. Using 4K video footage in a 1080p composition workspace allows for 200% digital cropping without pixelation.

4K (Ultra HD)

Pros:

- Superior Image Quality:
  - Four times the resolution of 1080p, offering crisper and more detailed visuals.
  - Enhanced camera sensors improve color accuracy and low-light performance. 4K cameras generally perform better with dynamic scenes and low-light situations.
- Future-Proofing:
  - Aligns with the growing trend towards higher resolution content, ensuring longevity.
- Greater Production & Post-Production Flexibility:
  - Allows significant zooming (up to 200%) without noticeable pixelation (in 1080p productions), enabling dynamic hero shots
- Higher Production Value:
  - Enhances the viewing experience with superior image quality, differentiating your content in a competitive market.

Cons:

- Larger File Sizes:
  - Requires significantly more storage space, increasing storage and management costs.

- Longer upload and download times, which can delay sharing and distribution.
- Higher Equipment Costs:
  - 4K cameras and compatible recording and switching equipment are more expensive.
  - Live streaming and instant replay setups in 4K demand advanced and pricier hardware.
- Increased Bandwidth Requirements:
  - Requires robust internet connections for smooth streaming and online distribution.
  - Potential accessibility issues for viewers with limited bandwidth, leading to buffering or reduced quality.
- Compatibility Challenges:
  - Some older devices and platforms may not support 4K natively.
  - May necessitate infrastructure upgrades to handle 4K content effectively.
- Complex Storage and Backup:
  - Managing and securing large 4K files can be more challenging and costly.
  - Requires extensive storage solutions for long-term archiving.
  - your target audience.

"As the demand for 4K video in sports analysis continues to grow, there's an increasing need to capture the full, wide-angle view of the game for team formation insights, while also zooming in on specific players or areas of the pitch. Thanks to its high resolution, 4K video makes it possible to do both."
– Ruben Saavedra, Metrica Co-Founder and CEO

Getting Started with Basic Techniques

Once you've chosen your gear and established a solid plan, the next step is to put your equipment to good use. Recording sports video effectively takes practice—just like playing the game itself. By focusing on a few fundamental techniques and skills, you'll set yourself up for success, ensuring that your footage is not only clear and stable but also genuinely helpful when it comes time to review, analyze or share.

Recording Practices and Matches for Improvement

Don't limit your filming to official games. Recording practices can offer valuable insights into a team's progress. Consistency is key—try to capture the same drill or exercise from the same angle each week. By reviewing these clips over time, coaches and players can spot improvements in technique, identify recurring mistakes and evaluate whether certain training methods are effective.

Matches themselves often provide the ultimate test. Recording full games ensures that you don't miss any important plays and having complete footage allows you to select the best moments for highlight reels or in-depth analysis. These recordings become a database of performance, a visual history of how a team evolves over the course of a season.

The Crucial Role of Video Editing in Team Improvement

While recording practices and matches provide a wealth of raw footage, the true value lies in how you edit and utilize that content. Effective video editing transforms lengthy recordings into concise, impactful clips that highlight key moments and areas for improvement. This process not only makes the footage more manageable but also enhances its utility for both coaches and players.

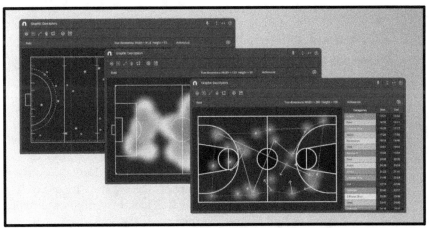

Nacsport heatmaps are generated from manually tagged data.

For this reason, many sports teams decide to use sports analytics software to "tag" games live, which eliminates the need for editing video. Sports analytics software such as Nacsport allows you to tag the game live or after the event. This allows you to create useful statistics and capture highlight clips at the same time.

Streamlining Long Video Files

Practices and games can result in extensive video files—imagine sifting through an hour-long practice session or a 1.5-hour game that includes numerous timeouts and halftime breaks. Editing these long recordings into shorter, more focused clips is essential for several reasons:

- **Enhanced Focus:** Shorter clips allow coaches and players to concentrate on specific drills, plays or moments that are connected such as all goals, blocks or rebounds.
- **Time Efficiency:** Reviewing concise clips saves time, enabling quicker feedback and more efficient use of practice or review sessions.
- **Targeted Analysis:** By isolating particular segments, you can perform a more detailed analysis of techniques, strategies and player performances.

Pro Tip: You can save a lot of time reviewing footage if you have timestamps or a scoreboard. Consider keeping track of time during practices and games if you are not yet using sports analytics tagging or using a graphics scoreboard.

Organize Edited Clips for Maximum Benefit

Once you've trimmed your videos into meaningful segments organizing them systematically is vital for easy access and comparative analysis throughout the season. Here are some strategies to consider:

1. **Categorize by Team Areas:**
   - **Offense:** Store clips that showcase offensive plays, strategies and player movements. This can include successful scoring attempts, passing drills and formations.
   - **Defense:** Organize defensive maneuvers, tackles, interceptions and positioning strategies.
   - **Special Teams:** If applicable, separate footage related to special teams play, such as kick-offs, punts and returns.
2. **Segment by Drill or Exercise:**
   - Create folders for specific drills or exercises performed during practices. This allows for tracking progress and identifying improvements or persistent issues in particular areas.
3. **Game Phases:**
   - **First Half / Second Half:** Breaking down game footage

by halves can help analyze performance trends and adjustments made as the game progresses.
- ○ **Specific Quarters or Time Periods:** For more granular analysis, especially in closely contested games.
4. **Player-Specific Folders:**
- ○ Sports management software allows teams to maintain player specific tagging of video. You can also create player-specific folders in a file sharing solution such as Google Drive or Dropbox.

Making Clips Accessible for Player Development

Ensuring that players have access to relevant video clips is crucial for their individual growth and for creating personalized highlight reels they can send to scouts. Here's how you can facilitate this:

1. **Centralized Storage Solutions:**
- ○ Utilize cloud-based platforms like Google Drive, Dropbox or specialized sports video analysis tools (e.g., Hudl, Krossover) to store and organize video clips. This ensures that players can access the footage anytime, anywhere.
2. **Structured Sharing:**
- ○ Share organized folders with players, ensuring that each player has access to their specific clips as well as team-wide footage for a comprehensive understanding of team dynamics.
3. **Highlight Reel Creation:**
- ○ Encourage players to create their own highlight reels by selecting clips that best showcase their skills and improvements. This not only boosts their confidence but also aids in personal scouting and recruitment opportunities.
4. **Interactive Review Sessions:**
- ○ Incorporate video review into team meetings and individual sessions. Use edited clips to illustrate points during coaching, allowing players to visualize and understand feedback effectively.
5. **Consistent Updates:**
- ○ Regularly update the video library with new clips from each practice and game. This ongoing process ensures that the video database remains current and continues to reflect the team's evolution throughout the season.

Best Practices for Effective Video Management

To maximize the benefits of your video editing and organization efforts, consider the following best practices:

- **Maintain Consistency:** Always capture and edit videos using the same angles and formats to ensure comparability over time.
- **Label Clearly:** Use clear and descriptive naming conventions for your video files and folders (e.g., "Offense_Drill_Passing_2024-04-15"). This will make searching for your videos much easier.
- **Incorporate Metadata:** Add tags or notes to clips with relevant information such as date, drill type, player involved and specific observations.
- **Encourage Player Engagement:** Motivate players to regularly review their clips and provide feedback on the video resources to continually enhance their effectiveness.

By prioritizing video editing and establishing a robust organizational system, you transform raw footage into a powerful tool for continuous improvement. This approach not only aids in tactical and technical development but also fosters a culture of accountability and self-improvement within the team.

Video Tutorial: In the included online course, there is a tutorial showing how to create player spotlights in your videos. You may have seen this type of video annotation on TV. With the free files and tutorial videos, you can do it too!

The Value of a Team Viewing Room in Sports Video Analysis

To fully leverage the power of video analysis, many teams establish a dedicated team viewing room where coaches and players can review footage together. This collaborative space fosters deeper insights by allowing everyone to engage with key moments and analyze performance in a focused environment. A team viewing room equipped with a large screen, annotation tools and playback controls creates an immersive experience that aids in breaking down plays, discussing strategies and addressing areas for improvement. By centralizing video reviews in one location, teams can make analytics-driven adjustments more effectively, ensuring that both coaches and players are aligned in their efforts to improve performance.

Estimating File Sizes in Sports Video Recording

When planning for sports video recording, it's essential to estimate the length of each game and the quality of the video to determine the necessary SD card or available hard-drive space. Factors such as the number of cameras, whether not you're ISO recording individual cameras, video resolution, frame rate and bitrate significantly influence the file sizes. By calculating the total recording time and understanding your video settings, you can choose SD cards (or hard drives or SSDs) that ensure you have enough storage with some extra space for unexpected needs.

Scenario	# of Cameras	Resolution	Frame Rate	Game Duration	Estimated File Size	SD Card
Basic Recording	1	1080p	30fps	70 minutes	5.25 GB	8 GB
Dual Camera Setup	2	1080p	30fps	70 minutes	10.5 GB	16 GB
4K Single Camera	1	4K	30fps	70 minutes	13.1 GB	16 GB or 32 GB
Dual 4K Cameras	2	4K	30fps	70 minutes	26.3 GB	32 GB or 64 GB
(4) 4K Cameras	4	1080p	60fps	70 minutes	52.5 GB	128 GB

These estimates are for each camera you want to record and a "switch" or "mixed" video recording with a scoreboard and other graphics is also important to record. By using this simplified guide and table, your sports video team can efficiently select the right SD card size or computer hard-drive space to ensure seamless recording of all your games. This approach helps in avoiding storage issues and ensures high-quality video capture tailored to your specific recording setup.

With these basics under your belt, you're ready to take the next step. Chapter 4 introduces the world of sports analytics, showing you how to transform raw footage into insightful data that can drive strategic decision-making. You'll learn how to integrate video with analytical tools, breaking down plays and player performance metrics to pinpoint strengths and weaknesses. As you refine your production techniques and incorporate analytics, your recordings will transcend simple documentation—they'll become powerful instruments that inform coaching strategies, enhance player development and deepen fan engagement.

Embrace this journey step by step. By continually honing your camera work, experimenting with new technologies and combining visuals with analytics, you'll emerge as a more confident and capable sports videographer. The skills you've developed in this chapter are just the beginning of a much larger toolkit—one that will serve you well, whether you're capturing the joys of a local youth tournament or producing top-tier content for an international audience.

4 IMPROVING YOUR TEAM WITH SPORTS ANALYTICS

Sports analytics doesn't have to be complicated or require expensive technology. Whether you're a coach, player or team analyst, you can begin enhancing your game strategies with tools as simple as pen and paper. As you become more comfortable, you can gradually incorporate more advanced methods to take your analysis to the next level.

Metrica sports provides insightful graphics and statistics via their software platform.

The Role of Video in Sports Analytics

Sports analytics, at its core, is about transforming raw data into actionable insights. This data is traditionally collected through metrics like player statistics, scoring patterns and game outcomes. However, when combined with video, the scope of analytics can expand exponentially.

Starting with Low-Tech Solutions

You don't need high-end systems to begin using sports analytics. Even these low-tech solutions can help you improve your video editing workflow by simply noting the time of keyplays and other analytics you are tracking. Here's how you can start with simple, low-tech tools:

- **Pen and Paper Scorekeeping**
  - Keep track of scores, player statistics and key moments

during games.

- ○ It's easy to set up and doesn't require any special equipment. You can quickly jot down important details that can be reviewed later.
- **Basic Notebooks**
  - ○ **How It Helps:** Record observations about player performance, team formations and strategies.
  - ○ **Why It's Good:** Having a dedicated notebook allows you to organize your thoughts and track progress over time.
- **Simple Spreadsheets**
  - ○ **How It Helps:** Use programs like Excel or Google Sheets to log data such as scores, player stats and game outcomes.
  - ○ **Why It's Good:** Spreadsheets are user-friendly and can help you identify patterns and trends without needing advanced technical skills.

Download this template here.

Gradually Incorporating Technology

As you become more comfortable with basic analytics, you can start introducing more advanced tools to enhance your analysis:

- **Video Recording**
  - ○ Capture games and practices to review plays, study formations and analyze player movements.
  - ○ Visual footage allows for a clearer understanding of what happened during the game and helps in providing concrete feedback.

o   You can synchronize your notes to the video footage by starting a stopwatch (on your smartphone) at the same time the recording starts and logging the stopwatch time with every note. As long as the recording doesn't stop, this loose synchronization will remain intact. If you're using a higher end system that records time*code* and can set the timecode generator to "time-of-day" timecode or free-run timecode (set manually to match the time-of-day) then you can use your watch or phone's clock - even if the recording is paused and restarted.

- **Simple Analytics Software**
  - o   Use affordable software to organize and visualize your data, such as creating charts or tracking player performance over time.
  - o   Software tools can automate some of the data analysis, making it easier to draw meaningful conclusions.
  - o   Dig deeper into analytics that you can't capture during the game.

Building Your Analytics Toolkit

Here's a step-by-step approach to developing your sports analytics system:

1. **Start with What You Have**
   - o   Begin by using pen and paper or a simple notebook to record basic information during games and practices.
2. **Organize Your Data**
   - o   Use spreadsheets to input and organize the data you've collected. This can include scores, player statistics and key events.
3. **Review and Reflect**
   - o   Regularly review your notes and spreadsheets to identify strengths and areas for improvement. Discuss these findings with your team.
4. **Incorporate Video Analysis**
   - o   Start recording games and practices. Use the footage to provide visual feedback and deeper insights into your team's performance.
5. **Advance to Digital Tools**
   - o   As your needs grow, explore more advanced analytics software that can help you create detailed reports, heat maps and player path analyses.

Live tagging during a sports game can generate useful analytics and reduce time spent editing recorded video.

Sports Analytics: Defining Key Performance Indicators (KPIs)

When incorporating sports analytics into your video production workflow, defining the right KPIs is essential for maximizing team performance. The key is collaboration between coaches, analysts and video producers to determine which statistics will have the most meaningful impact on strategy, training and player development.

How to Define KPIs for Your Team

Here's a step-by-step guide for defining KPIs in sports analytics:

1. Understand the Team's Goals

Start by clarifying the team's overarching objectives:

- Are you focused on improving offensive or defensive performance?
- Is player development a priority or are you more concerned with in-game strategy?
- Do you need real-time stats for coaching adjustments during games?

2. Collaborate with Coaches and Players

The coaching staff and players have firsthand experience with the game's nuances. Ask these questions:

- **What stats would help you better understand team strengths and weaknesses?**
- **What specific events or moments should be tracked in-game?**
- **Which player actions or plays determine the game's outcome most frequently?**

3. Select Relevant Metrics

Choose KPIs based on the sport's critical performance factors. Here are some common examples by sport:

- **Basketball:** Points per possession, shooting percentage, turnovers, player efficiency rating (PER).
- **Soccer/Football:** Shots on goal, pass completion rate, expected goals (xG).
- **Baseball:** Batting average, on-base percentage, earned run average (ERA).
- **Hockey:** Save percentage, face-off win percentage, goals against average.
- **Tennis:** First-serve percentage, unforced errors, net points won.

4. Make KPIs Actionable

Choose KPIs that can inform real coaching decisions. Metrics should be specific, time-bound and player-focused where possible. For example:

- **"Defensive rebounds per game"** informs defensive adjustments.
- **"Passing accuracy in the final third"** can improve attacking strategies in soccer.

5. Use Video to Support Analysis

Combine video footage with tracked KPIs. Consider these approaches:

- Use **slow-motion replays** to review key plays.
- **Tag and catalog plays** by action type, allowing for post-game review.
- **Overlay stats on video footage** during playback for context.

Checklist for Defining KPIs:

- Clearly defined team goals
- Collaboration with coaching staff
- Key moments and actions identified
- Real-time vs. post-game analytics needs
- Player-specific vs. team-wide KPIs
- Video integration for visual review
- Historical data for trend analysis

Example KPI Questions by Sport

Basketball Example:

- Are we winning the rebound battle consistently?
- How effective are we in transition defense?
- Which lineups produce the highest scoring runs?

Soccer/Football Example:

- Are we completing passes in dangerous areas?
- How often are we creating goal-scoring opportunities?
- Are players tracking back effectively on defense?

Baseball Example:

- Is our pitching rotation maintaining a consistent ERA?
- Are our batters hitting against left-handed pitchers effectively?
- How efficient is our base-running?

By defining KPIs using these steps, sports teams can transform raw game footage into actionable insights that fuel player development, improve in-game decision-making and drive long-term success.

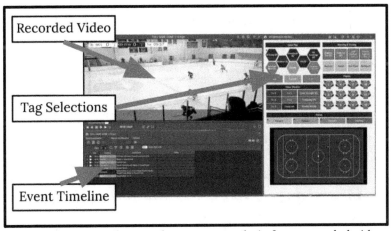

NACSPORT is used to produce sports analysis from recorded video.

Presenting Data Effectively: Turning Numbers into Actionable Insights

The integration of video technology into sports coaching has become a fundamental component at every competitive level, providing a strategic edge that extends beyond conventional methods of instruction. High-quality footage can reinforce verbal and on-field directives, highlight key moments and formations and serve as an objective source of performance data for evidence-based coaching decisions. Yet, the mere act of recording does not ensure that players will understand and benefit from the information captured. Effective communication depends not only on the technical quality of the footage but also on how the content is presented, contextualized and connected to the athletes' roles and responsibilities within the game.

Achieving this level of clarity requires drawing on principles from the science of learning. Coaches who consider cognitive load, motivation and retention strategies can create an environment in which data and visuals become meaningful rather than overwhelming. The goal is to translate raw metrics and video segments into a clear narrative that players can internalize and apply on the field. In other words, it's not enough to show a player their shot chart or passing accuracy; the key is guiding them to understand what these indicators mean for their positioning, decision-making and future performance. By combining the strengths of modern videography with evidence-based communication strategies, coaches and analysts can ensure that every frame of footage and every piece of data contributes to ongoing development and tangible competitive gains.

"Video enables discussion, reflection and visualization and I believe it is the most powerful tool sports coaches have to support the delivery of feedback and performance information to athletes.

Translating performance statistics from data into wisdom, supplemented with video evidence should be something every coach seeks to utilize in their practice at any level of sport, helping their teams and athletes unlock their full potential."
-Darren Lewis, Director Codex Analysis.

Here are strategies and scientific principles for presenting data so that it resonates with athletes:

1. Provide Context and Relevance

- **Contextualize the Metric:** Instead of just stating a KPI like "Your passing accuracy is 82%," add context by comparing it to a target benchmark or a league average. For example, "Your passing accuracy is 82%, which is just below the league average of 85%. Closing that gap by focusing on shorter, safer passes in high-pressure areas could create more scoring opportunities."
- **Link to Game Situations:** MySkyCoach is a great tool you can use to create and tag live video clips and deliver them to a wireless tablet in the hands of a coach. By tagging the video, you can quickly filter through video clips and review gameplay moments live or at a halftime break. Giving coaches the ability to pause, rewind and replay moments in slow-motion has become much easier with touch screen tablets. This connection between numbers and real-world scenarios helps the athlete visualize how to adjust their decisions.

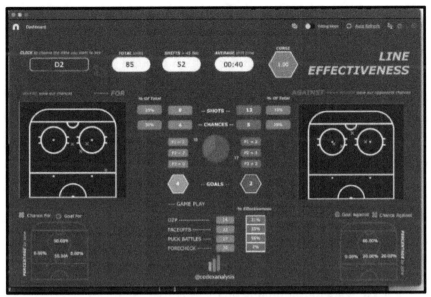

Line effectiveness charts built by Codex Analysis using Nacsport.

2. Use Visual Aids Wisely

- **Simplicity in Visualization:** Charts and diagrams should be easy to read. Highlight key figures with contrasting colors or callout boxes. Avoid cluttered dashboards with too many metrics at once.
- **Before-and-After Comparisons:** Show players how a slight change in technique or positioning impacted their stats over time. For instance, "Here's your shooting accuracy before you adjusted your foot placement and here's after," tied directly to video clips for a visual cause-and-effect relationship.

3. Relate Data to Player Roles and Responsibilities

- **Role-Specific KPIs:** Tailor data presentations to what the player needs to excel in their role. A central midfielder may benefit most from data on passing choices and interceptions, while a striker needs insights into shot selection and movement off the ball.
- **Highlight Individual Strengths and Weaknesses:** Emphasizing where the player excels can build confidence and buy-in. For example, "You're already among the top three on the team for defensive rebounds—imagine how effective you'd be if you improve your defensive positioning by just 5%."

4. Incorporate Learning Science and Cognitive Principles

- **Chunking Information:** Cognitive load theory suggests that breaking information into smaller, manageable segments helps players process and retain it. Present data in short sessions focusing on one or two KPIs rather than overwhelming them with every metric at once.
- **Guided Discovery:** Players are more likely to retain information if they actively engage with it. Ask questions like, "What do you think might improve if you raised your passing completion rate in the final third?" Encouraging players to draw their own conclusions improves internalization.
- **Storytelling and Narratives:** Humans are wired to remember stories better than standalone facts. Frame the data as part of a narrative: "Last season, you struggled under high-pressure situations, but this year your decision-making speed improved by 10%. Let's see how that helped us control the midfield during our last match."

5. Tie Data to Actionable Steps

- **Action-Oriented Feedback:** After presenting the data, give clear, specific instructions for improvement. Instead of "You need fewer turnovers," say, "In pressure situations, try making your first pass simpler—look for the nearby midfielder instead of attempting a long diagonal."
- **Short-Term Goals:** Setting immediate, quantifiable targets gives players something tangible to work toward. For instance, "In the next game, let's aim for a 5% increase in successful tackles near the sideline."

6. Reinforce Through Repetition and Follow-Up

- **Progress Tracking:** Show players their improvement over several games or training sessions. This visualization of progress not only motivates them but also confirms that the data-informed strategy is working.
- **Regular Check-Ins:** Periodically revisit the KPIs and video highlights. Reinforcement through repetition helps players incorporate the changes into their muscle memory and decision-making patterns.

7. Culturally and Individually Tailored Communication

- **Player-Centric Language:** Explain data in terms that resonate with the player's understanding of the game. Some athletes respond best to data-driven logic, others to visual and narrative explanations. Tailor your approach accordingly.

- **Cultural Sensitivity and Communication Styles:** Some players may prefer direct, concise instructions, while others benefit from more conversational, exploratory discussions. Adapt how you present data to match individual learning preferences.

Example Scenario:

A soccer coach wants a winger to improve decision-making in the final third. After running analytics, the coach finds that the player's pass completion rate in dangerous areas is lower than average, often due to overly ambitious forward passes against double coverage.

Step-by-Step Presentation:

1. **Contextualize the Data:** "Your pass completion rate in the final third is 60%. The league average for a winger in your role is about 70%. Just closing that gap would create 2–3 more scoring chances per match."
2. **Visualize with Video:** Show a clip of a recent match. Freeze the frame at the moment the player makes a risky pass. Annotations can be used to highlight specific areas and draw athlete's attention to specific areas.
3. **Relate to Role:** "As our main wide attacker, finding the midfielder who can switch play inside will open space for your runs behind the defense. That's your advantage—your speed is a real threat, so let's use it by making a safer pass that leads to a give-and-go."
4. **Chunk the Information:** Focus only on passes in the final third this session. In a future session, address crossing accuracy or dribbling decisions.
5. **Actionable Steps:** "In the next match, try aiming for two simpler passes back into the midfield when pressed. If we see that work, we'll expand on that approach."

Scientific Rationale:

- **Cognitive Load Theory:** By presenting only one or two metrics at a time, players are less mentally burdened, improving comprehension and retention.
- **Self-Determination Theory (SDT):** Involving players in interpreting their own data fosters autonomy and intrinsic motivation, making them more likely to adopt the suggested improvements.
- **Visual Learning Principles:** Intuitive controls such as "pinch

and zoom" make visual learning and instructions more natural.

By using these methods—contextualizing stats, employing clear visualizations, tying data to specific roles and actionable steps and leveraging learning science—coaches can turn raw metrics into meaningful insights. This approach ensures that players don't just see the data, but understand it, internalize it and apply it effectively in competition.

5 Capturing the Bigger Picture: Tactical Camera Use in Sports

A tactical camera serves a distinct role in sports analysis, differing fundamentally from broadcast cameras. While broadcast cameras follow the action closely, focusing on the ball and key players for viewer engagement, tactical cameras provide a zoomed-out, comprehensive view of the field. In soccer, for instance, a tactical camera or "main camera" captures the middle 20 players, enabling coaches to analyze team formations, defensive alignments and offensive strategies.

Oftentimes, broadcasters will collaborate with sports analytics teams and they will provide the "Main" camera feed over the network to the sports analytics software. IP video has enabled many new video workflows that allow software solutions like sideline instant replay tablets and sports analytics software to easily access video feeds over WiFi or ethernet connections to the network. The "Main" camera is essentially the camera view that follows the middle 2/3rds of the field which isn't used for close ups. It's very likely that the cameras used for the sports live streaming can be used for sports analytics too. You can decide to connect with these video feeds in real-time or access the recordings after the game. Working with the video production team to understand your sports analytics goals can help the team better understand the dual-purpose use of video.

Using the broadcast "main" camera feed as a baseline for sports analytics provides immediate, structured reference points that are already verified by officials and integrated into the flow of the game. This feed typically includes the official scoreboard, timeouts, penalty flags and other essential data markers that define the narrative of the match. By utilizing an SDI to RTSP encoder, analytics professionals can seamlessly import this broadcast-quality feed into their analysis software. Once integrated, they can enrich the data stream with sophisticated tagging and metadata that go beyond standard metrics—highlighting specific player actions, tactical formations and situational insights. This combination not only saves time by ensuring critical time-based data is already present, but also empowers teams to layer more advanced analytics on top of a rock-solid baseline, ultimately delivering a more nuanced understanding of player performance and strategic execution.

ISO-RECORDING

Recording each camera for sports analytics

Capture Every Goal
Capture Every Save
Capture Every Faceoff

2/3rds	1/3rds / Faceoff	Goal 1 / Fan Cam	Goal 2
Main Camera.	Close-up Camera.	Camera 3	Camera 4

Iso-recordings are "isolated" recordings of each camera, often used for post production or sports analytics.

The Four Camera System

A four-camera sports analytics system provides comprehensive coverage of the field, capturing critical gameplay moments from multiple perspectives. Each camera serves a specific purpose, enabling detailed post-game analysis for coaches and players. While not all teams can set up a four camera system for sports analytics, consider partnering with your school broadcast club or the video streaming team to capture more video for your coaching analysis.

2/3rds Wide Shot   1/3rd Close Up

Camera 1 - 2/3rd View of the Field: This camera provides a broad overview of the majority of the playing field. It captures team formations, transitions and overall game flow. Coaches can analyze player positioning, strategic movements and team dynamics from this wide-angle perspective.

Camera 2 - 1/3 View - Close-Up Action: Focused on a smaller portion of the field, this camera offers a more detailed look at individual offensive and defensive plays. It highlights key one-on-one battles, critical passes and defensive strategies, helping coaches assess individual player performance and tactical decisions.

Goalie Camera 1   Goalie Camera 2

Camera 3 - Goal Camera 1: Positioned behind one of the goals, this camera closely monitors goalie action and any offensive attempts within the goal area. It captures every shot on goal, saves and key defensive maneuvers, making it essential for analyzing goalkeeping performance and offensive execution.

Camera 4 - Goal Camera 2: Similar to Camera 3, this camera covers the opposite goal. It ensures that every offensive and defensive moment near the goal is documented, providing a complete view of scoring opportunities and defensive stops.

Close Up Face Off   Use Presets

Most sports have moments where additional viewpoints are important and the 1/3rds cameras can be used to capture these when necessary. By combining footage from all four cameras, coaches can review game highlights, break down critical plays and create focused training sessions. This multi-angle approach supports detailed player feedback, tactical adjustments and improved game strategy development.

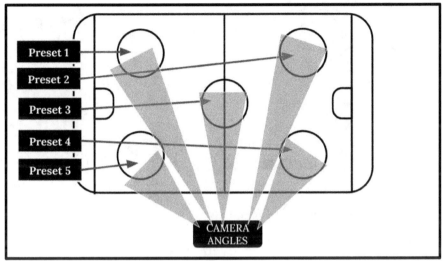

This diagram shows five PTZ presets set up for the faceoff locations in hockey.

PTZ cameras can quickly recall specific areas of a space with PTZ presets. Once your cameras are set up and in place, you can move the camera to these positions and save the location in a "PTZ Preset". This way camera operators can quickly move the camera to a specific area with the click of a button.

Why Tactical Cameras Matter

1. **Team Shape and Structure:** Coaches can evaluate how defenders respond to attacking plays, how midfielders reposition when possession changes and how strikers create space.
2. **Off-Ball Movements:** Tactical cameras track off-ball player actions, which are crucial but often missed in broadcast footage.
3. **Complete Play Analysis:** Seeing the entire play as it unfolds enables better assessments of team dynamics and decision-making.
4. **Training and Development:** Tactical footage supports targeted training by highlighting gaps in coverage, defensive breakdowns or missed opportunities for through balls or crosses.

This iPad is being used to annotate on top of an instant-replay.

Video analysis allows teams to:

Break Down Player Movements

Video footage captures every movement players make. Coaches can analyze:

- **Positioning:** Tracking how players hold or adjust their positions during plays.
- **Speed Changes:** Monitoring acceleration and deceleration.
- **Defensive Maneuvers:** Understanding individual and collective defensive reactions.

Track Tactical Formations and Plays

- **Formations:** Video analysis reveals how formations adapt throughout the game.
- **Strategy Insights:** Integrating real-time data helps assess the impact of tactical adjustments.
- **Decision Reviews:** Coaches can revisit plays to evaluate what worked and what didn't.

Assessing Player Fatigue and Injury Risk

Combining video with biometric data helps:

- **Spot Fatigue Indicators:** Identify reduced speed or improper mechanics.
- **Prevent Injuries:** Detect risky movements before injuries occur.
- **Manage Workloads:** Tailor training schedules to individual player needs.

Specific players and jersey numbers can be added to your sports analytics software, customizing the input area for quick play tagging.

Video as a Data Source

Video is no longer just for spectators—it's a valuable data stream for analytics teams. By capturing multiple angles and camera feeds, broadcast video offers a comprehensive view of every event during a game. Integrating this footage into a sports analytics system can be done in several ways:

1. **DIY Manual Tagging and Annotation:** Teams can manually tag key moments in a game, such as goals, fouls or turnovers. These tagged moments can be linked to statistical data for further analysis, helping teams understand not just what happened but why it happened.
2. **Automated AI Video Analysis:** With advancements in AI, machine learning and computer vision, automated systems can now analyze game footage in real time. These systems can identify player positions, classify actions (e.g., a pass, a shot, a tackle) and even assess the outcome of each play.
3. **Sports Stats Services:** You can hire professionals such as PrestoSports or Hudl to review your game video and return complete game analytics. These analytics can include presentation ready information to share with the team.

Video Tagging for Sports Analytics: Real-Time vs. Post-Game Analysis

In the world of sports analytics, video tagging plays a crucial role in providing coaches with actionable insights. Whether it's for tactical adjustments during halftime or for a comprehensive review after the game, understanding the options for tagging video footage can help teams maximize their competitive edge.

Option 1: Real-Time Tagging

Real-time tagging involves marking key events such as goals, assists, fouls or turnovers as they occur during the game. This process requires a dedicated staff member or analyst using specialized software to tag moments in real-time. The tagged data is immediately available for analysis, allowing coaches to review critical plays during timeouts or at halftime.

Benefits of Real-Time Tagging:

- **Instant Insights:** Coaches can adjust strategies on the fly.
- **Halftime Review:** Teams can make tactical adjustments based on the first-half performance.
- **Post-Game Efficiency:** Since the video is already tagged, less post-game work is required.
- **Ease of Use:** Software such as Nacsport allows you to tag the game without having to access the video. You can then sync up the video afterwards, which can sometimes be easier and more realistic.

Challenges of Real-Time Tagging:

- **Resource-Intensive:** Requires dedicated personnel and reliable hardware.
- **Technical Requirements:** Stable internet and seamless integration between tagging software and video systems are essential.

Option 2: Post-Game Tagging

Post-game tagging involves analyzing the recorded video after the game has ended. This option is ideal for smaller teams with limited staff or those focused on in-depth, data-driven reviews rather than immediate feedback.

Post-game tagging involves analyzing the recorded video after the game has ended. This option is ideal for smaller teams with limited staff or those focused on in-depth, data-driven reviews rather than immediate feedback.

vMix is a professional video production software running on a Windows laptop. being used to simultaneously record four video signals for sports analytics.

The ISO-Corder Advantage:

Many video production teams typically record a single "Program" video output, which switches between multiple cameras for the live stream or viewer experience. However, this approach doesn't align well with the needs of sports coaches and analysts.

Coaches require continuous, uninterrupted footage from each camera angle for effective analysis. An ISO-corder system (known as a "multicorder" in Vmix) solves this problem by recording each camera independently and simultaneously. This ensures that no critical play or movement is missed due to camera switching and no overlays or graphics are shown on top of video meant for analytics.

This "Quad Split" was used to record four camera views during a varsity hockey match.

Quad-split video recording is convenient because coaches can look at one video recording and look at four unique camera angles. You can also record a "quad split" of the four cameras (in vMix and other software). And if you record at 4K, each part of the quad split will have a resolution of 1920x1080 pixels. This means that you can blow up each quadrant when viewing and still see high quality images.

Alternatives to software solutions are hardware solutions like the AJA Ki Pro GO2 that can also record four (1080p/60) cameras at a time.

Four Blackmagic Design Hyperdeck Studio 4K recorders (4K-2160p/60) that can each record a single camera.

If you go the hardware route, be careful that you select hardware that is capable of recording at the resolution and frame rate you want.

By recording multiple cameras, teams can upload the separate video files into sports analytics software for tagging, analysis and annotation. Each camera's unique perspective offers valuable insights—whether it's a wide-field view, a close-up of player interactions or goal-specific action.

Switching between angles during live production can be distracting and even frustrating when reviewing footage for teaching purposes. With a multi-corder setup, coaches can focus on the exact plays and angles they need, streamlining the review process and enhancing player development through precise, angle-specific video analysis.

Benefits of Post-Game Tagging:

- **Resource Flexibility:** No need for live tagging staff during the game.
- **Detailed Analysis:** Analysts have more time to review footage, ensuring precise tagging.
- **Scalability:** Works well for teams of all sizes.

Challenges of Post-Game Tagging:

- **Delayed Insights:** Coaches miss the opportunity for mid-game

adjustments.
- **Time-Consuming:** Detailed post-game reviews can require significant time and effort.

Wireless Video Review for Sideline Access

Many sports analytics platforms, such as Hudl Sideline, SkyCoach and Vuestation offer wireless video review systems designed for sideline use. These systems allow coaches to access tagged plays in real-time using tablets or laptops. With features like instant replay, coaches can quickly navigate through recorded footage, helping players adjust during breaks.

How Wireless Review Works:

- **Live Sync:** The tagging software syncs with the team's video capture system.
- **On-Demand Access:** Coaches can search by play types or specific tags.
- **Performance Analysis:** Real-time feedback enhances tactical awareness.

Choosing the Right Approach

The decision between real-time and post-game tagging depends on the team's resources, staff availability and competitive goals. Larger teams with dedicated analytics staff may benefit from live tagging and sideline video review systems. In contrast, smaller teams can achieve great results by focusing on detailed post-game analysis.

By understanding these options, coaches can better integrate sports analytics into their workflow, ensuring that every game is an opportunity for growth and success.

Real-World Applications

Several sports teams and organizations are already using video for analytics. For example, in basketball, coaches use video analysis to examine defensive setups and offensive plays in minute detail, leading to more refined game strategies. In football, video analysis helps track player positioning and movement, offering insights into how players can maximize their effectiveness on the pitch.

Even in individual sports like tennis or golf, video combined with analytics can help athletes improve their technique. Tennis players, for instance, can use slow-motion replays to analyze their serve, looking for areas to improve speed or spin.

Top Sports Analytics Solutions

Sports Analytics Software Use Case Chart

Category	Primary Purpose	Who Uses It	Key Features
Game Play Analysis	Improve coaching & strategy	Coaches, Team Analysts, Performance Staff	Play breakdowns, tactics review, motion tracking
Stats Creation & Intelligence	Generate real-time insights	Broadcasters, Journalists, Sports Analysts, Scouts	Live stats, player insights, event tagging
Presentation & Analysis	Post-game reports & reviews	Coaches, Front Office, Marketing, Sponsors	Interactive charts, data visuals, summaries

Top Solutions for Gameplay Analysis

Hudl

Overview: Hudl offers an all-in-one platform for video analysis and performance tracking, widely used by sports teams at all levels, from amateur to professional. Hudl's software allows coaches to upload, review and analyze video footage of games and practices. Their tools focus on player development through video breakdown and custom tags for key plays.

Key Features:

- Video editing and sharing platform for teams
- Custom tagging for specific plays and game events

57

- Detailed player performance stats and review tools
- Cloud storage for easy access and sharing of game footage
- Ability to live stream the game directly to Hudl.

Catapult Sports

Overview: Catapult is one of the leading sports analytics platforms, specializing in wearable technology and video analysis for performance tracking. Their solutions help teams monitor player movement, workload and physical output through GPS trackers, accelerometers and heart rate monitors, giving coaches real-time insights into player conditioning and injury prevention.

Key Features:

- Wearable technology for athlete performance tracking
- Video analysis integration
- Detailed metrics for player workload, speed and injury risk
- Cloud-based analytics platform for data visualization

Dartfish

Overview:
Dartfish is leading video analysis software designed for coaches, athletes and sports analysts across various disciplines. It enables users to capture, analyze and share performance footage, making it a powerful tool for improving technique, enhancing strategy and optimizing team performance. Dartfish is trusted globally by sports organizations, educational institutions and professional teams.

Key Features:

- **Advanced Video Analysis**
- **Annotation Tools**
- **Data Integrations**
- **Cloud Storage & Sharing**

Nacsport

Overview: Nacsport is a comprehensive sports video analysis software designed to assist coaches, analysts and athletes in enhancing performance through detailed video breakdowns. Suitable for various sports, including football, basketball, rugby and hockey, Nacsport offers a range of tools to capture, analyze and present game footage effectively. Its user-friendly interface and customizable features make it accessible for teams at all levels, from amateur to professional.

Key Features:

- **Customizable Tagging Windows**
- **Comprehensive Timeline Analysis**
- **Advanced Presentation Tools**
- **Data Visualization Dashboards**
- **Multi-Angle Video Support**

Nacsport's scalable solutions cater to a diverse range of users, from grassroots teams to elite sports organizations, providing the necessary tools to elevate performance analysis and strategic planning.

Solutions for Presentation Analysis

Opta Sports (Stats Perform)

Overview: Opta Sports provides detailed sports data for professional teams and broadcasters. Known for their in-depth statistics across various sports, including soccer, rugby and cricket, Opta focuses on providing live data feeds and historical analysis for better decision-making during and after games.

Key Features:

- Real-time and historical data feeds
- Detailed player performance metrics and team stats
- Integration with video and broadcast solutions for real-time analytics
- Tactical insights and statistical modeling for team strategy

KlipDraw

Overview: KlipDraw is a video analysis tool designed for sports analysts and coaches who need to break down footage to illustrate tactics, formations and key player movements. KlipDraw allows users to annotate videos with graphics, arrows and drawings, making it easy to highlight key points during review sessions.

Key Features:

- Annotated video analysis for tactical breakdowns
- Tools for drawing, arrows and graphics on video
- Integration with other video analysis platforms
- Easy-to-use interface for coaches and analysts

Metrica Sports

Overview:

Metrica Sports offers advanced video and data analysis solutions tailored for coaches, analysts and teams across various sports. Their platform, Play, integrates cutting-edge technology to streamline the analysis process, enabling users to gain in-depth performance insights and enhance strategic planning. Designed with input from industry professionals, Metrica Sports' tools are accessible to teams at all levels, from grassroots to elite organizations.

Key Features:

- **Customizable Coding Tools**
- **Telestration**
- **Automated Player & Field Tracking**
- **Cloud-Based Video Management**
- **Pattern Detection Algorithms**

Metrica Sports' solutions are utilized by over 800 teams worldwide, reflecting their commitment to making professional-level analysis accessible across all levels of sport.

The modern coaching landscape has evolved dramatically and the power of sports analytics puts a world of insights at your fingertips. Instead of relying solely on intuition or post-game debriefs, you now have the capacity to make adjustments on the fly and communicate more effectively with players who crave instant, evidence-based feedback. As you refine your approach, this blend of real-time analysis and comprehensive video review not only elevates in-game performance, it also strengthens the overall culture surrounding your team. With every strategic pivot and carefully edited highlight reel, you're not just sharpening your tactics—you're enhancing the experience for everyone involved.

Yet, before you dive deeper into the realm of sports video production—where capturing, editing and sharing compelling footage can bring your story to life—there's an essential stepping stone: ensuring that the basics of team information are well-managed and widely accessible. The next chapter, *From Field to Fanbase: Preparing Your Team for Sports Video Success*, will explore how to build a strong informational framework. By clearly communicating schedules, rosters, streaming options and more, you'll lay the groundwork for broadening your audience, engaging loyal fans and even attracting sponsors. In short, managing the fundamentals sets the stage for your video content to truly resonate when it's time to press "record."

6 ELEVATING PLAYER PROFILES: CREATING CONTENT THAT ATTRACTS SCOUTS

As the sports world becomes increasingly digital, athletes now have unprecedented opportunities to shape their personal narratives and stand out to college recruiters, professional scouts and talent evaluators. No longer is it enough for a player's talent to remain confined to a local field or court; with the right approach to video content creation, that talent can be shared with anyone, anywhere, at any time.

This is where coaches, analysts, educators and sports content creators have a crucial role to play. While players may be the stars on the field, they often need guidance and structure off it—especially when it comes to making their skills visible to scouts. A well-coordinated sports video program doesn't just serve the needs of the team as a whole; it can also empower individual athletes to showcase their abilities in a polished organized fashion.

SPORTS CONTENT WORKFLOW

Record Video	Review Footage	Edit Video	Distribute Content
Start by capturing video or retrieving recorded files.	Review footage and use sports analytics software to generate supporting statistics.	Edit video to create highlight reel or include graphics with supporting statistics.	Upload to recruiting platforms, social media, direct outreach

The Role of Coaches, Analysts, Educators and Content Creators in Supporting Player Showcases

Coaches and analysts understand what scouts look for in prospective recruits. They know that a highlight reel isn't just about flashy goals or dramatic dunks; it's about consistently good decision-making, strong fundamentals, versatility and steady improvement over time. Educators and academic advisors can also help highlight the student aspect of "student-athlete," ensuring that videos feature not just athletic prowess but a player's intellectual engagement, team leadership and academic discipline. Meanwhile, the sports content creation team can shape raw footage into compelling narratives: organizing camera coverage, selecting the best angles, editing for clarity and even incorporating analytics or graphics that underscore a player's unique strengths.

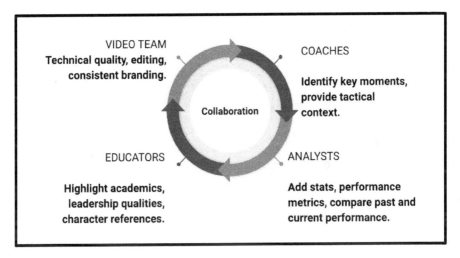

Together, these professionals create a support system that allows players to focus on what they do best—perform on the field—while a structured workflow transforms raw footage into a strategic scouting tool.

Why Player-Generated Content Matters: Personal Branding, Self-Promotion and Visibility to Scouts

For athletes aiming to continue their careers at the collegiate or professional level, personal branding has become an essential piece of the puzzle. While coaches and scouts still network through traditional channels, they increasingly rely on digital platforms—like recruiting websites, social media and video-sharing services—to discover new talent. A well-crafted highlight reel, combined with longer-form content that shows full games or training sessions, can give scouts a multifaceted understanding of a player's skill set, athleticism and potential.

By taking an active role in producing their own content, players learn to present themselves professionally and strategically. Instead of leaving their futures solely in the hands of chance, they can proactively build a portfolio of performance clips, interviews and training footage. When these assets are expertly produced and thoughtfully curated, they resonate more strongly with scouts, who often sift through countless profiles and videos in search of the right candidate.

Here are some of the key piece of content players should create:

Highlight Reel

- **Primary Purpose:** Provide a quick, impactful overview of top skills and standout moments.
- **Key Scout Takeaways:** Immediate skill level, athleticism and game-changing abilities.
- **Best Practices:**
  - Keep it short (2–3 minutes)
  - Lead with strongest plays
  - Clearly identify the player (e.g., arrows, spot shadows)
  - Maintain high-quality visuals and stable footage

Full-Game Footage

- **Primary Purpose:** Show consistency, decision-making and how the player performs over an entire match.
- **Key Scout Takeaways:** Tactical awareness, off-ball movement, stamina, adaptability and mental resilience.
- **Best Practices:**
  - Include offense, defense and transitional play
  - Highlight critical match situations (pressure moments, end-of-game scenarios)
  - Use stable, wide-angle shots for better context
  - Ensure good lighting and camera placement

Training/Workout Clips

- **Primary Purpose:** Demonstrate commitment to improvement, work ethic and technical skill development.
- **Key Scout Takeaways:** Progress over time, dedicated training habits and willingness to refine technique.
- **Best Practices:**
  - Show a variety of drills and exercises
  - Document progression (before/after comparisons)
  - Maintain consistent framing and clear angles
  - Ensure adequate lighting and minimal background distractions

Intro/Interview Segment

- **Primary Purpose:** Showcase personality, communication skills, academic achievements and character.
- **Key Scout Takeaways:** Attitude, leadership potential,

coachability, cultural fit within a team.

- **Best Practices:**
  - Keep it concise and authentic (1–2 minutes)
  - Maintain professional tone and attire
  - Include simple graphics or captions for key info (GPA, honors, leadership roles)
  - Ensure good audio quality and a quiet setting

How the Sports Video Team Can Facilitate Organized, High-Quality Player Content

A player's raw talent is only as visible as the quality of the video that captures it. While automated, AI-enabled cameras can record games and follow the action at a basic level, these systems often provide just one angle and limited context. By contrast, a dedicated sports video team—comprising camera operators, content creators and editors—can produce richer, more dynamic footage. These professionals understand how to highlight the precise details scouts care about: footwork, positioning, off-ball movements and adaptability in various game situations.

Moreover, the sports video team can implement a workflow that makes it easy for players to request clips, share highlight reels and update their portfolios regularly. This might involve a cloud-based storage system for footage, a tagging system that identifies player involvement in key plays and direct collaboration with coaches and analysts to ensure the right moments are captured. Platforms like Hudl can simplify this process by providing tools for video analysis, tagging and sharing, while Krossover and VidSwap offer advanced features like play breakdowns and easy player-specific clip creation. For teams looking to streamline their process even further, Trace uses AI to automatically generate personalized highlight reels for each player, eliminating the need for manual sorting. Similarly, Veo employs AI tagging to identify key plays, making it a breeze to find and share standout moments. With such tools in place, the sports video team can ensure that the final products are not only polished and scout-ready but also delivered efficiently—no more scrambling through random files or low-quality phone recordings to find that perfect clip. These purpose-built platforms not only save time but also enhance the professionalism of the team's media output.

By forming an alliance among coaches, analysts, educators and content creators, today's sports programs can provide players with the tools and expertise they need to shine on camera. The result? Players who step confidently into the spotlight, prepared to impress scouts with not only their athletic ability, but also the strategic, skillfully presented content that tells their story.

Understanding Scout and Recruiter Priorities

When it comes to attracting the attention of scouts and recruiters, pure athletic ability is only part of the equation. While they certainly appreciate a hard swing of the bat, a lightning-quick sprint down the sideline or a perfectly placed free kick, those searching for the next generation of college athletes or professional prospects often look deeper. They're hunting for well-rounded players who can excel in demanding environments, adapt to various game situations and contribute positively to a team's culture—both on and off the field.

Highlight Reels for Quick Impressions

Highlight reels are a staple for any aspiring athlete looking to catch a scout's eye. Short and engaging, these condensed videos should feature the player's most impressive moments: goals, tackles, assists, saves or standout technical skills. The key is **selectivity—quality over quantity**. You can save yourself a lot of time editing video, if you know what you are looking for and notate it during the video recording. The easiest way to do this is scrub through the video timeline looking for scoreboard changes. Another way to quickly scan video for specific plays is to reference timing notes you took during the game.

Pro Tip: While AI tools can automate much of the highlighting process, learning how to edit a sports highlight reel in video-editing software allows you to get exactly what you are looking for. When the AI fails, consider how much time it would take to simply sit down and get the job done by hand.

Long Form to Short Form

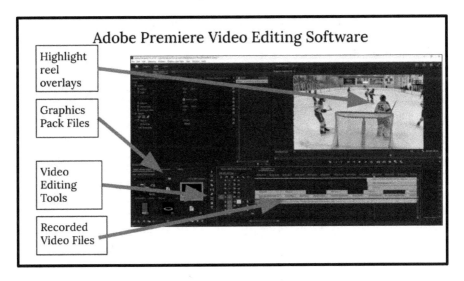

Adobe Premiere is a commonly used video editing software which is used in the *Sports Video* online course. Once you have your entire game footage, it's useful to break down smaller sections for your team, athletes and eventually scouts to review. Video editing can be outsourced to freelancers easily who can repackage "long form" content into more organized "short form" video.

Coaches often use these shorter video segments to focus on specific aspects of gameplay. For instance, a soccer coach might compile clips highlighting a striker's positioning during goal-scoring opportunities or a basketball coach might create a reel showcasing a player's defensive movements. These curated clips make it easier for athletes to focus on areas for improvement and refine their techniques. Additionally, such edits can serve as motivational tools, emphasizing an athlete's strengths by showcasing their top plays.

For scouts, these clips are invaluable. A baseball coach might send scouts a video featuring a pitcher's most effective strikeouts, complete with slow-motion analysis of their throwing mechanics. Similarly, a football coach might use game footage to create a highlight reel of a quarterback's most strategic passes to attract college recruiters.

Video editing also plays a critical role in preparing for upcoming games. Coaches can dissect opponents' strategies by creating breakdowns of key plays, such as a volleyball team's service patterns or a hockey team's power-play formations. These targeted videos allow teams to study their opponents in detail, adjust their strategies and execute game plans more effectively.

By leveraging tools like Adobe Premiere and engaging freelancers for editing, coaches can ensure their video resources are both professional and impactful.

In soccer, the possibilities for video compilations are vast, reflecting the diverse aspects of the game that coaches, players and analysts focus on. Here are some examples:

1. **Player-Specific Performance Reel Ideals**

   o A striker's **goal-scoring opportunities**: Highlighting shots on target, off-the-ball movements to create space and positioning during set-pieces.
   o A midfielder's **passing accuracy**: Clips showing key passes, through-balls and long-ball distributions that led to goal-scoring chances.
   o A defender's **tackling and interceptions**: Moments where they successfully stopped counterattacks or won one-on-one duels.

2. **Tactical Analysis Clips**

   o **Team shape during transitions**: Show how the team moves from defense to attack or vice versa, focusing on maintaining width and depth.
   o **Pressing sequences**: Highlight collective pressing efforts to win back possession high up the field.
   o **Set-piece strategies**: Break down corner kicks, free kicks or defensive setups during dead-ball situations.

3. **Match Highlights for Review**

   o **Goal analysis**: Highlighting the buildup leading to goals, both scored and conceded, to assess what worked or went wrong.
   o **Missed opportunities**: Clips focusing on moments where better decision-making could have resulted in a goal.
   o **Critical mistakes**: Highlighting errors in positioning, passing or marking that led to opposition goals.

Free 4K Sports Video Graphics Pack

Included with this book is a **Sports Video Graphics Pack**, a free set of 4K graphics designed specifically for sports productions. Whether you're crafting highlight reels in post-production or spicing up your live broadcasts, these professionally designed assets can elevate your video content to new heights.

What's Inside

- **Player Spotlight Rings**: Draw attention to a specific athlete, perfect for replays and highlight reels.
- **Countdown Shot Clock**: Keep viewers informed with an on-screen countdown for basketball or other timed sports.
- **Stinger Transitions**: Add dynamic, branded transitions between replays and live camera angles.
- **Scoreboard Template**: Provide real-time score updates during live streams or post-production edits.

Download the free sports graphics pack here.

The pack includes finished video files ready for quick integration, as well as editable Adobe After Effects projects for teams that want full customization—swap in your team colors, logos or unique stylistic elements. You'll also find tutorials on using these graphics with popular live video production software like OBS and vMix, as well as detailed instructions in the companion online course on Udemy.

This picture shows one of the highlight rings video files available in the free graphics pack.

By incorporating these graphics into your highlight reels, you can add a professional look that helps your athlete stand out. With minimal time and effort, you can transform a simple clip compilation into a polished presentation—one that quickly communicates your player's identity and skills to scouts, coaches or fans.

Personal Introductions and Soft Skills Videos
Lastly, consider including a more personal, human dimension. Short interview clips or self-narrated segments allow players to talk about their goals, academic interests, leadership experiences and the values they bring to a team. Educators can help shape this content, ensuring players articulate their commitment to academic excellence and community involvement, while coaches and content creators can guide them in presenting themselves confidently and authentically.

Scouts appreciate seeing who a player is beyond their stat line. Demonstrating communication skills, humility and an understanding of team culture can give a player an extra edge over similarly skilled athletes. When it comes to scholarships or choosing a recruit who fits into a program's long-term vision, character matters just as much as talent.

By producing a range of content—highlight reels for instant impact, full-game footage for context, training clips for evidence of improvement and personal segments for character insights—players can present themselves as complete packages. Coupled with the organizational and technical support of coaches, analysts, educators and the sports video team, this multifaceted approach maximizes a player's chances of making a powerful and lasting impression on scouts.

Involving the School's Media Club, Broadcast Team or Volunteers to Ensure Quality Footage
Relying solely on a single stationary camera or an AI-driven system often limits the depth and nuance of your footage. Instead, consider tapping into existing resources. Many schools have a broadcast club or a student media team eager to gain real-world production experience. These budding videographers can handle multiple cameras, capture various angles and react dynamically to the flow of the game.

Volunteers—such as parents, alumni or even injured players looking to stay involved—can also lend a hand. With a brief training session, they can learn basic shooting techniques and positioning strategies. Over time, these contributors become part of the production ecosystem, ensuring a steady flow of high-quality, context-rich video.

Editing for Clarity and Efficiency
Good editing is about telling a cohesive story that respects both the viewer's time and the player's goals. Editors should start by organizing footage and identifying standout moments aligned with the player's strengths. Cutting out dead time, irrelevant plays and repetitive actions keeps the narrative tight and engaging. Scouts are more likely to watch an entire highlight reel if it feels purposeful and well-paced.

Subtle graphics, such as player identification, stats overlays or branded bumpers, can lend a professional touch. Keep visuals clean and unobtrusive—scouts should never struggle to see the action because of cluttered screens. Captions or simple annotations can highlight key moments, such as "Excellent passing sequence" or "Demonstrated leadership under pressure," reinforcing the narrative you want the viewer to remember.

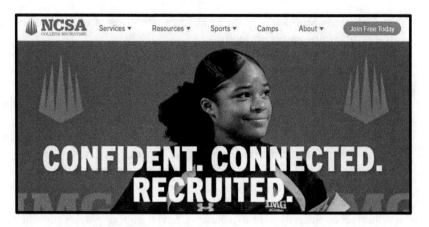

NCSA is a college sports recruiting solution.

Distribution Strategies for Maximum Visibility

Capturing and editing exceptional video content is only half the battle—making sure the right people see it is equally important. Scouts and recruiters navigate a sea of online profiles, highlight reels and social media posts in search of standout athletes. Purpose-built platforms like Hudl, widely used by teams and athletes, allow players to create polished highlight reels and share them directly with recruiters. NCSA (Next College Student Athlete) provides a comprehensive recruiting network where athletes can upload videos, manage their profiles and connect with college coaches. Similarly, BeRecruited focuses on providing a centralized space for athletes to showcase their skills and share videos with potential recruiters. FieldLevel, another recruiting platform, emphasizes collaboration between athletes, coaches and scouts to help players find the right opportunities. By choosing platforms like these, formatting content to suit various audiences and using direct outreach effectively, players and their support teams can ensure that their videos rise above the noise and reach the decision-makers who matter most.

Social Media Channels (Twitter, Instagram, YouTube, TikTok)
Modern scouting increasingly begins online, making social media a powerful tool for players. Platforms like Twitter and Instagram, with their strong sports communities, allow athletes to share short clips, training snippets and personal updates that build familiarity over time. YouTube offers a home for longer-format highlight reels and full-game footage, enabling scouts to dive deeper when something catches their eye. TikTok's brief, high-energy format can be ideal for showing off a player's speed, skill or personality in bite-sized segments.

Adapting content to each platform's strengths is key. On Twitter, a concise highlight of a crucial play paired with an engaging caption and relevant hashtags can spark interest quickly. On Instagram, well-edited Reels and Stories keep content fresh and interactive. YouTube's flexible format accommodates a player's full portfolio, from highlight compilations to "day in the life" vlogs, demonstrating dedication and growth.

Incorporating Sports Photography to Elevate Player Profiles

As you seek to showcase the multifaceted talents of your student-athletes, video often takes center stage. It's dynamic, immersive and offers a clear look at an athlete's skills in real time. However, there's another component that can make these profiles even stronger: sports photography. Beyond simply impressing college recruiters and scouts, still imagery can serve a broader range of audiences and purposes—think school newspapers, social media spotlights, personal keepsakes and promotional materials for the team.

The Versatility of Still Images

A single photo can capture an emotion or pivotal moment in a way that adds depth to an athlete's story. While highlight videos are crucial, complementary still shots are often more shareable on social media, eye-catching in a school newspaper article or ideal for printing on posters and banners. Photos deliver a quick visual hook, encouraging viewers to learn more and engage with the athlete's journey.

Extracting High-Quality Stills from Video

If you're already recording games and practices in high resolution, you have an untapped resource for compelling photography. Most video editing software allows you to export individual frames as still images. Here's how this adds value:

- **Never Miss the Moment:** Instead of relying on a single burst of photos from a dedicated camera, you can scan through your footage to pinpoint the exact split-second of a decisive play—whether it's a last-minute goal or a gravity-defying jump shot.
- **Consistent Look and Feel:** By extracting stills from the same camera that captures your video content, you ensure the images match the overall aesthetic of your highlight reels and team branding.

73

AI - Generative Fill and AI Upscaling

Editing photos has become much easier with generative fill and AI upscaling.

Leveraging AI for Generative Fill and Upscaling

Modern photo editing tools such as Adobe Photoshop, Lightroom, Topaz Photo AI and Gigapixelcan significantly enhance the overall quality and presentation of your sports photography:

1. AI Generative Fill
   - Remove background clutter or distractions in a few clicks.
   - Seamlessly fill in or extend parts of the image to highlight specific players and make each shot more engaging.
2. AI Upscaling
   - Perfect for creating large-format prints, banners or posters by enhancing resolution and clarity.
   - Retain crisp details, even when enlarging an image well beyond its original size.

These AI capabilities ensure every still image—whether destined for a social media feed, a school newspaper spread or a player's personal keepsake—looks polished and professional.

Benefits and Uses of Sports Photography

1. Social Media Engagement
   - Eye-catching photos on Instagram, Facebook or X (Twitter) quickly generate likes, shares and comments. Players, friends and family can repost and expand the team's reach.
2. School Newspaper and Yearbook Features
   - High-quality images are essential for editorial pieces,

player spotlights and end-of-season recaps. A striking photograph in the school paper can boost an athlete's presence in the local community.

3. Promotional and Branding Materials
   - Photos can enhance flyers, banners and programs for upcoming games or special events. They also provide visually appealing content for websites and newsletters.
4. Memorabilia and Personal Keepsakes
   - Families and players often cherish professional-quality action shots. These photos become lasting memories and can help build an athlete's personal brand.
5. Highlight Reels with Complementary Stills
   - Interspersing photographs within a video or adding them to thumbnails can draw attention to your highlight reels and provide a more comprehensive look at an athlete's performance.

Sports-Specific Recruiting Platforms (Hudl, NCSA, MaxPreps)
While social media can attract a broad audience, sports-specific recruiting platforms cater directly to coaches and scouts. By maintaining a polished, up-to-date profile on services like Hudl, NCSA or MaxPreps, players put their best foot forward in virtual environments designed for talent discovery. Here, recruiters can easily view integrated stats, access practice footage and compare athletes against their peers.

Coaches, analysts and educators can assist players in filling out detailed profiles—highlighting academic achievements, test scores, volunteer experiences and other personal attributes that might appeal to college programs looking for well-rounded recruits. Scouts value the efficiency of these platforms: they can filter based on position, level of competition and key performance metrics, ensuring that a well-maintained profile is never lost in the shuffle.

Direct Communication with Recruiters and Coaches
Even with well-optimized social media profiles and recruiting accounts, direct outreach still holds significant power. Sending personal emails with a brief introduction, key highlights and links to highlight reels allows players to control their narrative. Coaches and analysts can guide athletes on crafting professional, concise messages that emphasize strengths, character and fit with the target program. Including contact information for references—like a head coach or a mentor—further bolsters credibility.

Timing and follow-through matter. Sending highlight reels after a strong performance, along with a short note summarizing the player's recent improvements, can keep scouts engaged. A polite follow-up, if initial contact goes unanswered, demonstrates persistence and organization—traits that often translate well onto the field.

By strategically distributing video content across social media platforms, recruiting websites and direct communication channels, players expand their visibility and increase the likelihood of connecting with the right recruiter. Coaches, analysts, educators and content creators all have roles to play: guiding platform selection, curating content length and style and helping players present themselves professionally. With a smart distribution plan in place, the countless hours spent recording, editing and organizing video don't go to waste—they become stepping stones toward scholarships, roster spots and the next stage in a player's athletic journey.

Collaboration Unlocks the Future

Crafting player-focused video content that impresses scouts isn't a solo endeavor. It's a team effort that draws on a range of expertise, from on-field strategy to video production and academic mentorship. Sports video platforms such as Hudl are making it easier to make video accessible directly to athletes, coaches and scouts. When coaches, analysts, educators and content creators come together with a shared goal, they ensure that each athlete's footage not only looks good but also tells a compelling, well-rounded story.

Coaches: Identifying Key Moments and Providing Tactical Insights

Coaches know their players best—where they excel, where they need improvement and what moments in a game truly reflect an athlete's potential. By working closely with the video team, coaches can specify which plays deserve the spotlight. They can highlight a midfielder's improved passing accuracy, a defender's positional awareness or a forward's off-ball movement that opens space for teammates. This tactical direction ensures that every clip in a highlight reel or full-game analysis is purposeful, underscoring strengths that scouts value.

Beyond the technical side of the sport, coaches can share insights into a player's work ethic, attitude and coachability. This may seem like a lot for an already busy coach to handle, but new sports video tools are making it easier to share responsibility for accessing and creating sports video for these use cases.

Analysts: Integrating Data and Performance Metrics

Analytics add depth and credibility to a player's profile. Analysts can supplement raw footage with metrics like pass completion percentages, defensive clearances, shot accuracy or sprint speeds. Visual aids—heat maps, possession stats and comparison charts—can appear as simple, integrated graphics during key sequences.

This data-driven approach appeals to scouts who appreciate evidence that a player's impact goes beyond what the naked eye can see. Contextualizing a highlight reel with performance metrics transforms it from a "best-of" compilation into a nuanced analysis tool, showing steady improvement, reliability under pressure and the ability to influence the game in measurable ways.

Educators (Teachers, Academic Advisors): Highlighting Academic and Personal Traits

For collegiate recruiters, academic performance and personal maturity often matter just as much as athletic skill. Educators can contribute by recommending which honors, grade point averages or extracurricular activities to feature in a player's profile. They might also suggest including brief interviews where the athlete discusses balancing schoolwork with training, illustrating responsibility and time management skills.

By collaborating with educators, the video team can incorporate a player's academic achievements into their highlight package or online profile. A player who can handle rigorous coursework while excelling on the field demonstrates that they're ready for the demands of collegiate life, increasing their appeal to college programs.

The Sports Video Team: Coordinating Efforts, Maintaining Production Quality and Ensuring Timely Delivery

The sports video team plays the crucial role of orchestrating all these inputs. They listen to coaches' tactical insights, incorporate analysts' statistics and integrate educators' recommendations, all while maintaining a high standard of production quality. With clear communication channels and defined workflows, the team ensures that raw footage moves smoothly through the pipeline—from initial capture, to refinement, to final delivery.

They also manage scheduling: setting deadlines for editing, review sessions with coaches and feedback from educators or analysts. This coordinated approach helps prevent last-minute scrambles and ensures that players receive their updated highlight reels or full-game packages well before any scouting deadlines.

In a well-coordinated system, coaches sharpen the storytelling with athletic insights, analysts enrich it with data, educators elevate it with academic context and the sports video team stitches it all together into polished, professional content. Such collaboration doesn't just produce better videos—it ensures that players are presented as whole individuals, balancing athletic prowess with intellectual promise and character strengths. The result is a player profile that resonates more deeply with scouts, improving the athlete's chances of landing scholarships, roster spots and other career-advancing opportunities.

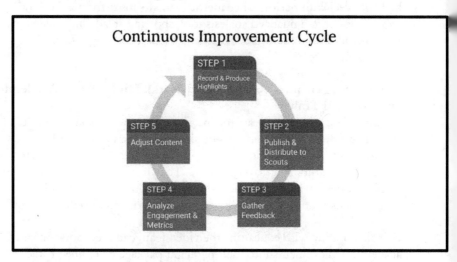

Continuous Improvement and Review

Even the most polished highlight reel or perfectly curated video profile isn't a one-time effort. Athletic performance is dynamic—players evolve, gain experience and refine their skills season after season. Similarly, the process of producing, sharing and leveraging video content for recruiting success should remain fluid and adaptable. By embracing feedback, monitoring results and adjusting strategies accordingly, players and their support teams can ensure that their content remains relevant, persuasive and aligned with their long-term goals.

Gathering Feedback from Trusted Advisors—Coaches, Mentors, Recruiters

One of the most valuable steps after sharing highlight reels and full-game footage is seeking constructive criticism. Coaches can identify areas where footage could better reflect tactical growth. Mentors and former players, who have navigated the recruiting process themselves, can offer insights on what resonated with scouts during their own experiences.

In some cases, players may receive direct or indirect feedback from recruiters. While not always possible, when a scout does share thoughts— perhaps praising certain angles, pointing out missing elements or noting that they'd like to see more defensive plays—it's an invaluable opportunity to fine-tune the approach. Incorporating this input quickly can turn a "maybe" into a "yes" down the road.

Monitoring Engagement and Interest: Views, Inquiries and Communication from Scouts

Digital platforms make it easier than ever to track engagement. By monitoring views, likes, shares, comments and direct inquiries from coaches or scouts, players and their support teams gain tangible data on what's working and what's not. For instance, if full-game footage consistently garners more interest than a sizzle reel or if certain types of plays spark conversations with recruiters, that information can guide future content decisions.

This ongoing evaluation transforms video production from guesswork into a data-driven practice. Just as analysts use performance metrics to measure on-field improvement, the video team can measure off-field success by how often scouts respond, request additional footage or invite a player for in-person evaluations.

Adjusting Content Based on What Resonates with Scouts

The sports landscape is always shifting. A year ago, a player's long-range shooting might have been their greatest strength; now, their defensive tenacity or playmaking ability might steal the show. As players mature, improve technique and maybe even change positions, their video content should reflect these developments.

If feedback suggests scouts want to see more complete matches or more evidence of leadership qualities, incorporate those elements in the next set of highlights. If the data shows that short clips on social media generate more engagement than full YouTube compilations, prioritize quick-hit, high-impact content. Flexibility and responsiveness help ensure that each new iteration of content is more aligned with recruiter expectations than the last.

Encouraging Players to Reflect on Their Growth and Update Highlights Each Season

Players shouldn't view video content as something created once and forgotten. Regular updates—each season, at the midpoint of a tournament or after a significant improvement in a key skill—keep content fresh and ensure that scouts always see the athlete's current level of performance.

Reflection is a powerful tool. By reviewing their own footage, players develop self-awareness about their strengths and areas for improvement.

They learn what scouts find compelling and can target those aspects in their training. This mindset transforms video production into a cycle of growth: athletes film, analyze, train, improve and then film again—each cycle building toward a more complete, more convincing athletic profile.

By embracing continuous improvement, players and their support teams transform video production from a static task into an evolving strategy. Through feedback, data-driven adjustments and regular content refreshes, they ensure that every highlight reel, every training montage and every full-game breakdown increasingly reflects the player's best and most relevant attributes. The result is a dynamic, ever-improving portfolio that continues to engage scouts, inching players closer to the scholarships and opportunities they've worked so hard to earn.

7 SPORTS VIDEO ESSENTIALS - LEVEL 1

When it comes to sports video, your equipment has to be ready for action and ideally easy enough for the people you have available to use. From capturing fast-paced plays on the field to delivering crystal-clear commentary, the right tools determine the quality of your stream.

Outdoor portable system.
(Tripod Warrior)

Indoor video system.
(Installed System)

This chapter will focus on easy to use technology that even kids can set up and use. The next chapter will focus on mobile systems, which I call "Tripod Warriors" which include larger tripods that are often used to capture the "birds eye view" so popular in sports video. After testing many different sports video systems, I have concluded that it's often best to simplify your technology setup so that "a kid could operate it." This is ideal, because you may often find yourself relying on untrained volunteers to operate your system. The best part about video production equipment is its versatility; the same tools used for video recording can be used for live streaming.

Four levels of live streaming gear

When it comes to live streaming sports, your setup can range from basic to advanced, depending on your needs. Here's a breakdown of the four main levels of equipment, starting from the most accessible and working up to pro-level setups.

- **Level 1**: Mobile streaming, recording, scorekeeping and automated statistics. Battery-powered, touchscreen video production switchers.
- **Level 2**: Camera systems for sports analytics and sideline replay.
- **Level 3**: Multi-camera sports video production systems. Camera operators, instant replay and iso-recordings for each camera.
- **Level 4**: Broadcast quality television production with everything you would expect in professional TV.

Gamechanger smartphone sports streaming app.

Level 1: Streaming with a Smartphone or Tablet

At the most basic level, live streaming can be done using just your smartphone or tablet. With apps like *GameChanger* and *Padcaster*, it's amazing what you can accomplish. These apps have improved so much that you can now use your phone's camera (which keeps getting better) or even add extra cameras over your network using protocols like RTSP or NDI.

How it looks:

Single camera smartphone video can look good, especially if you have graphics. This is why apps like GameChanger are so popular. Smartphones have high definition video cameras and there are plenty of mounting options to attach a phone to a fence or a tripod system. The drawback is that your viewpoint is usually limited. The further your camera is from the action the harder it is for viewers to see what's going on. Smartphones often capture a nice wide angle, but can't provide video switching or close ups.

Professional sports broadcasts have conditioned viewers to expect close ups and instant replays that are available in level 2, 3 and 4 systems.

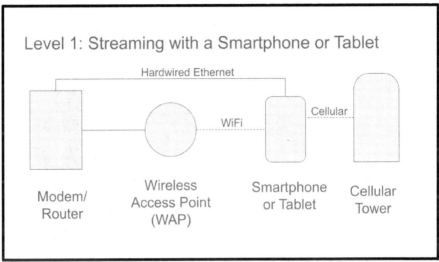

Level 1: Streaming with a Smartphone or Tablet

Hardwired Ethernet

WiFi

Cellular

Modem/ Router

Wireless Access Point (WAP)

Smartphone or Tablet

Cellular Tower

Level 1 live streaming system example.

When live streaming with a wireless device you generally have three connectivity options: WiFi, Cellular and Ethernet. Bonding is the use of multiple bandwidth sources used together to create a single more reliable connection.

The first and most common internet connection for streaming with a mobile device is WiFi. WiFi, short for Wireless Fidelity and there have been several versions of WiFi that continue to become faster and more reliable. The second option for wireless streaming is the use of cellular data, which can be less reliable but is often more widely available. 3G networks were the first to offer broadband-like speeds for mobile devices. While it can support basic streaming, it's generally too slow for high-quality live video. 4G networks offer much faster data speeds, making them suitable for HD video streaming in many areas. 4G LTE (Long-Term Evolution) is particularly effective for mobile broadcasting. The latest cellular technology, 5G offers extremely high speeds and low latency. It's capable of supporting multiple 4K streams simultaneously, making it ideal for high-quality sports broadcasts from remote locations.

Pro Tip: Test your internet speeds before attempting to live stream. If your internet connection isn't great, consider recording the game and uploading it later. This way you can record a much higher quality video.

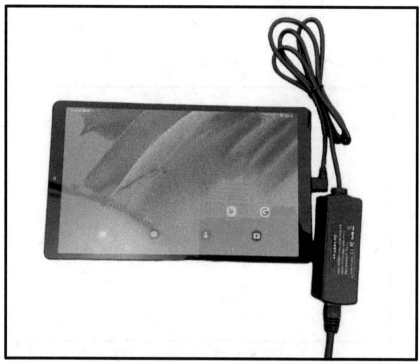

Ethernet to USB-C adapter from PoE Texas.

The third and most reliable option is to make use of hardwired ethernet connections. There are a variety of adapters that will allow smartphone devices to connect to your network switch or router through an Ethernet cable providing a reliable and robust internet connection. PoE Texas makes a USB-C to ethernet adapter I have tested that provides data and power over ethernet which is useful for streaming video during long events.

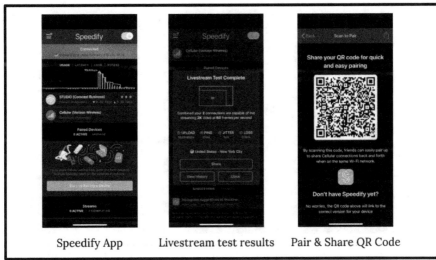

| Speedify App | Livestream test results | Pair & Share QR Code |

Speedify offers a bandwidth testing tool which provides suggestions on your live stream settings based on your available connectivity.

The most reliable option is the use of a bandwidth bonding service such as Speedify. A bandwidth bonding service is a technology which combines multiple internet connections into a single, more robust and reliable connection. This is particularly useful for live streaming, especially in situations where a single internet connection might be unreliable or insufficient. While Speedify does cost $14.99/month, it does offer a very useful tool called Pair and Share, which allows you to connect multiple phones together to leverage the shared connectivity. Pair and Share requires that each phone has the Speedify app and is connected to the same WiFi system. This is perfect for streaming a game from a field with no internet access, as long as there is WiFi. If there is no WiFi available you can use a mobile hotspot from one of the mobile phones you are using.

Smartphone Apps

The GameChanger App for live streaming, brings together team rosters, scorekeeping, live video streaming, highlight reels and athlete profiles.

GameChanger has become one of the most popular sports management apps available today. It offers integrated score-keeping and team management features that are controllable from any iOS or Android smartphone. The app continues to get better over time, offering scoreboards, custom athlete profiles and stats that you can build over the season. What makes GameChanger so convenient is that most of the core features are free for coaches to use. Once the coaches have the team roster loaded up and the game schedule in place, all the parents and players can easily login and participate. For example, one parent can help volunteer as a score keeper, another can help live stream the game.

Scorekeeping in GameChanger is easy and it allows for advanced statistics to be generated automatically.

While much of GameChanger is free to use it is a freemium app. This means that you can use the essential features for free but you'll have to pay $14.99/month for the premium features such as automated video highlight reels and player stats throughout the season. The automated video clipping leverages the scoring data you entered to know exactly where the highlights of the game are. This feature is only available after you have live streamed the game, so the system can match up the scores against the live video. This allows you to quickly post the highlights from the game for everyone to see. Live streaming on the app is a free feature and you can choose

GameChanger also allows you to grow your setup over time and add additional cameras such as those from Mevo, GoPro and PTZOptics. To live stream you can click the "Record Video" button and follow the instructions to record with your phone or an external camera that supports RTMP streaming. RTMP streaming is a standard streaming option from cameras such as the Mevo and Go Pro. This level is great for solo streamers or fans looking to produce a one-time event.

Another system I tested for "Level 1" is called the YoloBox. This small touch screen video switcher is available in several options starting at less than $1,000 USD. I consider this a "Level 1" system because it's a touch screen interface that you can put any novice in front of and they can operate the system. In the picture above, you can see the YoloBox Ultra with four HDMI video sources. In future productions, I started to use NDI video sources which connect over a single ethernet cable. This further simplifies the system for novices because you don't need to run additional HDMI cables for each camera.

The YoloBox scoreboard system is easy to customize and operate with the touch screen interface.

The YoloBox combines video recording, live streaming and instant replay into one simple to use touch screen system. The device has a built-in battery which I noticed can last for most sports events. The built-in scoreboard is a key feature sports broadcasters enjoy, because it's easy to customize the styling and operate the score live with a few taps on the screen.

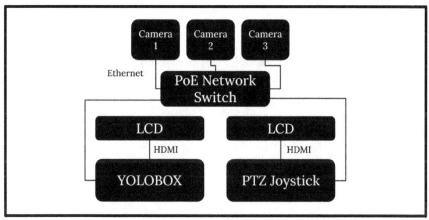

Simple 3 camera YoloBox and PTZ camera system.

The diagram above shows a simple power over ethernet (PoE) network switch being used to connect together a YoloBox, three PTZ cameras and a PTZ joystick controller. This is probably one of the easiest ways to set up multiple cameras for sports video and manage it all from a central location. This system can be operated by a single experienced person or more realistically managed by two dedicated people.

A young volunteer operates a PTZOptics SuperJoy Controller, while another volunteer operates the YoloBox.

From a camera placement perspective, I like to have one "tactical" camera in the center and one camera behind each goal on tall tripods. One person can be focused on following the play left and right while the other person can be focused on video switching and triggering instant replays. You can see that one LCD monitor is provided for each person to get a nice view of the action from the remote broadcasting location.

The YoloBox instant replay is very easy to use and really adds to the production quality. All you need to do is enable instant replay, choose the playback length and the speed. Once it's enabled you can simply click the "Replay" button in the top right corner and the replays will start to play. I tested this for Hockey and ended up choosing a five second replay that plays back at 50% speed. When choosing instant replay settings, you have to determine how quickly the game will start after a goal is scored. If you playback five seconds at 50% speed, it will take 10 seconds to play out. If you set up your YoloBox to play back two cameras it will then take 20 seconds total. In most sports, the teams are ready to start again in 20-30 seconds, so you have to consider this during instant replay playbacks. If you are using the YoloBox and the game resumes during the instant replay playback, you can always click a live video source to jump back to a live camera.

Pro Tip: Included in our Sports Graphics pack, are "instant replay" intro and outro video clips. You can set these up to play before and after your instant replays to give your production a more professional look.

Another reason the YoloBox is a "Level 1" video system is that it uses a simple SD card to record the video. This is ideal for transferring video to a computer for posting online or editing a highlight reel. I put the YoloBox in front of an 11-year-old volunteer, during a fast-paced hockey match and he was able to keep up with the video switching. With many other computer based solutions, including Open Broadcaster Software (OBS), more training is often necessary.

OBS is free software often used for recording and live streaming video.

Still, OBS is probably the most popular free video switching software in the world. While OBS isn't as easy to use as the YoloBox, it's free and you can install it on any Windows or Mac computer. You can make OBS easier to use by purchasing a StreamDeck which is a small USB connected keypad that you can use to program shortcuts for simple actions such as adding to the scoreboard or switching cameras.

Watch this tutorial on using OBS for Sports.

OBS is free open source software, so to add some of the functionality you might need for sports, you can install plug-ins and integrate hardware to expand what you can do. For example, to add instant replay, you can purchase a Roland P-20HD with a capture card and connect it to your computer as an input into OBS. You can also integrate PTZ cameras into OBS and control them to follow the action in sports. This can be done with a USB connection or via NDI, just like the YoloBox.

Check out the OBS SuperUser Guidebook.

In the video tutorial above, you can learn how to integrate sports graphics, PTZ camera controls and instant replay into OBS. OBS is a very flexible software and therefore, it can be used as a "Level 1" solution allowing you to take an existing computer and record and/or live stream sports. Because it's so flexible, it can also become more complicated and accommodate new workflows as you grow. If you decide to use OBS for your sports productions, I highly recommend reading another book I have published called *The OBS SuperUser Guidebook*.

In the next chapter, you'll learn about what I call the "Tripod Warrior" system which expands upon these simple level 1 systems and incorporates essential gear such as large tripods and the ability to control cameras remotely. While these systems do require more preparation, the video quality that you'll come away with will be superior in many ways.

8 PORTABLE SPORTS VIDEO SYSTEMS

Recording sports video in the field requires a portable, easy-to-use system that can be operated by a single person. Introducing the "Tripod Warriors" series, an example lineup of four mobile sports video systems designed for every level of production. Each system centers around a tall tripod setup that places the camera above players' and coaches' heads at 15 feet, ensuring a clear viewpoint. Whether you're a beginner or a seasoned videographer, there's a Tripod Warrior system for you.

Level 1: The Quick & Easy Tripod Warrior

Budget: $1,324 to $1,499

There are several entry level AI-camera systems that can be mounted on top of a tripod for recording and live streaming sports. VEO and Trace are two of the most popular. These easy to use cameras come with a subscription, but offer a complete cloud platform that makes it easy to share access with your team.

Key Components:

Product	Price
Camera: VEO Camera System	$1,299/year
Subscription: VEO platform. 1 Team, 30 users, 40 hours of recording per month.	Included
Tripod: A tall tripod/light stand (prices vary based on size)	$65-349
Total	**$1,364** to **$1,648**

How It Works:

The VEO camera is mounted atop a tall tripod, providing a clear vantage point above players and coaches. Using its dual-lens design and AI capabilities, the camera automatically tracks the ball and action throughout the game. After the match, recordings are uploaded to the VEO platform, where users can review, analyze and share game footage.

To set up, you only need to secure the camera to the tripod, connect it to a power source or portable power bank and ensure a stable internet connection for uploading the footage. The entire system is operated via the VEO mobile app, allowing you to start and stop recording with ease.

Advantages:

- **Fully Automated**: No camera operator required; the AI does all the work.
- **Portable and Easy Setup**: Lightweight and compact for easy transportation and quick assembly.
- **Professional Quality**: Captures games in high resolution with seamless ball and player tracking.
- **Cloud-Based Analysis**: Access the VEO platform for post-game review, highlight creation and team sharing.

- **Low Barrier to Entry**: Perfect for teams or individuals new to sports video production.

Tips:

- For improved portability, invest in a high-capacity power bank (like the Explorer 300 or larger from Jackery) to avoid relying on field-side electrical outlets.
- Use the VEO platform's analytics tools to generate highlight reels and focus on key gameplay moments.

The VEO Camera System is ideal for those looking for a turnkey, hassle-free solution that delivers high-quality video recordings and a straightforward workflow, all at a competitive price point.

Level 2: The Essential Tripod Warrior

Budget: $1,300 to $1,700

This entry-level system combines affordability and functionality, making it ideal for those just starting with sports video production who do not want to pay a monthly subscription. The 12X PTZ camera is ideal for tracking most sports up and down the field using a simple and affordable Xbox controller. OBS is a free software for recording the video and it can easily be used for live streaming or adding additional cameras in the future as needed.

Key Components:

Product	Price
Camera: PTZOptics Move SE 12X	$999
Recording Software: OBS (Open Broadcaster Software)	Free
Computer: Mac or PC computer (i5 or better recommended for 1080p)	Existing

Tripod: 13' to 26' tall for elevated views	$65-349
Accessory 1: Heavy-duty tray for Tripod stands. This is used as a computer stand.	$45
Accessory 2: PoE network switch. This is used to power the camera and connect the computer.	$60
Accessory 3: Power Station. If you do not have access to power you can get a battery with AC electrical outlets to power the PoE switch and your computer.	$130-250+
Controller: USB Xbox controller connected to a laptop with PTZOptics Software.	$40
Cables: (1) 12' ethernet cable and (1) 6' ethernet cable.	$30
Total	**$1,369** to **$1,653**

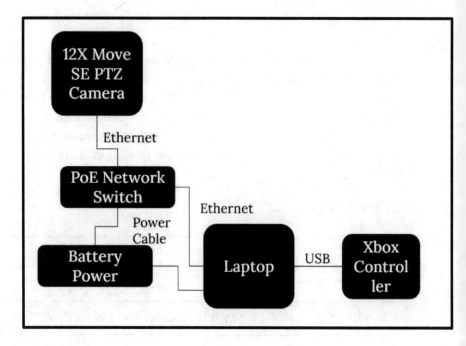

How It Works:

The 12X PTZ camera is mounted atop the tripod and connected to a simple PoE network switch. A laptop running OBS, a free video recording and live streaming software, is also connected to the same network switch. The Move SE camera supports NDI and can be connected to OSB with NDI (with the NDI plugin installed). OBS not only records high-quality video but you can use a plugin to display a scoreboard feature you can overlay on your recordings. This is especially helpful during post-game analysis, as you can quickly locate scoring moments by scrubbing through the timeline. If you want to create a highlight reel for the players, scrubbing through your videos based on the score is an effective way to edit the video.

PTZOptics offers a plugin for OBS which allows you to control the camera with an XBox controller connected to the computer via USB. The camera should have an IP address which you'll enter into the OSB plugin. An IP address is like a street address telling the software which camera you want to control over your network.

Tip: If you would like to include audio from the gameplay you can connect a line-level shotgun microphone (perhaps through a small mixer or adapter to become line-level) to the camera's 3.5mm audio input.

Tip 2: Using PTZOptics Hive, you can actually have someone else control the camera movements.

Level 3: The Advanced Tripod Warrior

Budget: $2,740 to **$3,024**

For advanced sports video production, the Level 3 system takes it to the next level with multi-camera capabilities and enhanced functionality.

Key Components:

Product	Price
Camera: Two cameras. Move SE 12X and wide angle HuddleCamHD Pro IP	$1,298

Recording System: YoloBox Pro (or better) laptop	$999
Tripod: A tall tripod (prices vary based on size)	$65-349
Accessory 1: Heavy-duty tray for Tripod stands. This is used as a computer stand.	$45
Accessory 2: PoE network switch. This is used to power the camera and connect the computer.	$60
Accessory 3: Power Station. If you do not have access to power you can get a battery with AC electrical outlets to power the PoE switch and your computer.	$130
Accessory 4: ¼-20 Camera Clamp. Used to connect the Atomos ZATO to your tripod.	$18
Cables: (3) 12' ethernet cables	$25
Total	**$2,029** to **$2,923**

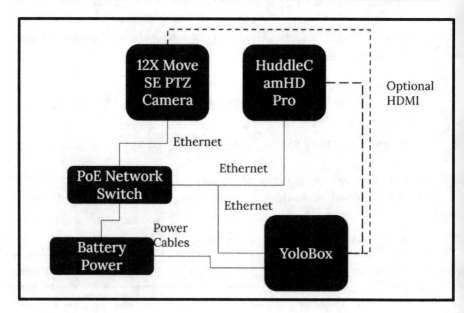

How It Works:

This system supports two cameras mounted on a single tripod, providing multiple angles for comprehensive coverage. The YoloBox serves as both the recording device and the PTZ controller. It accepts video feeds via HDMI or NDI and its built-in touch screen offers intuitive controls for scoreboards, instant replay and multi-camera management. If you have a wireless router you can use your smartphone for scorekeeping.

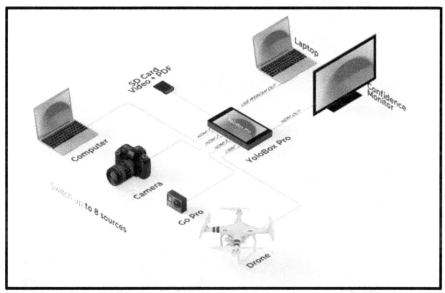

YoloBox Ultra used to record four HDMI video sources in 4K.

For those looking to take their sports video production to the next level, the YoloBox Ultra is a game-changer. This compact, all-in-one device is specifically designed for managing multi-camera sports streaming setups. Compared to using a laptop or computer, the Director Mini also offers several key advantages that make it my top recommendation for advanced setups.

Advantages:

- **Multi-Camera Capability**: Captures multiple angles seamlessly.
- **Advanced Features**: Includes scoreboards and instant replay functionality.
- **Integrated Solution**: Combines recording, control and playback in one device.

- **Tripod-Friendly Design**: Its small size and lightweight build make it easy to attach directly to your tripod, keeping everything compact and organized.
- **Battery Power**: Two NP-F Hot-Swappable Batteries.
- **Telestration Tools for Analysis**: The ability to draw on the screen during live broadcasts or replays.
- **Expandable**: Easily add an additional camera to your system by connecting it to your network switch. To capture a new angle all you need is a camera and an Ethernet cable.

The YoloBox Ultra is more than just a recording device—it's a complete solution for professional sports streaming. Its combination of portability, ease of use and advanced features makes it the ideal choice for anyone looking to elevate their production quality without the complexity of a traditional computer-based setup. If you're building a Level 3 "Tripod Warrior" system, the YoloBox is an investment that will pay off in performance, reliability and professional-grade results.

Level 4: The Advanced Tripod Warrior with SkyCoach

Budget: $3,733

For teams looking to combine professional video production with advanced coaching tools, the Level 4 Tripod Warrior system is an exceptional choice. This design integrates **SkyCoach**, a cutting-edge solution tailored for sports analysis and live review, allowing coaches to access video replays wirelessly while capturing multiple camera angles.

Key Components:

Product	Price
Camera: (1) PTZOptics Move SE 12X and (1) 20X	$2,098
Recording Software: SkyCoach 2 Camera Systems	$1,595/yr
Tablets: Provide your own wireless tablets for coaches	Existing
Tripod: Tripods are included with MySkyCoach Kit.	Included
Accessories: Accessories are included with the MySkyCoach Kit.	Included
Controller: USB Xbox controller connected to a laptop with PTZOptics Software. A wireless iOS app is also available.	$40
Cables: Cables are included in the SkyCoach Kit.	Included
Total	**$3,733**

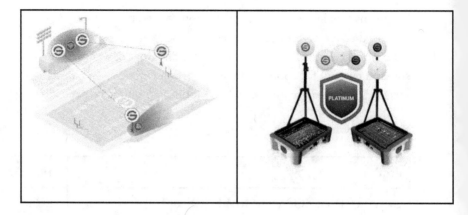

Why Choose SkyCoach?

SkyCoach brings a new dimension to sports video production by combining **live video capture**, **instant replay** and **wireless access for coaches**. It supports two camera inputs, allowing for versatile setups that provide comprehensive coverage of the field or court.

- **Wireless Access for Coaches**: Coaches can review live footage or instant replays from any location using tablets or smartphones connected to SkyCoach's wireless system.
- **Two-Angle Replays**: The system allows for seamless review of plays from two perspectives, offering a strategic advantage during games or practices.

The Two-Camera Setup

The Level 4 design features a two-camera configuration to maximize coverage and flexibility:

1. PTZ Camera on the Tripod

- **Position**: Typically placed at the 50-yard line or a central location on the sideline.

- **Purpose**: Provides dynamic coverage of the action with zoom and pan capabilities.
- **Connection**: The PTZOptics camera connects to the SkyCoach system via HDMI.
- **Control**: Operated using a **serial joystick controller**, enabling smooth pan, tilt and zoom movements for precise framing and tracking of plays.

2. Secondary Camera

- **Options**:
  - Mounted in the **end zone** for a unique perspective on goal-line plays.
  - Positioned in the **press box** to capture a wide-angle view of the entire field.
- **Connection**: Also linked to SkyCoach via HDMI.
- **Purpose**: This static camera ensures continuous coverage and complements the PTZ camera by providing a stable, overarching view.

Key Features of the SkyCoach System

1. Instant Replay from Multiple Angles

SkyCoach's built-in instant replay functionality allows coaches to view critical moments from two angles simultaneously. This feature is invaluable for:

- **Real-Time Analysis**: Evaluate plays as they happen, enabling quick adjustments.
- **Player Feedback**: Show athletes what went right—or wrong— immediately after a play.

2. Wireless Video Access

One of SkyCoach's standout features is its ability to stream video wirelessly to connected devices.

- **Coach Convenience**: Coaches can watch replays or live footage on their tablets or phones without being tethered to the system.
- **Collaboration**: Multiple team members can access the video feed simultaneously, fostering collaboration and in-depth analysis.

Kansas State versus middle Tennessee women's basketball game in St Joseph Missouri.

3. Seamless Integration with PTZ Cameras

The SkyCoach system pairs perfectly with PTZOptics cameras, leveraging their zoom and pan capabilities for dynamic, professional-grade footage. The joystick controller ensures precise control over the PTZ camera's movements, enabling operators to follow the action smoothly.

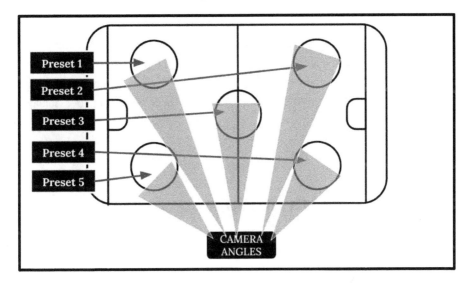

PTZ presets are a feature of PTZ cameras which are used to recall specific positions. To use this feature, you can steer a PTZ camera to a specific location such as a faceoff area on a hockey rink. Once you have arrived at the specific location, you can save the preset. These presets can then be recalled at any time to quickly move your PTZ camera to that location. Depending on the sport you are working with you, you may be able to make great use out of PTZ presets to quickly capture closeups. Having a plan and a map like the image shown above can greatly increase your PTZ camera operators efficiency during fast paced games.

Advantages of the Level 4 Design

1. **Comprehensive Field Coverage**: The combination of a PTZ camera and a secondary static (non-moving) camera ensures every angle is captured, from the wide field overview to zoomed-in, detailed shots.

2. **Wireless Access for Flexibility**: Coaches and staff can analyze footage on the go, whether they're on the sidelines or in the locker room.

3. **Dual-Purpose System**: While ideal for coaching analysis, the system's professional-grade video capabilities also make it suitable for live streaming games or creating highlight reels.

4. **Simple Setup**: SkyCoach's user-friendly interface and the ability to connect two cameras streamline the production process, allowing operators to focus on the game.

Practical Applications

Game-Day Advantage

Place one camera at the end zone and another on the sideline to capture the game's most critical angles. With SkyCoach's wireless functionality, coaches can adjust strategies in real-time based on replay feedback.

Practice Sessions

Use the system during practices to analyze player performance from multiple perspectives. Coaches can provide immediate, visual feedback to help players refine their techniques.

Versatility Across Sports

This setup isn't limited to football—it's ideal for any sport requiring multi-angle video analysis, such as soccer, basketball or lacrosse.

The Level 4 Tripod Warrior system with SkyCoach's combination of multi-camera functionality, instant replay and wireless accessibility offers unmatched value for teams seeking a competitive edge. Whether you're a coach analyzing plays or a videographer capturing game-day action, this setup provides the tools you need to succeed.

9 Sports Video Essentials - Level 2 - Sports Analytics

As sports production technology advances, level 2 focuses on sports analytics systems, which are designed to provide detailed performance analysis, game reviews and team presentations. This level leverages fixed cameras, typically high-resolution 4K cameras, positioned strategically around the playing field. These cameras capture wide-angle views ideal for analytics platforms that offer video breakdowns, annotations and player tracking.

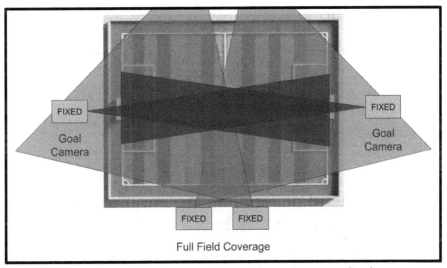

Full Field Coverage

Most sports analytics systems use a single wide-angle or two fixed camera angles to capture the full playing space.

In today's world of sports, data is as valuable as the game itself. Coaches, teams and analysts are increasingly relying on advanced sports analytics to gain insights into player performance, tactics and game strategies. One of the most powerful sources of data comes from video recordings, which provide an invaluable visual record of every movement on the field, court or track. When integrated with score keeping and play tagging, sports analytics can offer a deeper level of insight that traditional statistics cannot provide.

Cameras with an operator that move and follow players are still valuable to sports analytics systems and teams will often upload video from their broadcast/streaming system to their video analytics platform. For example, some teams like to have a PTZ camera following a specific key player. Other times teams like to have a single camera follow the action back and forth down a field.

Here are some example camera viewing angles used for sports analytics:

Breaking down sports analytics by camera angle is a great approach. Different angles provide unique perspectives that coaches can use for tactical analysis, player performance evaluation and game strategy development. Here's how you could structure it in your book:

1. Tactical (Wide) Angle

Primary Use: Team formation, tactical shape and overall gameplay structure.
Best For: Soccer, football, basketball, hockey, lacrosse.

- **Position:** High, centered view from the press box or elevated platform. Often cameras are on tripods or mounts at least 12' high.
- **Tip:** Using two cameras, one for each side of the playing area, often gives a higher level of detail. Video from static cameras are easier to use with telestration tools in most cases.
- **Key Metrics Captured:**
  - Team formation and spacing.
  - Tactical adjustments.
  - Player runs and passing lanes.

2. Sideline (Lateral) Angle

Primary Use: Play development, player tracking, sideline coaching reviews.
Best For: Football, soccer, lacrosse, track and field.

- **Position:** Near the field's sideline, parallel to the main play area. Often cameras are on tripods or mounts at least 12' high.
- **Key Metrics Captured:**
  - Player acceleration and movement.
  - Coaching interaction during timeouts.
  - Substitutions and tactical play adjustments.

3. End Zone (Goal/Behind-the-Net) Angle

Primary Use: Scoring analysis, defensive setups, goalkeeper performance.
Best For: Soccer, football, hockey, basketball.

- **Position:** Behind the goal or baseline.
- **Key Metrics Captured:**

- Goalkeeper/defender reactions.
- Offensive set plays.
- Scoring opportunities from different angles.

This PTZOptics Studio 4K camera is set up behind the goal of a hockey net.

4. Close-Up (Tight) Action Angle

Primary Use: Player technique, ball control, injury evaluation. Great for a camera specifically zoomed in for the goalie.
Best For: Baseball, tennis, soccer, basketball, golf (any sports with goal areas).

- **Position:** Above heads at field level, courtside or near the action zone.
- **Key Metrics Captured:**
  - Player technique and mechanics.
  - Ball/puck tracking.
  - High-detail review for slow-motion playback.

5. Overhead (Bird's-Eye) Angle

Primary Use: Positional awareness, full-field tracking and formations.
Best For: Indoor sports like basketball, volleyball and futsal.

- **Position:** Mounted on rafters or drones (if allowed).
- **Key Metrics Captured:**

- Player positioning and rotation.
- Team movements in dynamic play.
- Tactical strategy analysis.

6. Referee/Official View (Optional/Advanced)

Primary Use: For officiating reviews, addressing controversial calls and implementing systems similar to Video Assistant Referee (VAR) for accurate decision-making.

Best For:
High-level sports leagues and tournaments with access to advanced equipment. Examples include the FIFA World Cup, UEFA Champions League and other professional leagues.

Position:

- **Body Cameras on Referees:** Capture real-time footage from the referee's perspective, aiding post-game reviews and analysis.
- **Fixed Cameras in Key Zones:** Strategically placed near goal lines, penalty boxes and other critical areas for comprehensive coverage.

How Camera Angles Affect the Analysis Process

By selecting the right camera angles, coaches can gain better insights into their team's performance, spot tactical issues and enhance game preparation through comprehensive video analysis.

Pro Tip: Always opt for tall tripods when setting up your cameras, ensuring they can extend high enough to stay above the crowd's line of sight. It's a common rookie mistake to set up your cameras thinking you've got the perfect angle, only to have your view obstructed when fans fill the stands. Plan ahead to keep your shots clear and professional!

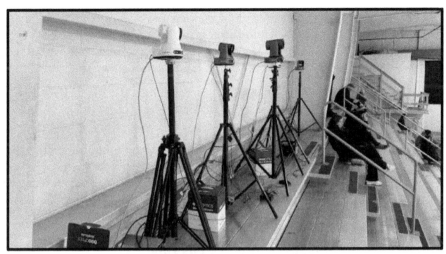

PTZ cameras set up out of the way of fans.

Camera Angle	Impact on Analysis
Wide Sideline View	Best for tactical and full-team analysis.
End Zone View	Highlights defensive structure and depth.
Corner View	Adds depth and situational awareness.
Close-Up View	Shows technical skill and player actions.

Understanding Field of View and Camera Distances for Sports Capture

When setting up cameras for sports capture, understanding the relationship between **field of view (FOV)**, **camera distance** and **image detail** is crucial. Here's a breakdown to help guide camera placement and system design.

Field of View (FOV) Explained

- **FOV** refers to the width of the area a camera can capture. A wider FOV means the camera can see more of the field but at a lower level of detail.
- **Camera Distance Impact:**
    - Moving the camera **closer** to the action **reduces FOV** but **increases detail** and **pixel density** (fewer pixels are

111

spread over the viewing area).

o Moving the camera **farther away increases FOV**, capturing a larger portion of the field but **reduces detail** since more area is captured using the same number of pixels.

Example:

- A soccer field captured from the sideline at midfield with a 4K camera might clearly show player movements.
- The same camera placed farther away from the field will capture the whole field, but individual players will appear smaller and less detailed.

Best Practice for Camera Placement

- **Wider Field Coverage:** Place the camera far enough to cover the entire playing area but close enough to maintain acceptable player visibility.
- **Optimal Pixel Density:** Consider the **intended use case:**
  o For **sports analytics**, focus on **full-field coverage** and **team formations**.
  o For **highlights** or **close-up action**, use a secondary camera with a narrower FOV.

How Optical Zoom Works

Optical Zoom uses the camera's lens to adjust the focal length, magnifying the image without reducing quality. This is **ideal for close-up views** when the camera is positioned far from the action.

- **Example Use Case:**
  o A PTZOptics camera with **30x optical zoom** can zoom in from the sideline to clearly see the goalie in a soccer match, maintaining high image quality.

Key Recommendations

1. **Full-Field Coverage**: Use fixed wide-angle 4K cameras at calculated distances for comprehensive coverage.
2. **Close-Up Shots**: Add a PTZ camera with high optical zoom for dynamic, detailed shots of key areas like goals, benches or scoring plays.
3. **Avoid Digital Zoom**: Digital zoom reduces quality by stretching

pixels, so rely on optical zoom for critical shots.

Nacsport integrates with live cameras and provides data analytics and presentation tools for coaching.

System Components:

1. **Cameras:** Typically two fixed 4K cameras with wide-angle lenses.
2. **Mounting Hardware:** Pole or tripod mounts near the sidelines, positioned according to calculated distances for optimal coverage.
3. **Analytics Platform:** Software for live recording, data processing, annotation and playback.
4. **Network Connection:** A stable wired or wireless network for data uploads if cloud processing is required.

When to Use This Setup:

Level 2 sports analytics systems are ideal for high school, college and professional teams focused on improving performance and game strategy. This setup can also serve dual purposes by integrating live streaming and video production for fans when paired with additional PTZ cameras or video switchers.

Challenges and Considerations

While integrating video into sports analytics offers numerous benefits, there are some challenges to consider. First, the quality of the video is essential for accurate analysis. High-resolution footage is necessary for tracking fine details such as ball movement or player positioning. Additionally, processing large volumes of video data requires significant computational power and storage.

What Is Pixels Per Foot (PPF)?

Pixels Per Foot (PPF) measures how many pixels fit into one inch of a video image.

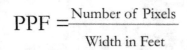

$$PPF = \frac{\text{Number of Pixels}}{\text{Width in Feet}}$$

Higher PPF = **Sharper, more detailed image**

Lower PPF = **Blurry, less detailed image**

Understanding Pixels per Foot (PPF) in Sports Video Analytics

When you watch a sports game on TV or online, you're actually seeing a grid of tiny dots called pixels. The more pixels there are in each inch of the video, the more detailed the image looks. This measurement is called Pixels per Foot or Pixels per Meter (PPF/PPM). For sports video, PPF/PPM tells us how clearly we can see important things like the ball, players and even the lines on the field.

Standards for Pixels per Foot / Pixel per Meter (PPF/PPM)

Use Case	PPF	PPM	Why It Matters
General Viewing	10-20 PPF	30-70 PPM	For wide field views (players visible but not detailed).
Broadcast TV	30-40 PPF	100-130 PPM	Clear enough for live broadcasts.
Sports Analytics (Players)	40-60 PPF	130-200 PPM	Recognize players and track movements accurately.
Sports Analytics (Ball)	60+ PPF	200+ PPM	Clearly track balls and small objects.

Facial Recognition (Ref/Coach)	75+ PPF	250+ PPM	Identify faces, read lips or track small hand gestures.

In sports video analytics, PPF or PPM is a crucial measure that determines how much detail a camera captures on the field. The higher the pixel count, the more detailed and clearer the video will be. This concept directly affects how well players, balls and even referee signals can be tracked during a game. Let's explore how this works using examples from a standard soccer field.

Imagine using a 1080p camera to cover a soccer field that is 225 feet wide. With this setup, each foot of the field only gets about 8.5 pixels. This means players appear as blurry figures and the ball might be nearly impossible to see, especially during fast gameplay. For live streaming or general viewing, this might be acceptable, but for detailed coaching reviews or sports analytics, it falls far short of what's needed.

Let's use the standard soccer field width of 225 feet and calculate PPF (Pixels per Foot) for both 1080p and 4K cameras.

Example 1 - Soccer Field

Field Width: 225 ft
Camera Resolution: 1080p (1920 width) vs 4K (3840 width)

PPF Calculation

$$PPF = \frac{1920}{225} \approx 8.35 \text{ PPF}$$

Zoom Camera In: If the camera covers only 60 yards (180 feet = 2,160 inches):

$$PPF = \frac{3840}{225} \approx 17 \text{ PPF}$$

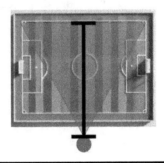

What These Calculations Mean:

1. **8.53 PPF (1080p):**
   - Too low for tracking small objects like the soccer ball.
   - Good for general field overview but not for detailed player analysis.
2. **17.07 PPF (4K):**

- ○ Better for streaming and gameplay review.
- ○ Still too low for precise ball tracking or facial recognition.

Switching to a **4K camera**, which has double the horizontal resolution of 1080p, improves the PPF to **17 pixels per foot** on the same field. While this is better, players are still not clearly defined and the ball can be difficult to track during long passes. This setup works well for streaming games to an audience but still lacks the precision required for professional sports analysis.

Example 2 - Zooming In

Field Width: 225 ft
Camera Resolution: 1080p (1920 width) vs 4K (3840 width)

PPF Calculation

$$PPF = \frac{1920}{100} \approx 19.2 \text{ PPF}$$

Zoom Camera In: If the camera covers only 60 yards (180 feet = 2,160 inches):

$$PPF = \frac{3840}{100} \approx 38.4 \text{ PPF}$$

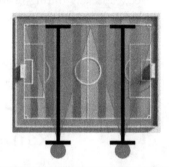

To capture more detail, consider moving the camera closer or zooming in on the action. If the camera only covers 100 feet of the field instead of the full 225 feet, the PPF improves dramatically. With a 1080p camera, the PPF jumps to 19 pixels per foot, making players easier to recognize and team formations clearer. Using a 4K camera in the same setup results in 38 pixels per foot, enough to see the ball clearly, track individual player movements and even detect referee gestures. While this limits the area you are covering, you can simply add more cameras to increase your coverage.

Example 3 - Goal Camera

Goal Width: 24 feet + 10 feet (extra space)
Camera Resolution: 1080p (1920 width) vs 4K (3840 width)

PPF Calculation

$$PPF = \frac{1920}{34} \approx 56\ PPF$$

Zoom Camera In: If the camera covers only 60 yards (180 feet = 2,160 inches):

$$PPF = \frac{3840}{34} \approx 112\ PPF$$

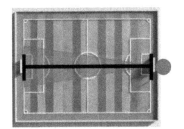

For specific areas of interest, such as a goal, you may want to use a camera with optical zoom to capture that area from a far distance away. For example, a PTZOptics 20X optical zoom camera can capture a 27' wide space from 390 feet away (the width of a standard soccer field). Using a camera with optical zoom can greatly improve your picture quality for sports analytics.

These examples show why PPF/PPM matters in sports production. For live streaming, a lower PPF/PPM might be acceptable, especially if the goal is simply to show the game to fans. However, for sports analytics, coaching reviews or broadcasting, a higher PPF/PPM is essential to ensure that every critical moment is captured in clear detail. This makes decisions like camera placement, resolution and field coverage critical when designing a sports video production system.

Signs That Your PPF/PPM Is Too Low

You may have a PPF/PPM that is too low if:

- Players appear blurry or hard to distinguish, especially when far from the camera.
- The ball is difficult to track, particularly during fast movements or long passes.
- Details like referee gestures or jersey numbers are unclear.
- The image looks pixelated or distorted during zoomed-in replays.

Options for Increasing PPF/PPM

If you notice these telltale signs, consider the following options to increase

PPF:

- Upgrade to a 4K Camera:
  - A 4K camera has twice the resolution of a 1080p camera, meaning more pixels cover the same field width. This instantly doubles the PPF, improving clarity for both players and ball tracking.
- Move the Camera Closer to the Field:
  - Reducing the field width captured by the camera increases PPF because the same number of pixels covers a smaller area.
  - Trade-off: Moving the camera closer reduces the overall field of view, meaning the camera can't capture the entire field.
- Use Optical Zoom:
  - Optical zoom allows you to magnify the field without losing resolution. This increases PPF by effectively "zooming in" on the action while keeping the original resolution intact.
  - Trade-off: Like moving the camera closer, this narrows the field of view, requiring additional cameras to cover the entire field.
- Add Dedicated Cameras for Critical Areas:
  - In high-value areas like goal zones, free-throw lines or key player positions, set up dedicated cameras with a narrow field of view and high PPF/PPM.
  - This setup is common in professional broadcasts where ball-tracking and player stats are essential.

Improving PPF/PPM comes with trade-offs. While upgrading to 4K cameras improves detail without sacrificing coverage, moving cameras closer or using optical zoom increases PPF/PPM but reduces the field of view. To balance this, consider using multiple cameras, including wide-angle views for the whole field and high-PPF cameras zoomed into critical areas like goals, free-throw lines or center court. This ensures optimal detail where it matters most while still capturing the overall game.

The Future of Video-Driven Sports Analytics

Looking ahead, the future of sports analytics is deeply intertwined with broadcast video technology. With the rise of AI, 4K/8K video and augmented reality, the level of detail available for analysis will only increase. We can expect to see more real-time analytics during live broadcasts, offering coaches and fans unprecedented insights into the game as it unfolds.

For broadcasters, this represents a new opportunity as well. By leveraging their video feeds as data sources, they can provide value not just for entertainment but also for enhancing the performance of athletes and teams. This blend of technology, sports and data will continue to reshape how we understand and interact with sports on every level.

10 FUNDAMENTALS OF LIVE-STREAMING

Live streaming has become an essential component of modern sports production, allowing fans worldwide to engage with their favorite teams and events in real time. Successfully live streaming a sports event involves understanding the various streaming methods, technical requirements and best practices to ensure a seamless and engaging viewer experience. This section delves into the different ways to live stream, the technical aspects of RTMP streaming and internet connectivity and practical tips to enhance your live broadcast.

Methods of Live Streaming

There are primarily three approaches to live streaming sports events: using a computer with streaming software, employing a hardware-based video switcher or using the cloud. Each method has its advantages and is suited to different production scales and requirements.

Computer-Based Streaming with Software

Overview: Using a computer with streaming software is a versatile and cost-effective method suitable for smaller productions or those just starting with live streaming.

OBS is one of the most popular free live streaming software solutions.

Pro Tip: The Sports Video online course includes a video tutorial on how to use OBS for sports streaming. To learn more, check out my book, *The*

OBS Superuser Guidebook.

Key Components:

- **Streaming Software:** Applications like OBS Studio, Wirecast or vMix allow you to manage multiple video sources, add overlays and control the broadcast.
- **Capture Devices:** Capture cards are used to convert an HDMI or SDI video signal into a USB connection you can easily connect to a computer running the software. Once connected, you can bring the video from a hardware video switcher or specific camera into your live streaming software just like a webcam.
- **Computer Specifications:** A robust computer with sufficient processing power, memory and graphics capabilities is essential to handle real-time video encoding and streaming. Depending on the amount of cameras and capabilities you require, an i7 processor or better computer is a good place to start.

Advantages:

- **Flexibility:** Easily customizable with various plug-ins and integrations. You can use your computer to live stream or simply record and edit your video after the game.
- **Cost-Effective:** Lower initial investment compared to hardware switchers. You can use a computer you already have and in this book you'll learn how to use IP-based cameras that don't require expensive capture cards and video extension systems.
- **Ease of Use:** Everyone knows how to use a computer. It's easy to navigate to YouTube, retrieve your RTMP server URL and stream key and enter that into your live streaming software.

Best For:

- Small to medium-sized events.
- Productions with limited budgets.
- Teams comfortable with software configurations.

Hardware-Based Video Switchers

Overview: Hardware-based video switchers provide a more streamlined and reliable solution for live streaming, particularly suited for larger productions with multiple video sources.

Key Components:

- **Video Switcher:** Devices like the Blackmagic Design ATEM series or Roland V-1HD allow for real-time switching between multiple camera feeds.
- **External Encoders:** Dedicated hardware encoders handle the encoding process, ensuring high-quality streams with minimal latency.
- **Professional Cameras and Accessories:** High-end cameras, microphones and lighting equipment enhance production quality.

Advantages:

- **Reliability:** Hardware switchers offer stable performance with less risk of software crashes or glitches.
- **Professional Quality:** Enhanced video and audio quality with dedicated processing hardware.
- **Efficiency:** Faster switching and smoother transitions between camera feeds.

Best For:

- Large-scale events and professional productions.
- Production that requires high reliability and minimal downtime.
- Teams with the budget for specialized equipment.

Pro Tip: You can use a video switcher with an HDMI or SDI capture card and bring the video output into a computer to add graphics, overlays and live stream to your preferred destination. Using a hardware switcher takes much of the video processing requirements off your computer and mixes everything down into one easy to handle video input for your computer to work with.

Cloud-Based Streaming

Overview:
Cloud-based streaming leverages internet-based platforms and services to manage the live streaming process entirely in the cloud. This method is ideal for productions that require scalability, remote collaboration and minimal on-site equipment. By utilizing cloud resources, you can reduce the need for on-site hardware and connect your cameras and audio directly to the cloud.

Key Components:

- **Cloud Streaming Platforms:** Services like Hudl, StreamYard and

PTZOptics Hive offer remote management of your cameras and live streaming settings.

- **High-Speed Internet Connection:** A reliable and high-bandwidth internet connection is essential to connect live video feeds to a cloud platform.
- **IP-Based Cameras and Network Infrastructure:** IP cameras can send video feeds directly to the cloud, eliminating the need for traditional capture cards. A robust network setup ensures seamless transmission of multiple video sources.
- **Cloud-Based Video Production Tools:** Tools like LiveU Studio (formerly EasyLive) allow producers to manage video sources, add graphics and overlays and control the live stream through web-based interfaces.

Advantages:

- **Scalability:** Easily scale your streaming capabilities up or down based on the size and demand of the event without significant upfront investments in hardware.
- **Remote Collaboration:** Teams can collaborate from different locations, managing the live stream through cloud-based interfaces without being physically present at the event site.
- **Reduced Hardware Dependency:** Minimize the need for expensive on-site equipment by leveraging cloud resources for encoding, processing and distribution.
- **High Reliability and Redundancy:** Cloud platforms typically offer built-in redundancy and failover options, enhancing the reliability of the live stream.
- **Global Accessibility:** Reach a wider audience with distributed CDN infrastructure, ensuring that viewers from around the world can access the stream with minimal latency and buffering.

Understanding RTMP Streaming and Internet Connectivity

RTMP Streaming: Real-Time Messaging Protocol (RTMP) is a widely used protocol for live streaming. It facilitates the transmission of audio, video and data from the encoder to the streaming platform.

You can retrieve your RTMP URL and stream key from live streaming destinations such as YouTube.

Key Points:

- RTMP is used by major streaming platforms like YouTube Live, Facebook Live and Twitch.
- Requires setting up the stream key and server URL provided by the streaming platform within your streaming software or hardware encoder.

Internet Connectivity: A robust and reliable internet connection is paramount for a successful live stream.

Best Practices:

- **Bandwidth Requirements:** Ensure you have sufficient upload bandwidth. For high-definition streams, a minimum of 5 Mbps upload speed is recommended.
- **Wired Connection:** Use a wired Ethernet connection instead of Wi-Fi to minimize latency and avoid interruptions.
- **Redundancy:** Consider having a backup internet source, such as a secondary ISP or a cellular connection, to prevent downtime in case of primary connection failure.
- **Testing:** Conduct thorough internet speed tests and stream rehearsals before the live event to identify and address potential connectivity issues.

Best Practices for Enhancing Your Live Stream

Implementing strategic practices can significantly improve the quality and viewer engagement of your live stream.

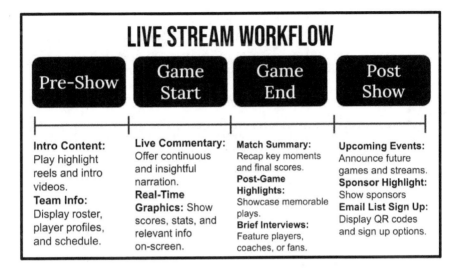

1. Start the Stream Early

Why: Beginning the stream 30-45 minutes before the game starts allows you to build anticipation and provide valuable pre-game content to your audience.

What to Include:

- **Introductory Videos:** Play highlight reels showcasing memorable moments from previous games or the season to engage viewers.
- **Roster and Schedule Display:** Present the team roster, player profiles and the game schedule to inform and excite fans.
- **Live Commentary:** Offer pre-game analysis and discussions to set the stage for the upcoming match.

2. Play Highlight Reels and Intro Video Clips

Enhancements:

- **Engagement:** Highlight reels and intro clips capture viewers' attention and provide context about the teams and players.
- **Professionalism:** High-quality video content reflects well on the production, making the stream more appealing and credible.

Implementation Tips:

- **Quality Content:** Use high-resolution footage and ensure smooth transitions between clips.
- **Timing:** Schedule highlight reels at strategic points, such as during breaks or before the game kickoff, to maintain viewer interest.

3. Show the Roster and Schedule Before the Game

Benefits:

- **Information:** Providing the roster and schedule helps fans familiarize themselves with the players and the event timeline.
- **Engagement:** Interactive elements, such as player statistics and upcoming game information, can keep viewers engaged while they wait for the game to begin.

Execution:

- **Graphics Overlays:** Use on-screen graphics to display the roster and schedule clearly and attractively.
- **Narration:** Complement the visuals with commentary that highlights key players and important game details.

4. Email the Live Stream Link to Fans

Importance: Direct communication ensures that your audience is informed about the live stream, increasing viewership and engagement.

Strategies:

- **Timely Distribution:** Send out the live stream link well in advance, preferably a day before and a reminder on the day of the event.
- **Clear Instructions:** Provide step-by-step guidance on how to access the stream, including any necessary platform information.
- **Personalization:** Tailor emails to different segments of your audience to make the communication more relevant and effective.

5. Utilize Multi-Streaming to Multiple Platforms

Advantages:

- **Wider Reach:** Broadcasting across multiple platforms simultaneously increases the potential audience, reaching fans who prefer different streaming services.
- **Flexibility:** Different platforms offer unique features and

audience demographics, allowing you to tailor content accordingly.

Implementation Tips:

- **Consistent Quality:** Ensure that the stream maintains high quality across all platforms to provide a uniform viewing experience.
- **Platform-Specific Adjustments:** Optimize settings and formats based on each platform's requirements and best practices.
- **Monitoring:** Keep track of each stream's performance and viewer engagement to identify which platforms are most effective for your content.

Mastering the fundamentals of live streaming in sports production involves choosing the right streaming method, understanding technical protocols like RTMP, ensuring a robust internet connection and implementing best practices to enhance viewer engagement. By leveraging computer-based software or hardware switchers, optimizing your streaming setup and strategically planning your broadcast content, you can deliver a professional and captivating live sports experience to fans around the world. Additionally, effective communication and multi-streaming strategies can significantly expand your reach and strengthen your connection with the audience. Embracing these fundamentals will empower you to produce high-quality live streams that resonate with sports enthusiasts and elevate your overall production quality.

Simplifying Tools for Coaches

Coaches need quick and straightforward control interfaces to review game footage under pressure. In high-energy environments, tools with one-click access to replays, zoom-ins and multi-angle switching help them respond quickly during timeouts or post-game analysis.

By integrating intuitive video tools and fostering strong communication among the entire production team, sports video production can seamlessly blend commentary, action and replays into a cohesive, professional viewing experience. This approach benefits both live audiences and sports teams aiming for improved performance through detailed video analysis.

Case Study Example: End Zone Camera

This example shows Sideline Power using a PTZOptics Move SE 12X on a very tall 20' tripod. The tripod features a joystick controller allowing the operator to control the camera which has a great bird's eye view of the end zone. This system is used for instant-replay and allows the production team to have close up video of key moments during the football game.

This system uses SkyCoach, an instant replay system which allows coaches and referees to review video footage from between one to four camera angles. The video is delivered wirelessly to an iPad or other touch screen device. The video from the camera is connected to the SkyCoach instant replay system via HDMI and it's connected to a PoE (Power Over Ethernet) network switch for video and control with the PTZOptics SuperJoy controller.

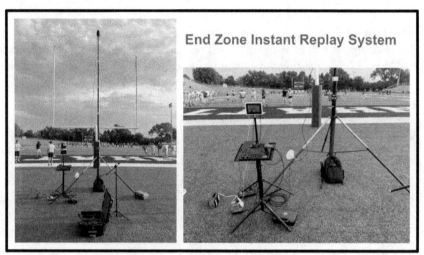

End-zone camera system from Sideline Power.

11 SPORTS VIDEO ESSENTIALS - LEVEL 3 - MULTI CAMERA PRODUCTIONS

At Level 3, things start to get more serious. This setup allows for more flexibility and growth, with a dedicated live streaming computer or network of connected devices like cameras and computers together. Here, many sports broadcasters typically start with basic camcorders or GoPro-style cameras, connected to an HDMI video switcher such as the Blackmagic ATEM Mini which supports four HDMI inputs. Most video switchers (that don't record and stream directly like the ATEM Mini) are connected to a computer with USB to record and stream the video output. This is ideal because instead of requiring a powerful computer capable of handling multiple cameras at once, the computer only needs to capture one "premixed" video source.

Multi-camera high school football production.

How it Looks:

At level three, the ability to switch between multiple cameras instantly improves the production quality. Professional sports broadcasts use dozens of cameras and you may only have two or three. Using PTZ cameras allow you to choose different areas depending on the players on field. Additionally the commentators can add value and interest to your videos.

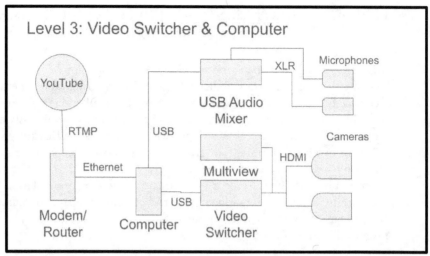

Level three live streaming system with a dedicated video switcher and audio mixer.

Most video switchers come with a "Multiview" video output which is ideal to have on a monitor for the operator. This way as you add multiple cameras, you can view them all at once and choose which video source to send to your live stream. At the computer, you have several software encoder options. Open Broadcaster Software (OBS) is, by far, the most popular solution for software encoding because it's free and open source. This is the software you'll use to bring your audio, video and graphics all together into a single scene that you can live stream.

Level three systems are easy to upgrade and many sports broadcasters do so to reduce their reliance on volunteers and add production quality with additional cameras or displays. Remotely controllable PTZ cameras, with a joystick controller are a nice upgrade. Adding new cameras or even extra computers to the production is simple, thanks to networking technologies like NDI. NDI has become the go-to method for linking cameras and video sources over a local network. A network is simply a collection of devices that are all connected to the same network switch and therefore available as resources for video, audio and control. By using a PoE (Power over Ethernet) network switch, you can power your cameras and connect them directly to your live streaming software without extra cables.

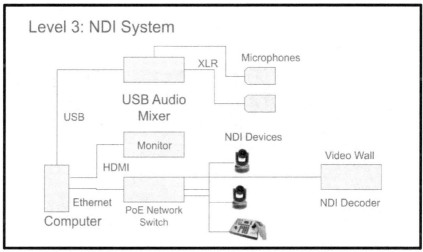

Level 3 live streaming system using a network and NDI.

One of things you'll notice in the level 3 NDI system, is that there is no hardware video switcher. With NDI, your network switch provides a way to get your cameras into your computer (over Ethernet), which would then need video switching software. Video can then be sent back out to additional monitors like an LED wall with an NDI Decoder. An NDI Decoder is a device that will take the video output from your live stream and convert it to HDMI so that you can connect it to any display. At level 2 the center of your production is your computer and because it's so important while you may start with a free software like OBS you may eventually upgrade to more advanced software like vMix or Wirecast. These programs allow for better control and offer built in support for graphics, overlays, recording and encoding for live streaming. This level is ideal for growing productions that need more features and flexibility than an app, especially if you're starting to produce sports events more regularly.

Level 3 does require some basic networking knowledge but it's much less expensive than level 3 which requires hardware video switching systems. An 8 port PoE network switch for example, will cost between $100-200, whereas an 8 input video switcher might cost $1,000-2,000. The difference being reliability and flexibility. If you know what you're doing and are willing to learn about IP video, you can save a lot of money and get a very powerful and flexible system.

At level 3, you can still use a smartphone. WiFi has become much more reliable over the past few years and you can now use the NDI camera app with a smartphone to capture new angles or send out reporters into the crowd. This type of production used to cost thousands for wireless video transmitters and receivers. Today, with WiFi and cellular connections becoming increasingly robust, placing wireless cameras in hard to reach areas is more common.

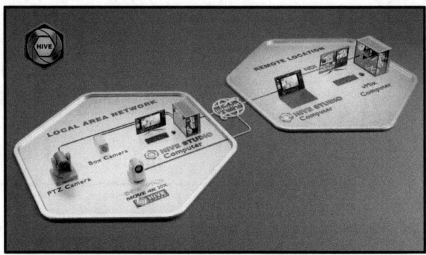

In this diagram, you can see a remote location producing controlling cameras and switching video.

Working with Cellular Bonding

Adding cellular bonding to your production setup can be a game-changer for live streaming in locations where hard-wired internet and even WiFi are limited or unavailable. In these environments, especially in outdoor sports venues, cellular bonding enables you to combine multiple cellular connections into a single, more robust internet link, enhancing both reliability and speed.

While smartphone cellular bonding is ideal for mobile streaming, a cellular bonding router (such as an MR·NET or the Miri router) may be the more professional solution your production requires. The YoloBox Ultra and Extreme video switchers also offer combined ethernet, wifi, usb and cellular bonding. This way, you're not solely dependent on a single cellular connection, which could be unstable or insufficient for high-quality video transmission. Instead, you're harnessing the combined strength of multiple signals, making it ideal for remote productions.

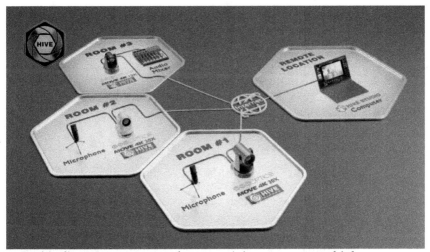

In this diagram, you can see how easy it is to manage multiple cameras across different locations.

The diagram above shows how you can set up just one or more remotely controllable cameras which can be set up for management at a remote location using the cloud. Setting up video systems with cameras like this can greatly reduce costs and set up times. By leveraging a cloud solution such as PTZOptics Hive, sports teams can greatly reduce the need for on-site hardware based video switching tools. PTZOptics Hive for example, allows you to remotely control PTZ cameras, record each camera and live stream out to multiple CDNs such as YouTube and Facebook.

Solutions like Speedify offer a software-based approach to cellular bonding, allowing you to use USB-connected cellular devices along with WiFi and Ethernet to ensure a stable connection. On the hardware side, systems like the MR·NET and MIRI cellular bonding routers and YoloBox Ultra & Extreme switchers provide dedicated hardware for multiple network connections, allowing you to connect everything from computers to cameras and other network devices. The MIRI cellular bonding system, in particular, integrates Speedify's technology with physical bonding hardware, delivering a comprehensive, managed network solution that ensures seamless connectivity and enables you to stream with confidence, even from challenging locations. With cellular bonding in your toolkit, you gain the flexibility to produce high-quality broadcasts from almost anywhere, expanding your reach without the restrictions of traditional internet infrastructure.

Multi-Camera Setups: Expanding Sports Video Coverage

Using multiple cameras is one of the most effective ways to enhance sports video production, whether you're live-streaming, capturing sideline instant replays or gathering footage for video analytics. A multi-camera setup allows you to capture different angles of the action, ensuring you don't miss key moments while creating a more dynamic, professional viewing experience. Even if one of your cameras is a basic webcam or smartphone, having an extra camera for a wide-angle "dump" shot can make a huge difference.

Benefits of a Multi-Camera Setup

1. **Comprehensive Coverage**
   A single camera often can't capture the full scope of a sports event, especially on larger fields or in fast-paced games. Multiple cameras allow you to cover every angle, ensuring no crucial plays are missed. For coaches, this means getting a complete view of formations and player positions.

2. **Dynamic Storytelling**
   Switching between cameras creates a more immersive experience by showing different perspectives. For example, during a soccer match, you can alternate from a wide field shot to a close-up of a player taking a penalty kick. In coaching sessions, you can review plays from multiple angles for deeper analysis.

3. **Professional Look**
   Multi-camera setups mimic traditional TV broadcasts, making your production look polished and engaging. This applies to both live-streamed events and recorded game footage for scouting and player development.

Choosing Camera Angles

In Chapter 4, we discussed camera placement for specific sports, but it's essential to consider how those angles work together during a live stream or video review session. Here's how to optimize your multi-camera setup:

1. **Main Wide Shot**
   - **Purpose:** Provides a full view of the playing area and acts as your primary feed. It helps fans follow the overall flow of the game and gives coaches a clear view of formations.
   - **Best Practice:** Use a wide-angle camera with a field of view (FOV) larger than 80 degrees. The exact FOV depends on your distance from the action.
   - **Tip:** Create a shortcut button (e.g., the spacebar or a

134

stream deck key) to quickly return to the wide-angle shot when switching views.

2. **Close-Up Camera**
   - **Purpose:** Focuses on individual players, scoring opportunities or reactions from the sidelines.
   - **Best Practice:** Use optical zoom for precise shots, reserving digital zoom for high-resolution sensors only.
   - **Tip:** Consider auto-tracking cameras that follow key players like a goalie or main tennis competitor. These cameras reduce the need for manual operation and deliver focused, zoomed-in views.

3. **Action or Mobile Camera**
   - **Purpose:** Moves with the play or offers sideline perspectives, adding energy and immediacy to the production.
   - **Best Practice:** Use wireless video transmitters to send footage to your video switcher with low latency.
   - **Tip:** Platforms like vMix and Wirecast offer integrated video calling features, allowing you to bring in smartphone video feeds over WiFi or cellular networks. For even greater reliability, consider a dedicated encoder backpack like LiveU.

4. **Specialty Cameras**
   - **Purpose:** Capture unique angles based on the sport, such as goal cams in soccer, backboard cams in basketball or end-zone cams for football.
   - **Best Practice:** Set these cameras to record continuously or trigger them for specific moments to enhance your sports video production or coaching review sessions.

5. **Fan Cam** *(PTZ Camera)*
   - **Purpose:** Highlights the crowd energy, mascots and other interesting sidelines elements to engage the audience and add character to the broadcast. It can also capture celebrations and cutaway moments that add color to the storytelling.
   - **Best Practice:** Utilize a PTZ camera with smooth pan/tilt motors and preset positions. This allows you to quickly move from a mascot shot to enthusiastic fans in the stands without shaky transitions.
   - **Tip:** Set preset angles for common fan reaction areas— like the student section or the mascot's "home" spot. With one button press, you can instantly cut to a lively reaction shot to enhance the viewing experience.

6. **Hero Camera** *(End-Zone or Corner PTZ Camera)*

- Purpose: Serves as a designated celebration camera where players know they can go after scoring a touchdown or making a big play. This camera angle provides a memorable moment for fans and a highlight-ready shot for post-game recaps.
- Best Practice: Position a PTZ camera at the end zone or a strategic corner of the field so it's easy for players to find. Ensure it has a slightly wide field of view to capture multiple players celebrating at once.
- Tip: Pre-mark the celebration spot on the field and communicate it to players before the game. Consider adding a branded backdrop or signage behind the Hero Camera for sponsor recognition or team branding, making celebrations even more visually appealing.

By combining these camera types strategically, you can create an engaging live stream or an insightful coaching video that covers every aspect of the game.

Video Switching & Communication in Sports Video Production

Effective video switching is at the core of successful sports video production, whether you're live-streaming a game, capturing footage for sideline instant replays or producing content for coaching and sports analytics. It involves precise timing, clear communication among production team members and the ability to align visuals with commentary and game flow.

Real-Time Switching for Live Action

During live gameplay, instant cuts are essential for keeping up with fast-paced action. These quick transitions maintain the energy and intensity of the game, ensuring that viewers remain fully engaged. A well-coordinated switching strategy lets producers follow the play seamlessly, shifting between wide shots, close-ups and specialty camera angles as needed.

Pro Tip: Use a dedicated hardware switcher like the ATEM Mini or a software-based switcher like vMix or Wirecast (with keyboard shortcuts or a Stream Deck) to allow for quick and intuitive switching and multi-camera management with minimal delay.

Switching for Replays & Analysis

In sports broadcasts, replays help highlight key moments for fans, while in coaching and training, they offer detailed performance reviews. For live productions, animated transitions like stingers create a clear visual break, signaling that the action is shifting to a replay. This keeps broadcasts professional and easy to follow.

For coaching sessions, instant replay systems like Hudl or SkyCoach let trainers analyze plays immediately after they occur. Smooth video switching ensures seamless integration of replays with original footage, helping coaches and athletes break down every move.

Pro Tip: Use stinger transitions with custom branding to enhance the professional look of your broadcast or training session. Consider adding slow-motion playback to provide a deeper analysis of crucial plays.

Communication & Workflow Management

Strong communication between camera operators, directors and announcers is critical to successful sports video production. Real-time coordination ensures that everyone knows where to focus and when to switch shots.

Best Practices for Communication:

- Use intercom systems like Clear-Com, Hollyland or Unity Intercom to maintain constant contact.
- Have a clear verbal cue system for calling camera shots, triggering replays and switching graphics.
- Conduct pre-game meetings to align everyone on key plays, camera angles and production goals.

By mastering video switching and fostering a collaborative production environment, you can elevate your sports video production—whether you're broadcasting live games, capturing coaching footage or creating content for sports analysis.

vMix system set up to capture six NDI cameras.

Communication & Control in Sports Video Production

Clear communication between camera operators, technical directors and commentators is vital for delivering polished sports video production. This applies to live broadcasts, sideline instant replays and coaching review sessions, where seamless coordination ensures that the right visuals match the action or analysis being presented.

Camera Operator Communication & Tally Lights

Camera operators need to know when their cameras are live or about to go live. Tally lights provide this critical feedback, showing a red light when live and a green light when in preview. This helps operators maintain steady shots and avoid making adjustments while on-air.

In more complex productions, intercom systems reinforce this communication, keeping operators and directors in sync. For coaching environments, software-based tally indicators can inform coaches using multi-camera setups when specific angles are active, streamlining footage review.

Pro Tip: Many live-streaming platforms and video switchers like vMix, OBS and Wirecast support software-based tally lights, which are cost-effective for smaller productions or coaching setups.

Previewing & Cueing Content

Before bringing any video, graphic or pre-recorded segment on-air, previewing is essential. The technical director must ensure that everything looks polished and aligns with the current game flow. This practice also applies to coaching video sessions where clips of recent plays can be cued and played back for detailed review.

Best Practices:

- **Use Hotkeys:** Assign hotkeys (aka "shortcuts") or stream deck buttons for frequently used clips, replays or camera switches.
- **Dedicated Control Panels:** For more advanced setups, hardware control panels make switching faster and more intuitive.

Listening to Commentary & Adapting Visuals

A well-synchronized production involves aligning visuals with what commentators or coaches are discussing. If a commentator analyzes a player's performance, the technical director can cut to a close-up or trigger a relevant replay. Similarly, coaches reviewing game footage can quickly bring up clips that illustrate key plays.

For coaching, intuitive control systems that allow fast clip selection and playback are essential. Instant replay tools like Hudl, SkyCoach or vMix Replay provide easy-to-use interfaces for coaches to quickly review critical moments without interrupting their teaching flow.

Timing & Precision

Switching at the right moment is a key skill in sports production. Cuts should happen at pivotal points, such as when a player makes a significant move or when a play climaxes. Working closely with camera operators ensures that relevant shots are ready to switch to, whether it's a wide shot, close-up or action-following camera.

Replays should also be well-timed, appearing immediately after key plays and ending smoothly with stinger transitions or a fade back to live action. Setting consistent replay durations—typically five to eight seconds—maintains a steady rhythm for both live-streamed broadcasts and coaching reviews.

Camera Switching Tips

Once you have multiple cameras set up, the key to a professional stream is the ability to switch between those camera feeds in real time. This process is called live switching and it helps keep the stream visually engaging.

Switching between cameras should be smooth and well-timed. Avoid sudden or rapid changes that can confuse the viewer or disrupt the flow of the broadcast. Here are a few tips:

- **Watch the Action**: Anticipate when key moments will happen and be ready to switch to the best angle. For example, switch to a goal cam or close-up camera just before a penalty kick, then return to the wide shot after the play.
- **Use Smooth Transitions**: Generally you should be using the "Cut" which happens instantly without any fancy graphics to maintain a professional look. Avoid jumpy transitions that could be jarring to viewers.
- **Use of Stingers**: Stingers are specific video transitions that overlay on top of the existing live video source before they switch to an instant replay. The use of stingers are almost exclusively used to signal to viewers that an instant replay is about to come up next.
- **Focus on Reaction Shots**: After a big play, like a touchdown or a game-winning shot, switch to close-ups of player reactions or crowd celebrations to capture the emotion and excitement.

Timing and Frequency of Replays in Sports Video Production

In sports video production, you never know when the next game-changing moment will occur. Whether you're producing a live broadcast, capturing sideline instant replays or recording footage for coaching analysis, continuously recording several minutes of footage is essential. This ensures that every critical play is available for review or replay.

However, striking a balance between live action and replay frequency is key. Showing too many replays can disrupt the flow of the game, causing viewers to miss important live moments. A good rule of thumb is to replay only significant events, such as:

- **Scoring Moments**: Goals, touchdowns or game-winning shots.
- **Game-Changing Calls**: Penalties, fouls or game-altering referee decisions.
- **Close Calls**: Controversial moments that need a second look.

Delivering a Complete Sports Video Experience

Producing a sports video isn't just about recording the action—it's about crafting an immersive, professional viewing experience that keeps audiences engaged and well-informed. Whether you're live-streaming for fans, producing content for coaching review or creating highlights for player recruitment, mastering key production elements is essential. These include:

- **Multi-Camera Setups:** Capture every angle of the game for comprehensive coverage.
- **Live Switching:** Seamlessly switch between views to maintain the game's intensity.
- **Graphic Overlays:** Display real-time scores, player stats and timekeeping.
- **Replays:** Highlight crucial moments without interrupting the game flow.

By combining these production techniques with thoughtful planning and precision timing, you can create a sports video experience that rivals traditional TV broadcasts while meeting the needs of players, coaches and fans.

12 SETTING UP FOR DIFFERENT TYPES OF SPORTS

Sports of all kinds require different approaches to camera placement, video switching and the overall look and feel of the broadcast. This is largely due to the unique nature of each sport, including the size of the playing field, the pace of the game and the key moments that viewers expect to see. Over decades of televised sports broadcasts, best practices have been established and refined, which we can learn from at all levels of sports production.

These established practices have effectively trained audiences on what to expect when watching a particular sport. For example, viewers of American football are accustomed to seeing a wide shot from high above the 50-yard line, while basketball fans expect to see shots from behind the backboard during free throws.

Capturing video for a tennis match.

This standardization is beneficial for several reasons:

- **Viewer Satisfaction:** By following these guidelines, we can meet viewer expectations and ensure their satisfaction with the broadcast.
- **Efficient Production:** These best practices provide a proven framework for camera placement and shot selection, streamlining the production process.

- **Leveraging Expertise:** We can benefit from the collective experience of generations of sports broadcasters who have refined these techniques.
- **Consistency:** Adhering to these standards ensures a consistent viewing experience across different broadcasts of the same sport.

While it's important to follow these established practices, there's also room for innovation. New camera technologies and creative shot compositions can enhance the viewing experience while still meeting the core expectations of the audience.

In the following sections, we'll explore the specific camera placement strategies for various sports, keeping in mind both the established best practices and opportunities for creative enhancements.

Why Camera Placement Matters

In sports live streaming, where you place your cameras is just as important as the type of cameras you use. Camera placement defines what the audience sees and how they experience the game. A well-placed camera can make your viewers feel like they're right there, on the sidelines or in the heart of the action. Poor camera placement, however, can result in missed moments, obstructed views or lack of engagement.

This chapter will guide you through the best camera placements for various sports, explain how to frame your shots to capture the energy of the game and show you how to adapt your approach based on the sport and venue.

How to Set Up Wireless Cameras

Camera placement is critical, but what do you do when your ideal camera spot is too far from your production hub for a standard cable connection? This is where a wireless setup becomes essential. Wireless camera systems allow you to position cameras wherever they're needed—whether that's high above the field, across the court or on the sidelines—without being tethered by cables.

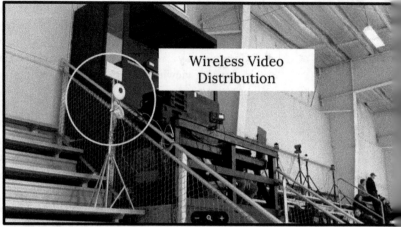

Ubiquiti point to point wireless networking system used to distribute video across an ice rink to the other side.

There are several technologies for transmitting video wirelessly and you may consider HDMI or SDI wireless transmission systems which can connect directly to traditional video equipment. Wireless video systems often lack the flexibility of wireless networking solutions, because they only handle video transmission. Wireless transmission systems such as the Ubiquiti point to point solutions, allow you to create a true wireless bridge that can be used for all kinds of sports video projects such as powering coach iPad, sending video from PTZ cameras and even controlling them with a joystick on the far side. In this section, you'll learn how to set up a wireless "bridge", which can be set up to handle wireless video transmissions between two locations just like a long ethernet cable.

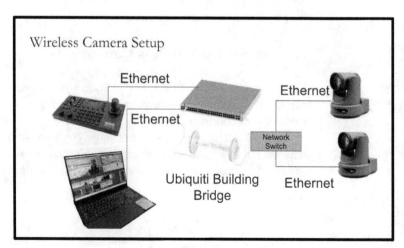

This diagram shows how the Ubiquiti Building Bridge solution can link together a network up to 500 meters (1,640 feet) away for remote camera connectivity.

Setting Up a Wireless Video System

To create a wireless link for your cameras, coach iPad and other devices, follow these simple steps:

1. Understand Your Wireless Needs

Start by evaluating your setup:

- **Distance**: How far is the camera from your main production area? For long distances, use equipment like the Ubiquiti PowerBeam or LiteBeam, capable of handling ranges up to 20 kilometers.
- **Bandwidth**: NDI|HX cameras require around 10-20 Mbps per stream depending on the bitrate you set. Ensure your wireless equipment can handle the combined bandwidth of all your cameras.

2. Choose the Right Ubiquiti Gear

Ubiquiti offers various solutions depending on your range and setup:

- **Short-range (up to 500 meters)**: UniFi Building-to-Building Bridge
- **Mid-range (up to 10 kilometers)**: LiteBeam 5AC Gen2
- **Long-range (up to 20 kilometers)**: PowerBeam 5AC Gen2

These devices create a point-to-point wireless connection, effectively replacing long Ethernet cables.

3. Install and Align the Wireless Devices

Wireless devices need a clear line of sight to function properly. Position one device near your camera and the other at your production hub. Use Ubiquiti's built-in alignment tools to fine-tune the connection for maximum signal strength. Ubiquiti includes flexible pole mounting options which you can use to secure the wireless transmitters to a sturdy tripod or speaker stand. Once secured, it's recommended to raise the transmitted up and over any obstacles to ensure a solid line of sight connection.

4. Connect Your Camera

Plug your camera into the Ubiquiti transmitter using an Ethernet cable. On the receiving end, connect the Ubiquiti device to your production computer or network.

5. Test Your Setup

Always test the connection. Check for latency, signal stability and video quality. You can log in to your cameras and other devices to adjust the video bitrate if necessary. You usually want to use a lower bitrate for wireless cameras than you would with hardwired connections.

Why Go Wireless?

A wireless camera system gives you the flexibility to place cameras in optimal positions, even in challenging venues. With Ubiquiti's high-performance gear, you can ensure a stable connection, giving your audience the best possible view of the action—no matter where it happens on the field or court.

In the next section, we'll explore specific camera angles for popular sports and how to frame your shots for maximum impact. Whether you're live streaming basketball, soccer or baseball, the right combination of camera placement and reliable wireless setup will take your production to the next level.

Understanding the Flow of Sports

Each sport has its own unique rhythm and flow and your camera placements should reflect that. Understanding how the game moves, where key moments happen and how to cover those moments will guide you in setting up the right shots. Here's a quick breakdown:

- **Field Sports (Soccer, Football, Rugby)**: These sports involve large playing fields with constant movement across a wide area. You'll need wide, sweeping shots that can capture the flow of the game, along with occasional zoom-ins for key moments.

- **Court Sports (Basketball, Volleyball, Tennis)**: These sports are faster-paced and confined to smaller areas. You'll need a mix of wide shots to show team dynamics and close-ups to capture the intensity of one-on-one moments.
- **Individual Sports (Swimming, Track & Field, Martial Arts)**: Here, the focus is often on one or two athletes at a time. You'll want to focus on tight framing and dynamic angles that emphasize the athlete's effort and skill.
- **Extreme and Action Sports**: These sports (such as skateboarding or snowboarding) often require a combination of stationary and action cameras that follow the athlete through fast-paced, unpredictable environments.

General Guidelines for Camera Placement

While each sport will have its own specific camera requirements, there are a few general rules to follow when determining camera placement for any live sports stream:

- **Cover the Entire Field of Play**: Ensure that no matter where the action happens, your cameras can capture it. For field sports, that might mean using wide-angle shots from a high vantage point, while for smaller courts, a central position may suffice.
- **Anticipate Key Moments**: Different sports have moments that fans always expect to see (e.g., goals, touchdowns, slam dunks). Make sure your cameras are positioned to capture these critical moments with a clear and unobstructed view.
- **Multiple Camera Angles**: Using multiple cameras allows you to capture different perspectives. A main camera for wide shots, secondary cameras for close-ups and mobile cameras for sideline or action shots are key to delivering a dynamic experience.
- **Avoid Obstructions**: Pay attention to potential obstructions like poles, scoreboards or referees that could block the view at key moments. Ensure that your cameras are placed where they can track the action smoothly without interruption.

- **Respect the 180 Degree Rule:** For sports that move primarily back and forth between two goals on the field (like soccer, football or hockey), it's crucial to follow the 180 degree rule. This means placing all cameras on the same side of the field, typically along one sideline. By adhering to this rule, you ensure that the direction of play remains consistent from all camera angles, making it easier for viewers to follow the action and understand which way the game is progressing.

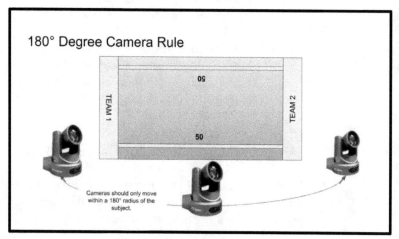

The 180-degree camera rule.

The 180-degree rule helps maintain spatial continuity for the audience. When all cameras are on the same side, a team moving left to right on one camera will always be moving left to right on all cameras. This consistency prevents disorientation and confusion that could occur if cameras were placed on opposite sides of the field.

While there may be exceptions for specific shots or replay angles, the main game action should generally be captured from cameras positioned within this 180-degree arc. This approach has become standard practice in sports broadcasting, creating a more coherent and enjoyable viewing experience.

Rule of Thirds

This timeless compositional guideline divides the frame into nine equal parts using two equally spaced horizontal lines and two equally spaced vertical lines. Placing important elements along these lines or their intersections creates balanced and aesthetically pleasing shots. This simple technique can significantly enhance the visual appeal of your videos.

The rule of thirds will help to guide your shot compositions.

Soccer video production camera and network layout.

Soccer/Hockey

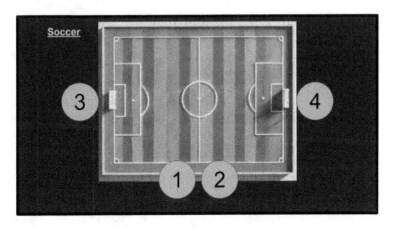

Camera Roles and Framing in Soccer Game Live Stream

This four-camera setup enables dynamic coverage of the soccer game, each camera strategically positioned for specific purposes to capture every critical angle and aspect of the gameplay.

1. **Center-Field Cameras**
   - **Cam 1 (Wide Shot):**
     - Positioned to capture a **broad view of the field**, this camera keeps between **25% and 50% of the field in frame**.
     - Primarily used for **general gameplay coverage**, ensuring the main movements and flow of the game are visible.
     - This wide shot helps to establish the game's overall context, allowing viewers to follow the ball and the teams' positioning as they move across the field.
   - **Cam 2 (Tight Follow):**
     - This camera focuses on a **head-to-toe shot** of the **player with the ball** along with 1–2 nearby defenders.
     - Used to capture intense, close-up shots following the **player at fault after a penalty** or to track the **scoring player after a goal** and the **goalie after a save**.
     - It provides an up-close perspective on individual player actions, highlighting key moments and celebrations and offering a more intimate view of player expressions and reactions.
2. **End-Field Cameras**
   - These cameras typically switch between **wide field views** and **tight follow shots**, depending on the situation:
     - **Wide Field View:**
       - Generally framed to show the **entire width of the field** (from sideline to sideline).
       - Ideal for tracking **players**

who are offside on the near
side, capturing **crowd
reactions** and framing
substitutions and **throw-ins**.

- **Tight Follow for Specific Scenarios**:
  - Primarily used for **corner
    kicks**, focusing on the players
    assembled near the goal and
    tracking the ball as it enters
    the frame and action unfolds.
  - Follows the **goalie for goal
    kicks**, staying wide enough to
    capture the play's
    development and the
    movement of players across
    the field.
  - Used for **hero shots** (low-
    angle shots that capture
    players as they prepare for or
    celebrate key moments) and
    capturing **coaches and
    benches** during key
    moments, as this setup often
    provides one of the only
    angles able to capture the
    sideline areas.

Together, this layout provides full coverage of the soccer game, balancing wide shots to track general play and tighter shots to emphasize individual players, goals and celebrations. This arrangement ensures an engaging viewer experience, allowing audiences to follow both the game's progress and its more personal, emotional moments.

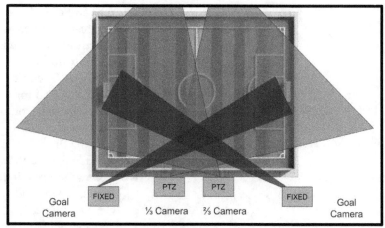

This layout shows four cameras from the "Broadcast" side of the field.

Example Equipment List

Cameras & Accessories

1. **Camera 1 (Center-Field - PTZ 20X)**
   - **Purpose:** Wide shot covering 25-50% of the field.
   - **Location:** Center of the field near the streaming equipment.
   - **Ethernet Cable:** 30 feet (for data and power through PoE).
   - **Tripod:** 15-foot tripod.
2. **Camera 2 (Center-Field - PTZ 20X)**
   - **Purpose:** Tight shot of players with the ball.
   - **Location:** Center of the field near the streaming equipment.
   - **Ethernet Cable:** 30 feet (for data and power through PoE).
   - **Tripod:** 15-foot tripod.
3. **Camera 3 (End-Field - PTZ 30X)**
   - **Purpose:** Goal-focused close-up from the opposite end.
   - **Location:** One end of the field.
   - **Ethernet Cable:** 300 feet (for data and power through PoE).
   - **Tripod:** 15-foot tripod.

4. **Camera 4 (End-Field - PTZ 30X)**
   - **Purpose**: Goal-focused close-up from the opposite end.
   - **Location**: Opposite end of the field from Camera 3.
   - **Ethernet Cable**: 300 feet (for data and power through PoE).
   - **Tripod**: 15-foot tripod.

Production Table & Accessories

1. **Foldable Table**: Sturdy folding table to house production equipment.
2. **Two Power Strips**: Multi-outlet power strip to supply power to multiple devices.
3. **Cart**: If you are setting up for an away game or simply bringing gear in and out of any space, a cart with wheels is a great accessory.

Network & Power

1. **PoE Network Switch**
   - **Purpose**: Supplies power and data to all cameras.
   - **Ethernet Cable to Router**: 5 feet.
2. **WiFi Router**
   - **Purpose**: Connects the WiFi tablet to vMix for instant replay access.
   - **Ethernet Cable to Network Switch**: 5 feet.
3. **Streaming Computer (Running vMix)**
   - **Purpose**: Central production system for receiving NDI feeds, streaming and controlling instant replays.
   - **Ethernet Cable to Network Switch**: 5 feet.

Control & Monitoring

1. **PTZ Controller**
   - **Purpose**: Controls PTZ cameras for manual adjustments and auto-tracking.
   - **Ethernet Cable**: 5 feet (if connected via Ethernet to the network).
2. **LCD Monitor**

- ○ **Purpose:** For viewing live feeds and monitoring production.
3. **Tablet (Touchscreen)**
   - ○ **Purpose:** Displays instant replays for coaches and referees via LiveLAN from vMix. Touchscreens are great for fast paced sports. They can be used for quick video switching, camera controls or annotations.
   - ○ **Connection:** Wireless, connected through the WiFi router.

Audio Equipment

1. **Audio Mixer**
   - ○ **Purpose:** Manages audio input from microphones and adjusts audio levels for the live stream.
2. **Shotgun Microphone**
   - ○ **Purpose:** Captures ambient sound from the field.
   - ○ **Microphone Stand:** For stable placement of the shotgun microphone near the field.

Replay & Streaming Systems

1. **Roland 20P-HD Instant Replay System**
   - ○ **Purpose:** Provides instant replays through HDMI output to vMix or the LCD monitor.
   - ○ **HDMI Cables:** Required for connecting the Roland 20P-HD to vMix and monitor.
2. **SkyCoach**
   - ○ **Purpose:** Provides sideline instant replays to wireless tablets for coaching.
   - ○ **Setup:** Requires wireless transmission system for each camera.
3. **Optional Cellular Bonding System**
   - ○ **Purpose:** For stable, high-quality streaming when a wired network connection is unavailable, ideal for remote locations.

Summary of Cable Lengths

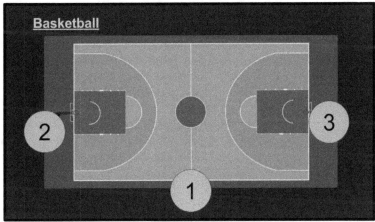

Basketball live streaming system set up.

Basketball

Suggested Camera Layout:

- **Main Camera**: High center court, capturing the entire court action from sideline to sideline.
- **Baseline Cameras**: One camera behind each hoop for capturing fast breaks, dunks and close-range shots. This is also great for foul shots.
- **Sideline Camera**: At ground level for sideline shots of coaches, players on the bench and court-level action.

This four-camera setup provides complete coverage of a basketball game, with each camera serving specific purposes to capture the fast-paced action, critical plays and close-up details of the gameplay.

1. **Camera 1 – Game Follow (Wide Shot)**:
    - Positioned to deliver **general coverage of gameplay** from a wide perspective, this camera is the primary on-air angle and remains active for most of the broadcast.
    - Smooth **pans from left to right** are used to follow the game's flow, with **slow zooms** in and out to reduce empty space, keeping the

action centered and dynamic.

○ When a team is setting up an offense, the framing should place the **basket on one side** and the **last offensive player on the opposite side** for balanced coverage of the court.

○ **Key Responsibilities**: Since this camera is on-air frequently, the operator should always anticipate being on tally, ensuring smooth, consistent movement.

○ **Example Clip**: An isolated recording of the Game Follow camera showcases its ability to track wide movements and capture the full context of plays.

2. **Camera 2 – Tight Follow (Close-Up)**:

○ This camera focuses on a **tight, head-to-toe shot** of the player with the ball and the nearest defender, capturing close-ups of intense interactions.

○ Used to track the **player responsible after a foul** and to highlight individual players after a **score or defensive stop**.

○ **Additional Uses**: Often follows players off the court during substitutions and provides tight shots that enhance what commentators are discussing during the game.

○ **Key Responsibilities**: Ideal for capturing player emotions, this camera must be ready to switch quickly between active players and ensure focus on individual movements for dramatic effect.

○ **Example Clip**: An isolated recording of the Tight Follow camera demonstrates its precision in capturing specific players and moments.

3. **Cameras 3 & 4 – Handhelds (Close Side and Under-Basket Action)**:

○ These cameras capture **head-to-toe shots of the player with the ball**, especially effective on the side closest to them, providing high-quality replays from under the basket.

○ **Primary Role**: Though less used in live action, these cameras are essential for **replays** and **close-ups** of key moments, such as fouls, baskets or crowd reactions.

○ Perfect for **capturing action under the**

basket, framing up shots of **players taking free throws** (typically waist-up) and gathering **crowd shots** when needed.

○ **Additional Uses**: During substitutions, these cameras show players entering or exiting the court and capture sideline shots of coaches or announcers as needed.

○ **Key Responsibilities**: Even when the players are on the opposite side of the court, these operators continue recording to provide valuable replay angles. They also maintain awareness of baselines for any out-of-bounds situations important for official replays.

○ **Example Clip**: Isolated recordings of these handheld cameras display their versatility in capturing up-close action, player reactions and providing dynamic shots for production highlights.

This multi-camera setup allows for seamless, engaging basketball coverage, balancing wide gameplay views, intense player close-ups and situational shots for commentary and replays, ensuring every aspect of the game is available to the viewers.

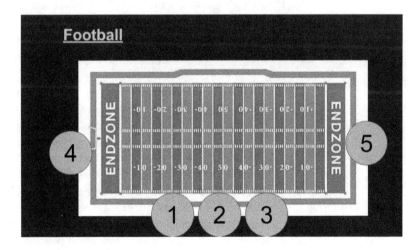

American Football

For covering an American football game, a five-camera setup provides comprehensive field coverage, focusing on essential game dynamics from various angles and distances.

- **Main Sideline Cameras:** Positioned high in the press box, three cameras span the length of the field. These offer sweeping coverage of plays, transitions and formations, capturing gameplay from a high vantage point that allows viewers to follow field positioning and player movements fluidly.
- **End Zone Cameras:** Two cameras, each mounted on a 15-foot-high tripod in both end zones, capture goal-line action and close-up views of touchdowns, player celebrations and defensive stands.

The Palmetto Tigers are a high school football team using two camcorders and a center PTZOptics camera.

Camera 1 – Wide Game Follow (Primary Shot):

- **Position**: Center sideline, high above the field in the press box area.
- **Function**: This camera provides a broad view (2/3rds) of the game, capturing the action for live coverage.
- **Use**: It follows the flow of the game, panning smoothly to track plays as they unfold across the field.
- **Key Responsibilities**: This camera operator should anticipate play direction, ensuring smooth panning and framing that maintains balanced coverage. Positioning should include both end zones when possible for a full-field perspective.

This PTZOptics 30X Move 4K camera is used as the main follow camera near center field.

Camera 2 – Tight Game Follow (Close-Up of Plays):

- **Position**: Sideline, high in the press box, focusing tightly on players involved in the play. Generall y focused on ⅓ of the field.
- **Function**: This camera captures tighter, head-to-toe shots of key players, particularly focusing on the quarterback, primary receivers or defenders closest to the action.
- **Use**: This angle is used for close-ups of player interactions, fouls and substitutions, capturing player expressions, reactions and individual achievements.
- **Key Responsibilities**: The operator must be ready to quickly switch focus, following individual players as needed to enhance the intensity of close plays and individual efforts.

Example Clip: A close-up shot displays the Tight Follow camera's focus on individual player movements, capturing precise details of tackles, passes and runs.

Static cameras can be used on the sidelines to capture large areas of the field.

Camera 3 – Secondary Sideline (Player Interactions and Benches):

- **Position**: Sideline, high press box, on the opposite side of the primary sideline camera.
- **Function**: This camera captures sideline interactions, player substitutions and coaches' reactions, providing an alternate angle for detailed analysis.
- **Secondary Function**: This camera can be used for a "fan cam" or used to capture half-time shows or other fan engagement opportunities.
- **Use**: This angle is often used to capture players and coaches on the sidelines and it can track out-of-bounds plays or incidents occurring close to the field boundary.
- **Key Responsibilities**: The operator should maintain a close watch on the sideline for out-of-bounds calls, player substitutions and reactions, capturing emotional or strategic moments off the field.

End zone cameras shown on 20' tripods connected to the Sky Coach instant replay system.

Cameras 4 & 5 – End Zone Views (Goal-Line Action and Key Replays):

- **Position**: Each camera is mounted on a 15-foot tripod in both end zones.
- **Function**: These cameras provide critical goal-line views, capturing touchdowns, defensive stops and end-zone celebrations from a unique, close-up perspective.
- **Use**: These views are essential for live coverage and replays of scoring moments, tracking the ball as it crosses the goal line and capturing celebrations and critical plays from the end zone perspective.
- **Key Responsibilities**: Operators should follow the ball's movement into the end zone and be ready to capture quick, decisive shots of the action near the goal line, which are particularly useful for replay reviews and scoring confirmation.

A six camera football video system shown in vMix.

This five-camera setup provides a dynamic and comprehensive view of the football field, covering all aspects of the game, from full-field formations to goal-line intensity. With coordinated camera angles, each position captures unique perspectives that enrich the viewing experience with live action, close-ups and replay capabilities.

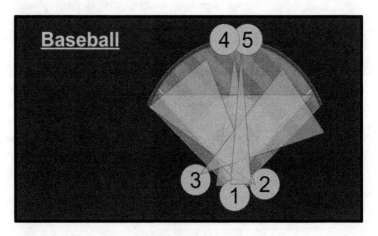

Baseball Suggested Camera Layout:

For baseball, a five to six camera setup provides comprehensive field coverage, highlighting the essential areas of action and maximizing viewer engagement. If you only have one camera the wide shot from a backstop is generally the best place to start.

- **Wide Shot from Backstop**: Positioned behind home plate, this camera captures the entire field, providing a complete view of the action as it unfolds.
- **First Base Camera**: Located near the first-base dugout or above, this camera captures plays at first base, a key area of action for defensive and offensive plays.
- **Pitcher-Batter Close-Up Camera**: Positioned directly between the pitcher and batter, this shot focuses on the exchange between the two, capturing pitches, swings and the batter's response.
- **Outfield Camera 1**: Positioned behind the pitcher, over the shoulder, this camera provides an iconic view of the batter and pitcher, often requiring a wireless transmitter and a stable tripod with a 20X or 30X zoom to maintain clear, stable shots.
- **Outfield Camera 2**: Positioned behind the pitcher, over the shoulder, but zoomed in further to show the batter close-up.
- **Third Base Side Camera**: Positioned near or above the third-base side, this camera captures plays at third base, the home plate and incoming runs, providing essential coverage for scoring plays.
- **Pitcher Camera**: Most professional broadcasts will include a camera dedicated to the pitcher.

Camera 1 – Wide Backstop Shot (Full-Field View):

- **Position**: Behind home plate, providing a wide-angle view of the entire field.
- **Function**: This is the primary camera for live coverage, capturing the whole field and giving viewers the context of each play's location and movement.
- **Use**: Ideal for tracking defensive alignments, player positions and base running, this angle ensures comprehensive coverage.
- **Key Responsibilities**: This camera can mainly

stay static and is used as a wide angle viewpoint and establishing shot.

Camera 2 – First Base Shot (Close-Up of Key Plays):

- **Position**: Near the first-base dugout or above, with a wide angle on first base.
- **Function**: This camera captures plays at first base, an area with frequent action as batters reach base or fielders attempt outs.
- **Use**: Perfect for replays and close-ups of plays at first base, this angle captures critical defensive actions, pick-offs and runners reaching first.
- **Key Responsibilities**: The operator should anticipate plays moving toward first base, framing shots to include the first baseman and runner as they approach, with tight zooms for replays when needed.

Camera 3 – Pitcher-Batter Close-Up (Pitching and Hitting Action):

- **Position**: Located between the pitcher and batter.
- **Function**: This camera focuses tightly on the interaction between the pitcher and batter, highlighting pitches, swings and the batter's response.
- **Use**: Essential for tracking pitch speed, ball movement and the batter's swing, this angle is crucial for capturing the intensity of each pitch and hit.
- **Key Responsibilities**: The operator should keep the pitcher and batter in frame, with precise focus and framing to capture close-up details of each pitch and hit.

Camera 4 – Outfield Over-the-Shoulder Shot (Long-Range Batter View):

- Position: Behind the pitcher from the outfield, over the shoulder, with a stable tripod and a 20X or 30X zoom lens.

- Function: This angle provides a unique perspective of the batter, often used for broadcast quality, capturing the batter and pitcher in line.
- Use: Used to emphasize batting sequences, this view requires a wireless transmitter for flexibility and a stable mount to handle the zoom level without shake.
- Key Responsibilities: The operator must maintain focus, accounting for the long zoom and ensure stability throughout the sequence to avoid camera shake.

Camera 5 – Third Base Side Shot (Home Plate Coverage):

- Position: Near the third-base side, angled toward home plate.
- Function: This camera captures plays from third base and home plate, offering a view for scoring plays and runners advancing.
- Use: Often used for shots of the batter's box, scoring plays and close-ups of players at third base, this angle provides flexibility for both live action and replays.
- Key Responsibilities: The operator should focus on capturing plays near home plate and third base, adjusting angles as needed to cover both areas of high activity.

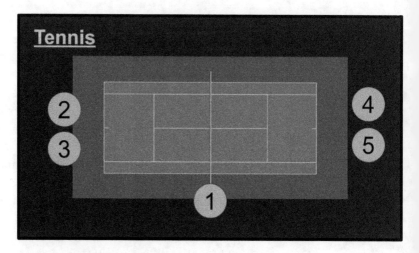

Tennis Suggested Camera Layout:

To capture the full intensity and athleticism of a tennis match, a multi-camera setup is ideal, going beyond the standard overhead view to include both wide and close-up perspectives at court level. This setup leverages PTZ cameras with automated tracking, which can follow players dynamically while maintaining appropriate zoom levels for each shot, giving viewers a detailed and immersive experience.

This PTZOptics Move 4K camera is powered over ethernet and is capable of auto-tracking.

Camera 1 – Overhead Wide Angle (Traditional Shot)

- **Position**: High above the court, positioned centrally to capture the full court.
- **Function**: This camera provides a traditional broadcast angle, displaying the overall play and player positioning on the court.
- **Use**: It captures both players and the entire court from above, ensuring a clear view of point progression and positioning.
- **Limitations**: While effective for showing the court layout, this angle misses the details of player movement, spin and pace, making it ideal for providing overall context but insufficient for highlighting intensity.

Cameras 2 & 3 – Court-Level Wide Angle (Side Shots for Each Half of the Court)

- **Position**: One camera on each side of the court, positioned at court level.
- **Function**: These cameras capture the match from each side, emphasizing player movement, the intensity of each shot and the ball's spin and net clearance.
- **Use**: Typically, each angle is used on its respective side of the court and only switched between points or during serve changes to avoid viewer confusion.
- **Key Responsibilities**: Operators should set fixed zoom levels that allow viewers to appreciate player positioning, movements and ball dynamics without needing to adjust during play.

The video production software vMix is being used for recording and instant replays.

Cameras 4 & 5 – Tight Angles of Opposing Players (Close-Up of Player Movements)

- **Position**: One camera on each side of the court, positioned for a close-up of the opposing player.
- **Function**: These cameras capture tight, close-up shots that focus on each player individually, showing the speed, spin and power behind each shot.
- **Use**: These close-up angles reveal intricate player actions, such as swing intensity, net clearance and footwork, allowing viewers to see the pace and athleticism involved.
- **Key Responsibilities**: The tight angle cameras should be positioned to avoid rapid switches during active play. Operators (or automated PTZ tracking) should maintain focus on individual players, creating immersive close-ups for replays and breaks.

PTZ Tracking and Automation

- **Feature**: Using PTZ cameras with automated player tracking can enhance the broadcast by maintaining focus on players dynamically.
- **Function**: PTZ cameras auto-track player movements based on their fixed position and maintain steady, controlled zoom levels for smooth transitions.
- **Use**: Automated tracking keeps players in frame, adjusts angles seamlessly based on player positions and

reduces the need for rapid manual adjustments, allowing the broadcast to keep up with the fast pace of tennis.

This multi-camera layout balances the traditional overhead view with dynamic, court-level perspectives. Each angle captures unique aspects of the game: the overhead shows the strategic layout, court-level wide angles highlight movement & ball dynamics and close-up shots give insight into the athleticism of each player. With PTZ auto-tracking, this setup provides comprehensive, engaging tennis coverage that captures every detail, speed and effort from each player.

Golf Suggested Camera Layout and Solution:

Covering a golf tournament requires a multi-camera setup that can capture wide, sweeping shots of the course, follow the ball's trajectory and zoom in on player technique and reactions. A successful layout for golf includes cameras strategically placed at the tee, fairway, green and key vantage points along the course. With PTZ cameras and wireless capabilities, automated tracking and stabilized shots can follow both the ball and players smoothly across varying distances.

Suggested Camera Setup:

1. **Tee Box Camera** – Close-Up of Players and Swing Technique
2. **Fairway Tracking Camera** – Following the Ball's Flight Path
3. **Green-Side Camera** – Capturing Approach Shots and Putting
4. **Hole Overview Camera** – High-Level Course Perspective
5. **Roving PTZ Camera** – Flexible, Wireless Option for Additional Angles and Player Reactions

Camera 1 – Tee Box Camera (Close-Up for Player Swings)

- **Position**: Positioned near the tee box on each hole.
- **Function**: Captures close-up shots of the golfer's setup, stance and swing mechanics.
- **Use**: This camera provides viewers with a clear view of

169

the golfer's technique, swing speed and focus, highlighting the initial ball launch.

- **Key Responsibilities**: With fixed zoom levels, this camera should follow the player through the swing and into the follow-through, capturing any immediate reactions.

Camera 2 – Fairway Tracking Camera (Ball Flight and Trajectory)

- **Position**: Positioned at a high vantage point along the fairway, aimed toward the landing area.
- **Function**: This camera follows the ball's trajectory after the tee shot, tracking its flight path and approximate landing point.
- **Use**: Ideal for capturing long shots from the tee to the fairway, helping viewers follow the ball's path and predict where it will land.
- **Key Responsibilities**: This camera needs strong zoom and tracking capabilities. PTZ automation is highly effective here, using pre-set tracking functions to follow the ball in flight.

Camera 3 – Green-Side Camera (Close-Up for Approach and Putting)

- **Position**: Near the green, positioned to capture approach shots and putting.
- **Function**: This camera zooms in on the player as they approach the green and follows their putts, capturing each putt's speed, roll and precision.
- **Use**: Critical for showcasing the skill and strategy of putting, along with the subtle undulations and speed control required to sink a putt.
- **Key Responsibilities**: With precise zoom and focus, this camera should capture both the ball's trajectory toward the hole and the player's reactions, switching smoothly between these perspectives.

Camera 4 – Hole Overview Camera (Wide Shot of Entire Hole)

- **Position**: Elevated position to capture the entire layout

of the hole from tee to green.
- **Function**: This camera provides a wide, high-level view of each hole, showing the layout, hazards and distance.
- **Use**: Great for context, this camera offers viewers an understanding of each hole's unique challenges, showing bunkers, water hazards and elevation changes.
- **Key Responsibilities**: The operator can switch between static wide shots or slow pans, emphasizing the player's journey from tee to green.

Camera 5 – Roving PTZ Camera (Player Reactions and Flexibility)

- **Position**: Mounted on a mobile cart or carried by an operator, with wireless capabilities for flexible movement across the course.
- **Function**: Captures additional angles, player close-ups and reactions, adding variety to the broadcast.
- **Use**: Used for player close-ups, crowd shots and spontaneous reactions, this flexible camera is ideal for capturing moments outside the standard play areas.
- **Key Responsibilities**: Operators can use this PTZ camera to zoom in on players between shots or capture reactions to highlight the emotional aspect of the game.

Archery, Riflery and other specialty sports

Covering archery, riflery, and similar precision sports requires a multi-camera setup designed to capture target accuracy, shooter technique, and the emotional intensity of the competition. These sports often demand high-definition, zoomed-in shots of targets alongside close-ups of participants' focus, form, and reactions. The right camera setup ensures viewers can follow every moment, from the calm precision before the shot to the triumphant results.

Cutting-edge broadcast system at the 2025 Lancaster Archery Classic, featuring wireless roving cameras.

Suggested Camera Setup for Archery, Riflery, and Specialty Sports

1. **Shooter Technique Camera** – Focus on Form and Precision
2. **Target Close-Up Camera** – Highlighting Shot Accuracy
3. **Overhead Context Camera** – Wide View of the Range or Competition Layout
4. **Official Review Camera** – Capturing Scoring and Adjudication
5. **Roving PTZ Camera** – Flexible Coverage for Dynamic Angles

Crane operated broadcast cameras are used to capture athletes at the 2025 Lancaster Archery Classic.

Camera 1: Shooter Technique Camera (Close-Up for Form and Focus)

Position: Positioned near the shooter, capturing their stance and actions.
Function: Provides detailed close-ups of the shooter's technique, focus, and actions during the shot.
Use: Ideal for training, coaching, and broadcasts where viewer engagement with the participant's skill is essential.
Key Responsibilities:

- Capture the shooter's setup, alignment, and release with clear focus.
- Zoom in on details like grip, hand position, and body alignment to emphasize skill.

One PTZOptics Move SE 20X camera was used for each target at the 2025 Lancaster Archery Classic. The video output is shown on a large indoor LED screen.

Camera 2: Target Close-Up Camera (Accuracy and Results)

Position: Positioned downrange, with a clear line of sight to the targets.

Function: Focuses on the target, capturing arrows or bullets striking the bullseye in real time.

Use: Essential for slow-motion replays and judging the precision of each shot.

- Utilizes optical zoom to show precise impact points on the target.
- Switch between wide and close-up views of multiple targets as needed.

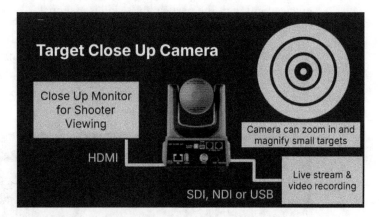

Camera 3: Wide Angle Context Camera (Range Layout and Events)

Position: Elevated position above the range or field of play.
Function: Provides a wide-angle view of the entire competition area, showing shooter lanes, targets, and audience areas.
Use: Offers context for viewers by showcasing the range layout, the positions of participants, and the overall event setup.
Key Responsibilities:

- Pan across the range to highlight different participants.
- Use zoom sparingly to maintain the broad context of the event.

Confidence monitors are used for each athlete and reviewed by officials.

Camera 4: Official Review Camera (Scoring and Adjudication)

Position: Near the scoring table or review station.
Function: Captures official reviews, scoring updates, and adjudication processes.
Use: Ensures transparency for viewers and provides close-ups of scoring decisions during live broadcasts.
Key Responsibilities:

- Zoom in on scorecards, judges, or reviews of target impacts.
- Maintain stability and clarity during scoring updates.

Camera 5: Roving Camera (Dynamic Angles and Reactions)

Position: Mobile, carried by an operator or mounted on a dolly for flexible movement across the venue.
Function: Captures spontaneous angles, player or team reactions, and crowd responses.
Use: Ideal for adding variety and energy to the broadcast by covering non-static moments and behind-the-scenes activity.
Key Responsibilities:

- Follow participants as they prepare or celebrate.

- Zoom in for emotional close-ups, crowd shots, or interviews.

Framing the Action

Once your cameras are in place, the next step is to frame the action correctly. Here's how to ensure your viewers stay engaged:

- **Wide vs. Tight Shots**: Wide shots help viewers see the overall action, while tight shots give focus to individual players or moments. Use a combination of both to keep the stream visually interesting.
- **Follow the Ball/Player**: Ensure your camera operators (or automation if using PTZ cameras) are trained to follow the ball, puck or key player. This keeps the audience focused on where the action is happening.
- **Focus on Key Plays**: For certain moments—such as a goal attempt, free throw or sprint finish—tighten your framing on the player or ball. Highlighting these key moments can build excitement.
- **Dynamic Angles**: If you have multiple cameras, switch between wide, mid and close-up shots for a more dynamic viewing experience. For example, switch to a close-up right before a goal attempt, then return to a wide shot to capture the celebration.

Remote Camera Control and PTZ Cameras

Using PTZ (Pan-Tilt-Zoom) cameras can give you greater flexibility when it comes to framing your shots. These cameras can be remotely controlled, allowing you to pan across the field, tilt up or down to track vertical action and zoom in or out depending on the play.

- **Preset Positions**: You can program PTZ cameras with preset positions, allowing quick transitions between different angles, such as a wide-field view or a close-up on a specific player.
- **Automation**: Many PTZ cameras, including those from PTZOptics, offer automatic tracking options, which can follow a player's movement without manual control, allowing for smoother transitions.

Proper camera placement and framing can elevate your sports live stream from ordinary to professional. Whether you're streaming a local high school game or a major tournament, understanding the nuances of camera angles, placements and dynamic framing ensures that your audience stays engaged and never misses a moment.

In the next chapter, we'll dive into best practices for operating cameras in sports production—a crucial step in elevating your broadcasts to a professional level.

13 Camera Operation Best Practices for Sports

The key to capturing great sports footage starts with understanding the sport itself. Each game has a unique flow and knowing this will enable you to anticipate critical moments. For instance, soccer is a fast-paced game where the action can shift quickly from one end of the field to the other. In contrast, football is more stop-and-go, with crucial moments of action followed by downtime. By learning the rhythm of the sport, camera operators can prepare for the best angles and anticipate where the action will unfold.

Positioning cameras is also sport specific. In basketball, you may want a mix of wide-angle shots to capture the flow of the game and tighter shots for player reactions. For soccer, overhead cameras that cover large portions of the field are essential to show passing strategies. Strategic camera placement is key to giving viewers a comprehensive perspective.

Camera Types and Setup

In a live sports production, choosing the right camera for the job can make a significant difference in the broadcast quality. PTZ (pan-tilt-zoom) cameras are a popular option in sports because of their auto-tracking functionality and remote control capabilities. They allow operators to adjust shots without physically moving the camera, which is particularly useful for covering large fields or arenas.

Fixed cameras also play an essential role, especially for capturing specific zones, like end zones in football or goal lines in soccer. These cameras provide reliable coverage of the most critical areas of the field and can be left in place without needing adjustment. Handheld cameras, often used on the sidelines or close to the action, offer dynamic, up-close shots that give viewers a more intimate view of the game, focusing on crowd reactions, sideline plays or post-game celebrations.

Best Practices for Camera Movement

Smooth camera movement is vital to maintaining a professional sports broadcast. Fast-moving sports like basketball or hockey require the camera to follow the action seamlessly, while slower sports like baseball allow for more deliberate camera movements. Whether using a PTZ camera or operating a handheld unit, camera operators should aim for smooth pans and tilts that keep the subject in frame without jarring or abrupt shifts. PTZ cameras can have pan and tilt limits put in place to avoid overshooting the end of a field or court area.

Anticipation plays a critical role in good camera operation. In fast-moving sports, an experienced operator will predict where the action will go next, allowing them to stay ahead of the play and avoid missing crucial moments. This requires both a solid understanding of the sport and real-time communication with other operators on the production team.

Using PTZ Cameras in Sports

PTZ cameras, with their remote-control capabilities, have become increasingly popular in sports production. One of the main advantages of PTZ cameras is the ability to set preset positions. These presets allow operators to instantly switch between critical areas of the game, such as goals, benches or the sidelines. By setting these PTZ preset positions in advance, operators can react quickly to changing game conditions without manually panning or tilting the camera.

Dynamic zooming is another advantage PTZ cameras offer even while in auto-tracking mode. When a PTZ camera is auto-tracking a specific player, you may want to have a wider zoomed out view most of the time. However, zooming should be done slowly and deliberately to avoid disorienting the viewer. Sudden or fast zooms can make the broadcast feel chaotic, so it's best to use these features strategically after while the camera isn't "live".

Finally, adjusting the camera's speed settings is essential depending on the type of sport being broadcast. For example, faster pan and tilt speeds are ideal for sports like hockey, where the action is fast and unpredictable, whereas slower movements work better for sports with more deliberate pacing, such as tennis or golf.

Two PTZ camera operators and one commentator are shown. A small touch screen video switcher is also used in the center.

Operating Your Cameras

Streaming sports with a portable PTZ camera system, such as the "Tripod Warriors," is an efficient way to capture the action on the field or court. To help you get the most out of your system, here are some essential tips for camera selection, operation and optimizing your video production.

1. Choosing the Right Camera for the Job

Main Camera (12X Zoom):

A 12X PTZ camera is ideal for capturing sports where the ball moves back and forth, such as soccer, basketball or volleyball. The moderate zoom level ensures you can follow the entire field or court without being overly zoomed in, making it easier to track fast-paced plays.

Secondary Camera (Wide Angle)

A wide-angle camera is ideal as a "dump" or "safety" shot giving you the ability to quickly switch to a wide angle when the action moves outside your main PTZ camera view. Wide angle cameras are great for giving the viewer a reference point for the entire space. Wide angle cameras are easy to manage because they are generally fixed and to widen the view, you simply need to move the camera further away.

Additional cameras (20X or 30X Zoom):

If you need close-up shots of specific moments, such as coach reactions or referee decisions, consider adding a 20X or 30X PTZ camera as a secondary angle. This level of zoom is perfect for highlighting key details or focusing on smaller areas of the field or court.

2. Mastering PTZ Camera Operations

Smooth Pan and Tilt Movements:

For most sports, you'll be panning more frequently than tilting. Set your pan and tilt speeds to create smooth, natural movements. Avoid settings that are too fast and jerky, as they can distract viewers, but ensure they are quick enough to follow breakaway plays.

- Pro Tip: Test different pan and tilt speeds during warm-ups to find the best setting for the pace of the game.

Use Pan and Tilt Limits:

To avoid overshooting your shot when tracking the action, set pan and tilt limits. These boundaries help you quickly move to the edges of the field or court without going too far, keeping the action consistently in frame.

3. Leveraging Joystick Controls

A joystick controller is an invaluable tool for sports streaming. It allows for quick, intuitive reactions to fast-paced gameplay. Use the joystick to make precise adjustments to your framing and smoothly follow the action.

4. Balancing Zoom for Maximum Coverage

When to Zoom Out:

If you're struggling to keep up with the play, zoom out. A wider shot ensures you capture the entire field or court, making it easier to track the action without missing critical moments. This is especially important if you're using only one camera.

When to Zoom In:

For detailed shots of players or specific plays, zoom in to bring your audience closer to the action. If you have multiple cameras, you can switch between wide and tight shots for a more dynamic viewing experience.

- Single Camera Strategy: Stick with a wider angle to keep all the action in frame.
- Multi-Camera Strategy: Use one camera for wide coverage and another for tight shots. Switch between the two as the play dictates.

5. General Sports Streaming Tips

- Practice Before the Game: Familiarize yourself with the camera's controls and test your settings during warm-ups or practice sessions.
- Anticipate the Action: Stay a step ahead by anticipating where the ball or players are headed.
- Stay Calm Under Pressure: If you lose track of the play, quickly zoom out to regain your bearings and refocus on the action.

PTZOptics Hive used for high school football camera management.

Live Adjustments and Remote Control

During a live sports broadcast, conditions can change quickly. Lighting may shift, especially in outdoor settings or the action may move to a different area of the field. Camera operators need to be ready to make real-time adjustments to ensure their shots stay crisp and well-composed. For this reason, operators must be familiar with their equipment and comfortable making on-the-fly changes to focus, exposure and framing.

With advancements in remote production technology, many sports broadcasts now incorporate cloud-based systems like PTZOptics Hive, which allow operators to manage cameras from anywhere in the world. This makes it easier to maintain a consistent, professional quality, even when the production team is spread across different locations.

Remembering the importance of shutter speed when shooting sports when camera operators are adjusting for lighting changes, they will generally adjust the iris setting. However, if your iris is already wide open pretty (not advised), you may need to slow down the shutter speed a bit, though try to keep it above 1/350 of a second - and higher if possible - to reduce motion blur. Remember too that the wider the iris (the lower the number) the shallower the depth-of-field (area in focus). It is a bit of a balancing act.

Instant Replay Camera Operation

Instant replays are a vital component of sports production, allowing viewers to relive the most exciting or controversial moments in the game. Camera operators should focus on capturing the key angles that will be used for replays. Wide-angle shots provide full context, showing how the play developed, while tight close-ups focus on specific moments like a goal or a player's reaction.

To capture smooth, slow-motion replays, cameras should be set to record at a higher frame rate, typically 60fps or above. This ensures that when the footage is slowed down, it remains clear and smooth.

Using a jog dial controller like the Xkeys XKE-64 or JLCooper ES SloMo allows operators to control the replay playback speed with precision. This gives broadcasters the ability to adjust replay timing in a way that aligns with the live commentary and storytelling.

Environmental Considerations

Outdoor sports production comes with its own set of challenges, primarily related to lighting and weather. As lighting conditions change, especially during day-to-night transitions or cloudy weather, camera operators need to adjust exposure and white balance settings to maintain image quality.

Weather can also be a factor, especially for cameras placed on tripods in potentially rainy or windy conditions. Using weatherproof enclosures or camera housings can help protect equipment from the elements. For larger events, operators should also consider the placement of their cameras in relation to the crowd to ensure that spectators do not block crucial shots or interfere with cables and equipment - and that cameras are not blocking the view of spectators and cables are placed (and held down) to minimize the risk of injury

Tips for aspiring Camera Operators

Know Your Camera Inside and Out

Become technically proficient with your camera. Whether it's adjusting ND filters, setting white balance or controlling depth of field, you should be able to handle it all. If you're using unfamiliar gear, don't hesitate to ask another operator for a quick tutorial. Confidence in your tools is crucial.

Framing is Everything

A well-framed shot is your bread and butter. Watch major broadcasts like ESPN and pay attention to how the pros do it. Too much headroom or unnecessary movement can break the flow. Don't track every little action — for example, don't follow a football during a punt; focus on where the action is headed instead.

Stay Active, Always Find the Story

Even if the action isn't on your camera, don't just sit idle. Find a shot that enhances the narrative. Whether it's crowd reactions or subtle moments between plays, there's always something interesting to capture. Your director will appreciate a great shot, even if it's unexpected.

Smooth Movements, Proper Drag Settings

The key to smooth camera operation is learning how to correctly set the drag on your tripod head. Too loose and your movements will be shaky; too tight and your pans will be stiff. It's also essential to check your camera is level in both axes, not just forward-facing.

Bring Your Own Essentials

A good camera operator is always prepared. Bring your own kit: gloves, extra clothes, gaffer tape, rain covers and even a small HDMI monitor. These essentials will make you more self-reliant and ensure you're ready for any situation, especially in unpredictable environments.

Understand the Game

Knowing the sport you're filming isn't optional — it's essential. Whether it's football, lacrosse or soccer, understand the rules and key players. Experienced operators keep cheat sheets of important players so they can quickly frame the action when the director calls for a specific athlete.

Let the Action Breathe

You don't have to chase every movement. Let the action take place within the frame. Constant panning and zooming can make your shots feel chaotic. Sometimes the best choice is to hold a steady shot and let the players move through it naturally.

Protect the Gear

Your job isn't just about filming; it's about keeping the equipment safe. Whether it's rain, sideline chaos or people tripping over cables (and causing a camera on a tall tripod to fall over), you need to be vigilant. A camera operator who loses or damages gear due to carelessness will earn a bad reputation quickly.

Help with the Teardown

When the broadcast is over, don't rush off. Stick around for teardown and handle the gear with care. This is where a little extra effort goes a long way in building trust with the crew. Being a team player during breakdown can make a lasting impression.

Build Relationships with Fellow Operators

Networking isn't just for directors — it's essential for camera operators too. Be kind and helpful to your fellow operators. Many of the best opportunities come from recommendations and having a solid reputation among your peers can lead to bigger and better gigs down the line.

Mastering these elements will make you a highly sought-after camera operator and set you apart as someone who knows not just how to capture great shots, but how to do so professionally and reliably.

Final Tips for Successful Sports Camera Operation

Flexibility is the key to any live sports production. Even with the best-laid plans, unexpected moments can arise that require quick thinking and fast action from the camera operators. Regular practice with the production team, thorough equipment testing and maintaining clear communication during the event can make all the difference between a smooth broadcast and one filled with missed opportunities.

By following these best practices, camera operators can ensure they are ready to capture the fast-paced, unpredictable action that makes sports production such an exciting and challenging field.

14 BUILDING A SPORTS PRODUCTION TEAM

Building a successful sports production team requires a well-structured crew, each member playing a distinct role to ensure a smooth and engaging broadcast. The size of your team will depend on the complexity of the event and the available resources. Below, we outline the roles for a solo, small, medium and large team, covering various responsibilities needed at each level.

Solo streaming setup for one-person with a PTZ camera and a camcorder.

Solo Team (Just You)

It's the way we all start, and you have probably been there longer than you'd like. When you are the only person running the entire live stream, you have a lot on your plate. Solo streaming is quite popular especially with the advent of smartphone streaming. It's common to see a smartphone or a go-pro clipped to a metal fence and connected to WiFi for a simple stream.

Being a solo sports stream producer means handling every aspect of the live stream on your own. This includes setting up the equipment, managing the camera angles, controlling the audio levels and ensuring the streaming software is running smoothly. You are responsible for capturing the action, engaging the audience with commentary and addressing any technical issues that arise during the broadcast. It's a challenging task that requires multitasking, quick decision-making and a good understanding of both the technical and creative aspects of live streaming.

Now let's be honest, as a solo streamer, you simply can't do everything. Many solo streamers simply set up a smartphone and hit the "stream" button. The next step in production quality is leveraging an app like GameChanger which can overlay the scoreboard. As you get more comfortable, many solo streamers start to reach into "Level 2" where they bring a small network switch to connect together a laptop and a few cameras. If those cameras are PTZ, the same person running the video switcher can easily set up PTZ presets to move the cameras as needed. Running cables and setting everything up is of course a main challenge for solo streamers. This is where cable reels and organization come into play. You will want to have your physical equipment organized along with your digital plan. On the networking side, you'll want to know your equipment well and have static IP addresses set for each device so you can easily connect to them and troubleshoot as needed. I like to have an organized Google Sheet with each device, the IP address and the general settings (example: Camera 1, 192.168.1.99, 1080p60).

The great thing about PTZ cameras and software like vMix and Wirecast is their ability to save PTZ presets with images to easily recall several important locations. This allows you to quickly click an image tile for where you want the cameras to move. An experienced solo streamer can operate a video switcher, update the scoreboard and move PTZ cameras as needed. Adding commentary and instant replay is usually a stretch for even the most advanced video producers. Enlisting volunteers and part-time help is always a good idea as your production grows.

Small 3-5 member streaming team with a large PTZ camera and tripod.

Small Team (3-5 Members)

A small team can handle basic live streaming setups, perfect for community sports, small venues or budget-conscious productions. Here are the key roles:

1. **Director/Producer (1 person)**
   - Oversees the entire production process, from planning to execution.
   - Directs the camera operators or PTZ cameras and ensures the streaming software is working correctly.
   - Manages live switching between cameras, graphics and replays (if applicable).
   - Responsible for monitoring the stream's quality and addressing any technical issues.
2. **Camera Operator (1-2 people)**
   - Operates cameras to capture the action. One operator might focus on wider shots while the other captures close-ups or specific angles (e.g., player tracking).
   - Could also be responsible for setting up and adjusting camera settings before the event.
   - Responsible for running cables and setting up tripods.
3. **Audio Technician (1 person, optional)**
   - Monitors audio levels, ensuring clear commentary and crowd noise.

- o Handles any microphones for commentators, players or crowd sound.
- o In small teams, this role could also update the scoreboard.

4. **Commentator/Announcer (1 person)**
   - o Provides live commentary to engage the audience and explain what's happening in the game.
   - o May double as a sideline reporter for quick interviews if needed.

5. **Technical Support (1 person, optional)**
   - o Available to address any connectivity or hardware issues.
   - o Can be a shared responsibility with the director/producer on smaller teams.

Larger 6-10 person streaming team in the press box.

Medium Team (6-10 Members)

A medium-sized team allows for more specialized roles, which can enhance production quality and viewer engagement.

1. **Director (1 person)**
   - o Focuses purely on directing the production without technical responsibilities, allowing for more creative decisions.
   - o Collaborates with the producer to ensure everything runs smoothly.

2. **Producer (1 person)**
   - o Manages logistics, communication and

production schedule.

o Responsible for coordinating with teams (e.g., commentators, camera crew) and monitoring the live feed.

3. **Camera Operators (2-4 people)**

o Dedicated operators for various camera positions; including a primary wide-angle camera, a roaming sideline camera and close-up shots.

o One operator may focus on a static shot while others follow the action closely.

o One camera operator could be roaming with a wireless camera. This camera could be a smartphone connected to a strong WiFi signal or a broadcast camera connected to a wireless transmitter.

4. **Replay Operator (1 person)**

o Handles instant replays using dedicated software like vMix or NewTek 3Play.

o Ensures smooth transitions between live footage and replay clips.

5. **Graphics Operator (1 person)**

o Manages on-screen graphics, such as scores, player stats and lower-thirds.

o Updates information in real time as the game progresses.

6. **Audio Engineer (1 person)**

o Dedicated to managing all aspects of the audio mix, ensuring optimal sound quality.

o May use a multi-channel audio mixer to balance microphones, crowd noise and music.

7. **Commentators/Announcers (1-2 people)**

o Multiple commentators can provide in-depth analysis and color commentary.

o One may focus on play-by-play, while the other adds strategic insights or historical context.

8. **Sideline Reporter (1 person)**

o Conducts interviews, provides updates from the field and reports on specific aspects of the game.

o Can double as a social media correspondent.

A large broadcast team with multiple camera operators and video producers.

Full Large Team (11+ Members)

A full large team is suited for professional-level productions, where multiple roles are essential to create a broadcast that rivals network sports coverage.

1. **Executive Producer (1 person)**
   - Oversees the entire production from a strategic level, ensuring all departments are coordinated.
   - Works with the director to achieve the broadcast's vision.
2. **Director (1 person)**
   - Focuses entirely on directing live camera feeds, replays and graphics, while communicating with the camera operators.
3. **Technical Director (1 person)**
   - Operates the video switcher to execute the director's commands, switching between camera feeds and graphics.
   - Manages the routing of video signals to different outputs.
4. **Engineer/Camera Control Operator (1-2 people)**
   - Engineer oversees and troubleshoots all technology and live stream operations.
   - Camera Control Operator color matches cameras and maintains that match throughout the course of a shoot.
5. **Camera Operators (4-6 people)**
   - Includes specialized roles such as jib/crane

operators, drone pilots or handheld camera operators for dynamic angles.

- o May have operators dedicated to high-frame-rate cameras for slow-motion footage.

6. **Replay Operators (2 people)**
   - o One operator handles the main replays, while the other manages highlight packages or multiple angles.
   - o Allows for more complex replay sequences, including slow-motion and different camera perspectives.

7. **Graphics Team (2 people)**
   - o One operator focuses on live graphics like scoreboards and timers, while the other creates or updates custom animations and lower-thirds.
   - o May include an additional role for social media or live stats integration.

8. **Audio Team (2 people)**
   - o Includes a primary audio engineer managing the live mix and a second engineer focusing on specific aspects, such as commentators or sound effects.
   - o May also involve a music director for background music or event-specific audio cues.

9. **Commentators/Analysts (2-3 people)**
   - o Play-by-play commentator, color commentator and expert analyst roles for deeper coverage.
   - o May include a guest commentator or former athlete providing insider perspectives.

10. **Sideline Reporter and Social Media Correspondent (2 people)**
    - o One focuses on field reports and interviews, while the other manages live social media updates or fan engagement.

11. **Production Assistants (2-3 people)**
    - Handle various tasks such as managing equipment, assisting the director or helping with graphics and audio needs.
    - Ensure the production runs smoothly by addressing any issues promptly.

1. **Post-Production Team (1-2 people, optional)**
   - Prepares highlight reels, edits footage for on-demand viewing and manages content distribution after the

event.

Conclusion

The size of your live streaming team will depend on the scale of your production, the event's requirements and the resources available. Starting with a small team allows you to cover basic needs, while scaling up to a medium or large team provides more room for specialization and improved production quality. The key is to ensure that each role is well-defined and every team member is trained for their specific responsibilities, ensuring a professional and engaging live streaming experience for viewers

CHAPTER 15: CHOOSING THE RIGHT EQUIPMENT

Choosing the right equipment is the foundation of successful sports video production. The right gear can make the difference between a professional-quality broadcast and a missed opportunity. In this chapter, we'll explore essential equipment for sports video, including cameras, audio gear, switchers and accessories. Whether you're working with a tight budget or building a high-end production setup, understanding your options and matching them to your production goals will set you up for success on game day.

The camera is an important piece of equipment for live streaming sports. Since sports involve rapid movements, dynamic camera work is crucial for capturing the action. Here are the primary camera types to consider:

- **Consumer Camcorders**: Handheld camcorders are often used in smaller, indoor venues or for sideline shots. They offer more direct control over framing and zooming but require an operator at all times.
    - **Advantages**: Flexible framing, portable, great for close-up action.
    - **Use Case**: Basketball, volleyball or close-up sideline shots for outdoor sports.
    - **Connection Type**: Camcorders often offer an HDMI output that can be connected to a video switcher.
- **Action Cameras (e.g., GoPro)**: Action cameras are compact, durable and capable of capturing unique angles. They are commonly used in extreme sports but can be useful in any fast-moving sport where standard cameras may struggle to keep up.
    - **Advantages**: Small size, durability, many mounting options, wide-angle shots.
    - **Use Case**: Mountain biking, skateboarding or mounted to a referee/player for POV shots.
    - **Connection Type**: Most record locally. Some feature WiFi and RTMP streaming capabilities.
- **PTZ (Pan-Tilt-Zoom) Cameras**: PTZ cameras are ideal for live streaming sports because they can be

remotely controlled, allowing operators to pan, tilt and zoom to follow the action. These are especially useful for larger fields or arenas where manual camera work would be challenging. Some PTZ cameras offer AI-based auto tracking.

- ○ **Advantages**: Remote control, wide coverage area, multiple preset positions, some automatic operations
- ○ **Use Case**: Soccer, football or larger sports fields where movement is widespread.
- ○ **Connection Type**: PTZ cameras offer a variety of connection options including HDMI, SDI, NDI, USB, RTMP, SRT.

- **DSLR/Mirrorless Cameras**: While not traditionally used for live sports, DSLRs and mirrorless cameras offer incredible video quality for stationary shots, such as interviews, pre-game footage or post-game analysis.
  - ○ **Advantages**: High-quality footage, versatile for photography and video.
  - ○ **Use Case**: Interview segments, pre/post-game shows.
  - ○ Connection Type: Mostly used for recorded video but also sometimes offer HDMI and USB outputs.

- **Prosumer Camcorders**: A step up from consumer camcorders and substantially less expensive than broadcast camcorders (often $2,000-$5,000+) these are often the choice for professional live streamers and reality TV producers.
  - ○ Significantly better image quality than their consumer counterparts.
  - ○ Long zoom ranges and/or interchangeable lenses.
  - ○ Professional audio (XLR) and video (SDI) connectors and increasingly, NDI and direct streaming outputs over Ethernet.
  - ○ Many recording format options including 60 frames/second.
  - ○ Manual controls for exposure, color settings, neutral density filters and much more.

- **Broadcast Cameras**: Professional-grade cameras specifically designed for high-end sports productions, broadcast cameras set the gold standard for capturing live-action events. These cameras are built to deliver

197

unparalleled image quality, reliability, and advanced features, ensuring the production meets the expectations of both broadcasters and audiences.

- **Advantages**
  - **Exceptional Image Quality:** Large sensors and advanced optics ensure sharp, vibrant visuals.
  - **Long Zoom Ranges:** Ideal for capturing action in large venues like stadiums or golf courses.
  - **Durable Build:** Weather-resistant for outdoor events.
  - **High Frame Rates:** Perfect for smooth motion and slow-motion replays.
  - **Professional Features:** Precise controls, HDR support, and internal stabilization.
  - **Use Case:** Broadcast cameras are essential for major sporting events like the Olympics or the Super Bowl, offering dynamic angles and professional results.
  - **Connection Type:** Typically use SDI and fiber optics for long-distance, high-quality signal transmission, with modern models supporting IP workflows for remote control.

The Importance of 60fps in Sports Streaming

When it comes to live streaming sports, frame rate plays a crucial role in capturing and conveying the fast-paced action. While 30 frames per second (fps) is standard for many video applications, sports benefit significantly from higher frame rates, particularly 60fps. Using higher frame rates will make fast moving objects appear clearer and more fluid. Most viewers are used to seeing live sports broadcast in 60fps, which gives the video a more immersive and realistic viewing experience.

- **Impact on Production Equipment:**
  - Cameras: Ensure your cameras have long zoom lenses and can capture at 60fps. Many modern cameras support this, but older models may not.
  - Processing power: Your encoding system (hardware or software) needs to handle the increased data throughput.

- o   Storage: Higher frame rates mean more data, requiring increased storage capacity for recordings.
- **Camera Settings:**
    - o   Shutter speed: While we usually start with the 180-degree shutter rule - setting shutter speed to double your frame rate (1/120 for 60fps) to ensure realistic movements, when shooting fast-moving subjects like sports, this rule doesn't apply. Start with 1/350 of a second to reduce motion blur. If planning to do slow-mo instant replay or take stills from your video, experiment with much higher shutter speeds (1/1000 and higher).
    - o   ISO and aperture: May need adjustment to compensate for faster shutter speeds, especially in lower light conditions since the higher the shutter speed the less light you're letting into your camera. In higher light conditions, like bright sunlight, you can go to higher shutter speeds too. Video cameras without ISO settings, like most PTZ cameras, may need to adjust gain instead.
    - o   Focus: Faster frame rates can sometimes make autofocus more challenging, so manual focus might be worth some experimentation.
- **Additional Processing and Bandwidth Needs:**
    - o   Encoding: 60fps requires more processing power to encode in real-time.
    - o   Bandwidth: Expect to use about 1.5-2 times more bandwidth compared to 30fps at the same resolution. Given the choice, many sports broadcasters will choose 720p@60fps over 1080p@30fps.

Bitrates and Their Impact on Video Quality

When it comes to live sports, bitrate plays a crucial role in determining the overall quality of your video. Bitrate refers to the amount of data transmitted per second, usually measured in kilobits per second (Kbps) or megabits per second (Mbps). Higher bit rates generally result in better video quality, but they also require more bandwidth and processing power.

- **The Importance of High Bitrates in Sports Streaming:**
  - Reduced compression artifacts: Higher bitrates allow for less compression, resulting in clearer images with fewer blocky artifacts, especially during fast-moving action.
  - Better detail preservation: Sports often involve quick movements and small details (like a ball or puck). Higher bitrates help preserve these details, making it easier for viewers to follow the action.
  - Improved color accuracy: With more data available, color information is better preserved, leading to more vibrant and accurate representations of team colors and the playing field.
- **Recommended Bitrates for Sports Streaming:**
  - 720p60: 3.5-5 Mbps
  - 1080p30: 4.5-6 Mbps
  - 1080p60: 6-8 Mbps
  - 4K (2160p60): 13-34 Mbps

Resolution	Frame Rate	Bandwidth
1280x720	30	2.5 Mbps
1280x720	60	5Mbps
1920x1080	30	4Mbps
1920x1080	60	8Mbps
3840 x 2160 (4K)	30	8 Mbps
3840 x 2160 (4K)	60	16 Mbps

It's important to note that these are general recommendations. The optimal bitrate can vary depending on the specific sport, the amount of motion in the frame and the encoding settings used.

- **Balancing Bitrate with Viewer Capabilities:**
  - Consider your bandwidth: While higher bitrates improve quality, ensure that you have the required upload speeds to support your bitrate.
  - Multiple quality options: Offer viewers the choice between different quality settings to accommodate various internet speeds and devices.

By prioritizing high bitrates in your sports live streams, you can significantly enhance the viewing experience, ensuring that fans don't miss any of the fast-paced action due to compression artifacts or loss of detail. However, always balance this with the practical considerations of your audience's internet capabilities and your own streaming infrastructure.

Tripods, Mounts and Stabilization

Keeping your shots steady is necessary for maintaining a professional-quality live stream. Sports, in particular, often involve fast movements that require careful camera work. Here's how to keep your shots rock-solid:

- **Tripods**: A stable tripod is essential for any camera. Look for tripods with fluid heads, which allow for smooth panning and tilting if you are using a camcorder or static camera. For PTZ cameras look for stable tripods recommended for sports which are between 10-20' in height.
  - **Use Case**: Stationary cameras for continuous coverage or PTZ cameras with a high viewpoint.
- **Monopods**: For a more mobile setup, especially for sideline shots, monopods offer support and flexibility, allowing the operator to move freely without sacrificing stability.
  - **Use Case**: Sideline or action shots requiring mobility.

- **Gimbals and Stabilizers**: For handheld or moving shots, a gimbal can help keep the footage smooth, even if the operator is moving. This is particularly useful in sports like basketball or soccer, where you may want to track the action up close.
  - Use Case: Dynamic sideline shots or action-focused sequences.

Audio Equipment: Capturing the Atmosphere

High-quality video is only half of the equation—clear and professional audio is just as important. Viewers want to hear the commentary, the cheers of the crowd and the sounds of the game itself.

Here's what you'll need:

- **Microphones**:
  - **Lapel Mics (Lavalier)**:
    - **Types**: Omnidirectional or cardioid pickup patterns.
    - **Features**: Small size, clip-on design, often wireless for mobility.
    - **Use Case**: Ideal for commentators, sideline reporters or interviewing players. Offers hands-free operation with clear sound pickup.
  - **Shotgun Mics**:
    - **Types**: Short, medium or long interference tube designs.
    - **Features**: Highly directional, can be mounted on cameras or boom poles.
    - **Use Case**: Perfect for capturing distant sounds like player interactions, referee calls or specific game sounds without picking up excessive crowd noise.
      - **Tip**: Shotgun microphones can be connected to many cameras and the audio can be transmitted through the NDI, HDMI or other video connections.

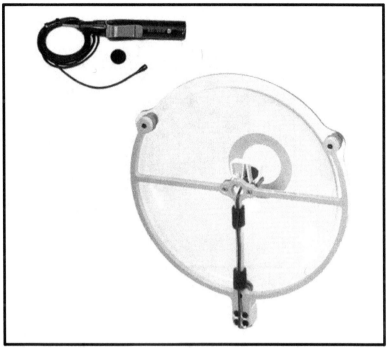

Klover Sound Shark Parabolic Mic with Equalized XLR Kit.

- ○ **Parabolic Mics**:
    - ■ **Types**: Plastic dishes (with or without mics included) that can support lavalier and often other mic types
    - ■ **Features**: Highly directional, long range, hand-held for use at sidelines (operator must wear headphones)
    - ■ **Use Case**: Even better (longer range and more directional) than shotguns for capturing distant sounds like player interactions, referee calls or specific game sounds.
- ○ **Crowd Mics**:
    - ■ **Types**: Omnidirectional or wide cardioid condenser microphones.
    - ■ **Features**: High sensitivity, often with wind protection for outdoor use.
    - ■ **Use Case**: Positioned near the stands to capture the atmosphere and crowd reactions, giving viewers a sense of being at the event.

Whirlwind THS4 Talkback Headphone Box - 1/4 Inch TRS and 3.5mm headphone jacks/ latching mic switch/ cough switch/ TB

o **Commentary Microphones or Headset Microphones**: High-quality vocal microphones for commentators are essential for clear and professional audio. These are typically used in press boxes or dedicated commentary areas with a clear view of the game.

- **Types**: Dynamic or condenser microphones with cardioid pickup patterns to reduce background noise. These are often combined with headphones. A separate "sports announcer" or "talkback" box is recommended to combine intercom and program audio into headphones (for communication with producer & other crew, along with a "cough" switch.
- **Features**: Look for models with built-in pop filters and shock mounts to minimize unwanted sounds.
- **Use Case**: Ideal for play-by-play commentary and analysis in a controlled environment.

- **Mixers and Audio Interfaces**: A good audio mixer
  will allow you to blend commentary, game sounds and
  crowd noise, creating a balanced audio experience.
  USB audio interfaces can help connect multiple
  microphones to your streaming setup.
  - **Use Case**: Balancing commentary and
    ambient sounds to ensure smooth audio
    transitions.

When mixing audio for live sports streaming, using
headphones is crucial. They allow you to hear exactly what
your audience will hear, helping you make precise adjustments
to levels and balance. High-quality, closed-back headphones are
recommended to isolate external noise and focus on the mix.

For more complex setups, consider using IP Audio systems
like Dante (Digital Audio Network Through Ethernet). Dante
allows for the transmission of uncompressed, multi-channel
digital audio with near-zero latency over standard Ethernet
networks. This can be particularly useful in large venues or
when dealing with multiple audio sources spread across a wide
area.

- **Benefits of Dante for sports broadcasting**:
  - Flexibility: Easy to route multiple audio
    channels over long distances without signal
    degradation.
  - Scalability: Allows for easy expansion of your
    audio setup as your production grows.
  - Quality: Maintains high audio quality with
    minimal latency.
  - Integration: Many professional audio devices
    now come with built-in Dante compatibility.

While Dante systems can be more expensive and complex to
set up initially, they offer significant advantages for larger
productions or venues where traditional analog audio routing
would be challenging.

Streaming Hardware and Software

Once you have a plan to capture video and audio, you need to
stream it live to your audience. A hardware or software encoder
is used to take these live video sources and stream them to

your chosen viewing destination.

- **Hardware Encoders**: A hardware encoder converts your video and audio into a digital stream. This can be done via standalone units or built into cameras like PTZOptics models. Hardware encoders are more reliable and stable for live streaming compared to software alone.
  - **Use Case**: High-end or professional setups where reliability and quality are critical.
- **Software Encoders**: Software like OBS (Open Broadcaster Software) or vMix can handle live encoding on your computer. This software offers flexibility and customization, making it ideal for smaller setups or those with a tight budget.
  - **Use Case**: Entry-level or budget-friendly setups. Offers features like multi-camera switching and graphics overlays.
- **Capture Cards**: If you're using a camera that doesn't natively support IP video streaming, a capture card will be required to route the HDMI or SDI signal into your computer and convert it into a streamable format. Brands like Elgato, Magewell and AVerMedia offer easy-to-use solutions.
  - **Use Case**: Converting DSLR, camcorder or other video feeds into a format compatible with streaming software.

Additional Displays

Additional Displays for Fan Viewing: Extending your live stream to additional displays around the venue can enhance the fan experience. Here are some methods:

- **HDMI over CAT-5**: Use HDMI extenders to send the video signal from your streaming system to displays over long distances using CAT-5 ethernet cables.
  - **Use Case**: Ideal for sending high-quality video to displays in different areas of the venue without signal degradation.
- **NDI over Network**: Utilize NDI (Network Device Interface) to send video over your local area network (LAN).

- ○ **Use Case**: Perfect for distributing video to multiple displays across a campus or large venue. An NDI decoder can convert the IP video back to HDMI for display.
- **Smart TV with YouTube**: For a simple setup, use Smart TVs to display the YouTube stream of your event.
  - ○ **Note**: While easy to implement, this method introduces significant delay and is not suitable for real-time viewing.

Additional Accessories: Building Your Complete Kit

There are a few additional accessories you'll need to ensure a smooth live stream:

- **Lighting**: For indoor sports or even some outdoor night games, adequate lighting is crucial for clear footage. Consider using LED lights or softboxes to illuminate commentators or specific areas of the game.
- **Cables and Power Supplies**: Having enough HDMI cables, SDI cables and power adapters is essential. Ensure your setup is powered for the entire duration of the game and always have backup cables. Portable power stations like those from Jackery and Anker with built-in 110v power inverters, some with solar charging options, can power your setup for an entire day.
- **PoE Switches**: Power-over-Ethernet (PoE) switches are ideal for powering PTZ cameras and other devices using a single Ethernet cable for both power and data.
  - ○ **Use Case**: Simplifies cable management and reduces clutter in multi-camera setups.
- **WiFi router or Wireless Access Point (WAP)**
  - ○ A WiFi router is a networking device that allows multiple devices to connect to the internet wirelessly within a certain range. It acts as a hub, managing the data traffic between the internet and the connected devices, such as smartphones, tablets, computers and smart home devices and assigns IP addresses to each device. Wireless access points (WAPs) and Network extenders

connect to existing wired or wireless networks to extend their range.

Building Your Kit on a Budget vs. Professional Setup

Whether you're starting with a limited budget or building a high-end professional setup, here's a breakdown of the gear you'll need based on your goals:

- **Budget Setup:**
  - Basic camcorder or PTZ camera.
  - OBS for streaming and/or recording.
  - Lapel mic for commentary.
  - Monopod or basic tripod.
  - Capture card for non-streaming cameras.
- **Mid-Tier Setup:**
  - Multiple PTZ cameras for multi-angle shots.
  - vMix or other professional software.
  - Wireless microphones and shotgun mics for crowd noise. A USB connected audio mixer with headphones.
  - PoE network switch to connect your computer and cameras together.
- **Professional Setup:**
  - 4K PTZ cameras with remote control capabilities.
  - Hardware encoder for high-quality streams.
  - Full audio setup with mixers, ambient mics and commentator headsets.
  - Tripods with fluid heads, gimbals for dynamic shots and dedicated PoE switches for network management.

Summary: The Right Tools for Success

Choosing the right equipment will make all the difference in the quality of your live sports stream. Whether you're working with a shoestring budget or aiming for a professional-level production, understanding the tools available and how to use them will give you a strong foundation.

16 AUDIO FOR SPORTS PRODUCTION

In any sports production, capturing high-quality audio is just as important as delivering clear visuals. Whether it's the thud of a basketball on hardwood, the crowd's roar after a goal or the subtle sound of cleats on grass, audio helps bring the viewer closer to the action and enhances the overall experience. In this chapter, we'll explore the essential elements of capturing audio for live sports broadcasts, including microphone types, USB audio capture devices and the importance of using copyright-free music for intros and outros.

Capturing the Essence of the Game: Live Audio

When broadcasting live sports, the goal is to transport your audience to the heart of the event. Capturing the raw sounds of the game—such as the athletes' movements, crowd reactions and environmental noises—adds depth and realism to the production. This type of ambient sound provides context and makes the audience feel as if they are right there, in the stands, watching the game unfold.

Key audio elements to capture during a sports event include:

- **Athlete Movement Sounds:** The sound of players' feet moving across the field or court, ball bounces, hits and other physical interactions are essential for immersion.
- **Crowd Reactions:** The dynamic reactions of the crowd (cheers, boos, chants) should be captured, as they reflect the emotional ebb and flow of the game.
- **Commentary and Announcements:** Clear and professional commentary is critical for explaining gameplay, key moments and statistics to viewers.
- **Environmental Sounds:** Wind, referee whistles and other game-specific sounds can enhance the audio texture of the broadcast.

To achieve this, a combination of carefully positioned microphones and professional-grade audio equipment is required.

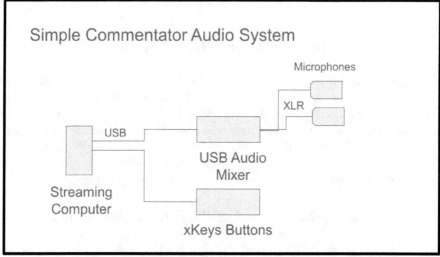

Audio connection diagram for sports commentators.

Technical Use of a USB Audio Capture Device

For smaller or more mobile sports productions, particularly those utilizing computers and live streaming software like OBS, vMix or Wirecast, a **USB audio capture device** can be a convenient and reliable way to capture high-quality audio. These devices serve as an interface between your audio sources (e.g., microphones, mixers) and your computer, converting analog signals into digital audio that can be processed by your streaming setup.

Steps to using a USB audio capture device:

1. **Connect the Microphone or Mixer:** Plug your microphones or audio mixing console into the USB audio interface. This could be a simple one-mic setup for smaller productions or a multi-mic feed via a soundboard for larger events.
2. **Connect to the Computer:** The USB audio interface is then connected to your computer via a USB cable. Most devices are plug-and-play, meaning your system will automatically recognize the hardware.
3. **Configure in Streaming Software:** In OBS or vMix, set the audio input to the connected USB capture device. From there, you can monitor levels, adjust gain and fine-tune your audio setup to ensure optimal sound quality.

Advantages of USB audio capture devices:

- **Portability:** Ideal for on-the-go setups, allowing you to capture professional audio without the need for bulky equipment.
- **Quality:** Converts analog signals to digital without sacrificing audio quality, ensuring clear, broadcast-ready sound.
- **Compatibility:** Works with various streaming and recording software, offering flexibility across different production environments.

Popular USB audio interfaces include the **Focusrite Scarlett 2i2**, **Behringer UMC22** and **PreSonus AudioBox USB 96**, each offering great options for different budget ranges.

Using Copyright-Free Music for Intros and Outros

Adding music to the intros and outros of your sports stream can elevate the production value and set the tone for the event. However, when using music in your streams, it's essential to avoid copyright infringement. Licensing issues can lead to streams being taken down or even legal penalties, so it's crucial to use **copyright-free music**.

Where to find copyright-free music:

- **YouTube Audio Library:** Free for commercial use, the YouTube Audio Library offers a wide variety of background music and sound effects.
- **Epidemic Sound:** A subscription-based service providing a vast library of high-quality, royalty-free music, ideal for stream intros and outros.
- **Artlist.io:** Another subscription service that offers access to a wide range of cinematic, sports-friendly music tracks that can be used in broadcasts.
- **Free Music Archive (FMA):** Provides a large collection of free music under Creative Commons licenses. Just be sure to follow the usage rights associated with each track.

Tips for using music in sports productions:

- **Match the Energy:** Choose music that matches the intensity of the sport. For instance, upbeat, energetic tracks work well for fast-paced sports like basketball, while more dramatic music may be suitable for soccer or football intros.
- **Volume Balance:** Ensure that the music volume is well-balanced with the commentary and live audio. Music should enhance the production, not overpower it.

- **Fade In/Out:** Use smooth transitions (fade-ins or fade-outs) when bringing music in or out of the broadcast to maintain a professional feel.

By using copyright-free music, you ensure that your broadcast remains legally compliant while still benefiting from the emotional and thematic lift that music can provide.

17 WORKING WITH COMMENTATORS

Commentators play a critical role in live sports broadcasts, bringing the game to life for viewers with play-by-play insights and expert analysis. Setting up a dedicated space for your commentators and ensuring they have the right technology is essential to a smooth broadcast. In this chapter, we'll explore how to prepare a commentary space, the best equipment to use and the communication systems needed for real-time collaboration between commentators and the production team.

One commentator and two camera operators working together to produce a simple three camera production with a touch screen video system.

1. Choosing the Right Headset for Commentators

When selecting a headset for your commentators, comfort and sound quality are paramount. Over the years, I've used various announcer headsets and I've found that not all are created equal. Here's my experience with some of the industry standards.

Sennheiser HMD280 (HMD300) Announcer's Headset

The Sennheiser HMD280 and its successor, the HMD300, stand out as solid, reliable headsets for professional sports broadcasting. I've used the HMD280 for years and I recently upgraded to the HMD300, which continues to impress with its durability and comfort.

Compared to earlier models like the Sennheiser HMD25 and HMD26, the HMD280/300 headsets have several advantages:

- **Durability:** The HMD25 and 26 were known for their excellent sound quality but suffered from poor physical construction, with exposed wiring and small, uncomfortable muffs. In contrast, the HMD280 and HMD300 have no exposed wires and the larger ear muffs offer far superior comfort, especially during long broadcasts.
- **Comfort:** The large muffs reduce ear fatigue, making these headsets perfect for extended use.
- **Audio Quality:** Both headsets provide crisp, clear sound, ensuring your commentators can hear every detail, whether they're communicating with the director or listening to the program feed. The microphone delivers high-quality voice capture, ideal for professional sports broadcasting.
- **Recommendation:** When purchasing, look for the "XQ" suffix model. This version includes both a 1/4" connector for the headphones and an XLR output for the microphone, making it compatible with most professional broadcast setups.

While the Audio-Technica BPHS1 may be an attractive option due to its lower price point, its boom arm is prone to breaking and it doesn't offer the same comfort or durability as the Sennheiser models. For long-term reliability and professional performance, the HMD280 and HMD300 are worth the investment.

2. Setting Up the Commentary Station

A commentator's station is far more than just a headset plugged into a mixer—it's a thoughtfully organized workspace that enables announcers to excel at their job while staying connected with the production team. To deliver engaging and informed commentary, announcers often rely on pre-event research, giving them access to detailed backgrounds on athletes. This allows them to share compelling stories, such as an athlete's hometown or key moments in their journey, adding depth and context that captivate the audience.

Commentary station at the 2025 Lancaster Archery Classic.

Announcer Stations: More Than Just a Mixer

Announcer stations are standalone systems that allow commentators to communicate with the director and other crew members while on-air. These stations are crucial for managing who can talk to whom and when. For example, during a broadcast, your announcers should be able to communicate with each other and the director without interrupting the live program.

One of the most respected brands in the industry for announcer stations is **Studio Technologies**. Their announcer stations are highly recommended for several reasons:

- **Internal Compressors:** These stations include built-in compressors to maintain consistent audio levels, preventing sudden volume spikes from the commentators.
- **Talkback and Cough Switches:** These features allow commentators to mute their microphones (using the cough switch) or communicate off-air with the director (using the talkback switch), ensuring smooth communication during live broadcasts.
- **Intercom Integration:** Studio Technologies' announcer stations double as intercom stations, allowing seamless communication between the commentary team and the production crew. They're powered over XLR intercom cables, simplifying the setup.

Commentator station with headsets and graphics control.

High School Commentary Case Study

The image above shows a two person commentary audio and graphics system. It can make sense to give the commentary team access to a controller which can overlay graphics for specific players. In this example, Salesianum High School allows the commentators the ability to overlay graphics and statistics about any player on the home team. There is a small display that shows the output of the live stream and the graphics. The 94 button Xkeys controller allows them to select any player by their number. The commentators can reference a roster which allows them to quickly know the names of players and bring up an image and graphic for that player. By labeling each button the same as the player's number, the commentators only need to consider which player number they want to display. A statistician sits next to each of the commentators and includes stats about each player which is brought in through a Google Sheets integration. This provides a professional level of graphics and control to a student run broadcast.

Defining Communication Channels

Before the broadcast, you need to define who needs to communicate with whom. In a typical setup, commentators will need to talk to each other, the director and possibly other team members like sideline reporters or camera operators. Here are a few common configurations:

- **Commentators ↔ Director:** Commentators should always be able to communicate with the director during the broadcast. This helps the director cue up replays, switch camera angles or make other live adjustments based on the commentary.
- **Director ↔ Camera Operators:** If your broadcast involves multiple camera angles, the director will need a direct line of communication with the camera operators to coordinate shots.
- **Producer ↔ Director:** In some setups, the producer may also need to communicate with the director, especially when coordinating graphics, replays or sponsorship elements.

This is where **intercom systems** come into play.

3. Intercom Systems for Real-Time Communication

Intercom systems are the backbone of real-time communication during a live sports broadcast. A well-configured intercom allows everyone involved in the production to stay in sync without causing confusion or interrupting the live broadcast.

Clear-Com Intercom Systems: Industry Standard

Clear-Com is one of the leading manufacturers of intercom systems for live broadcasts. Installing a 2 or 4-channel Clear-Com intercom headend allows you to manage communication across multiple channels.

- **Multiple Channels:** With a multi-channel intercom system, you can create separate communication lines for different groups. For example, you might have one channel for commentators and the director, another for the camera crew and a third for the production team. This keeps communication organized and prevents information overload.
- **Party Line Mode:** Clear-Com systems allow you to set up "party line" communication, where everyone on the intercom can talk to each other simultaneously. This is useful for large broadcasts where quick, group-wide communication is necessary.
- **Program Audio Feed:** The intercom system also allows you to feed the program audio to the commentators, ensuring they can hear what's happening on-air. This is crucial for commentators who need to respond to replays or other live events.

Cost Considerations

While professional intercom systems like Clear-Com can be expensive—ranging from $7,000 to $10,000—they are a worthwhile investment for serious live sports productions. These systems provide reliable, real-time communication, reducing errors and improving the overall quality of the broadcast.

If you're working on a tighter budget, there are more affordable solutions available. However, these often limit the number of communication channels or require workarounds that can introduce complexity. For smaller productions, a simpler intercom system may suffice, but for larger broadcasts, it's worth investing in a professional-grade system.

1. **Centralized Communication Room:** Keep all team members in the same room to facilitate communication. Utilize the mute button to manage audio and employ remote PTZ cameras to eliminate the need for direct communication with camera operators.
2. **Unity Intercom System:** Use a Unity Intercom system that leverages smartphones. This approach significantly reduces costs while maintaining essential features, although it requires a Unity subscription.
3. **Video Communication Platforms:** Consider using a video communication platform like Zoom or Discord. While not specifically designed for sports productions, they offer low-latency communication. You can connect your main live streaming computer to Zoom or Discord via virtual audio cables and others can join the communication via the app, provided they have a stable internet connection.

In conclusion, successful sports broadcasting relies heavily on effective communication and the right equipment. By selecting reliable headsets, setting up well-organized commentary stations and using professional intercom systems, broadcasters can ensure smooth and engaging live broadcasts. Investing in quality technology and clearly defining communication channels will enhance the collaboration between commentators and the production team, ultimately improving the viewer's experience.

18 GRAPHICS FOR SPORTS

When live streaming sports, the graphics you display significantly enhance the viewer's experience by providing critical information and adding a layer of professionalism. Let's start by ranking the types of graphics commonly used in sports broadcasts by their importance, from essential elements like scoreboards to more specialized graphics like social media callouts and team rosters.

Overlays -Uno graphics system embedded into OBS with a browser input.

Scoreboard (Highest Priority)

The scoreboard is the most crucial graphic in any sports broadcast. It shows the score, time, period/quarter and other basic game information like penalties or timeouts. Viewers constantly rely on the scoreboard for game context. It keeps them informed and engaged, helping them follow the action.

Here's a breakdown of common types of scoreboard graphics used in sports broadcasts:

1. **Standard Score Bug**

    The score bug is the small graphic typically positioned in a corner of the screen, showing the current score, time remaining and sometimes the period or quarter. It's designed to stay on screen throughout the game without obstructing the action. Scorebugs keep viewers informed on the game status at a glance.

Simple scorebug from Overlays.uno.

2. **Lower Thirds**

Lower thirds are graphics that appear across the bottom third of the screen. They're often used to display additional information, like player statistics, quick game summaries or recent scoring plays. Lower thirds are flexible, as they can appear and disappear as needed without covering too much of the game.

Full screen takeover graphic from Overlays.uno

3. **Full-Screen Takeovers**

A full-screen graphic temporarily replaces the game feed with a detailed scorecard or stats breakdown. Full-screen takeovers are used during breaks, timeouts or pre- and post-game segments to provide deeper insights, including team comparisons, player stats and scoring summaries. These are often animated and visually rich to enhance engagement.

4. **Ticker or Scrolling Scoreboard**

Tickers are horizontal scrolling graphics, usually at the bottom or top of the screen, that display scores, updates or stats in a continuous loop. This type is used to share quick updates or show scores from multiple games. Tickers are popular in multi-game broadcasts, like major tournament coverage.

5. **Animated In-Game Pop-Ups**

These smaller, momentary graphics appear briefly on the screen to highlight specific information, such as a scoring streak, player performance milestones or important game statistics. They provide context without interrupting the live view and are often used to emphasize key moments without taking over the screen.

Implementation Tips:

- **Automation:** Use software that can pull live data directly from the scoreboard controller, reducing manual updates. Genius Sports and ScoreLink from Sportzcast are solutions that can take the output from scoreboard systems and convert them into usable data for live streaming software such as Wirecast, vMix or a TriCaster.
- **Manual Input:** If automation isn't possible, assign a team member to update the scoreboard manually in real time, ensuring consistency throughout the game. You can use a keyboard, a custom xKeys interface or a web-browser for data input. You can also use a simple Google Sheet for keeping score, which can sync the data with your live streaming system. This allows you to have your data come from anyone watching the game willing to update the Google sheet that is synced with your virtual scoreboard. SuiteCG is a solution for manually inputting graphics that is designed for inputting data with a touch screen or computer interface. SuiteCG is a subscription that makes it easy to capture scoreboard data and output that data via NDI or XML which is

easy to use with vMix, Wirecast, OBS, Livestream Studio, xSplit and video switchers like those from Blackmagic Design.

- **Computer Vision:** It's possible to point a camera at a scoreboard and extract the data from the physical scoreboard for use with digital graphics. These systems pull data from the video and output the data in a readable XML or TXT file. Scoreboard OCR recognizes digits from physical scoreboards and sends them directly to your graphics software. All you need is a laptop with a connected camera (or you can use your existing live production computer). It's a great solution for basketball, hockey, handball, floorball, futsal, volleyball and other sports.
  - **Pro Tip:** If you don't have a scoreboard to pull data from, you can use an optical zoom camera to zoom into the score board and overlay a video feed from the actual scoreboard on your broadcast.

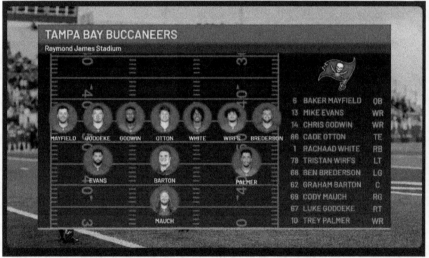

Field placement and player roster graphic.

Informational Sports Graphics

Here's a breakdown of common informational sports graphics used in broadcasts to deliver in-depth game context:

1. **Match Stats**

   Match stats graphics show essential game metrics—such as possession percentages, shots on goal, turnovers and fouls. These graphics are often displayed during pauses in play, giving viewers a quick summary of team performance without disrupting live action.

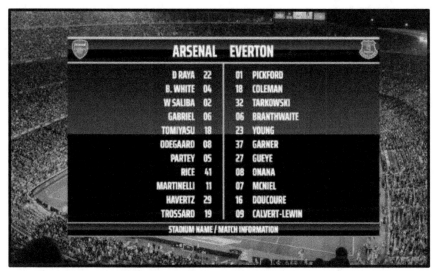

Lineup panel from Overlays.uno.

2. **Lineup Panels**

Lineup panels introduce the starting players and their positions for each team. They're often shown pre-game and include player names, numbers and sometimes key stats. Lineup graphics help viewers familiarize themselves with the players on the field or court.

3. **Field Formations**

Field formation graphics illustrate each team's tactical setup, showing the positions and structure (like 4-3-3 or 3-4-3 in soccer). These are typically displayed before the game starts or after major changes (like a substitution), helping viewers understand strategic choices.

4. **Leaderboards**

Leaderboards are used in individual or seasonal sports to show rankings based on cumulative stats. They display the top performers in various categories, such as points, goals or wins, offering context on where each player or team stands in the competition or season.

5. **Scoreboards with Stats**

These are enhanced scorebugs that add key in-game stats alongside the score, such as top scorers, assists and shooting percentages. They provide extra insights while remaining relatively unobtrusive and can be used as mini recaps during game breaks.

6. **Fullscreen Player Bio**

A fullscreen player bio takes over the screen to highlight details about a specific player, such as height, weight, age and career stats. These are used to spotlight notable players during breaks, providing fans with a closer look at star athletes or rising talent.

7. **Final Score Overlay**

The final score overlay appears at the end of the game to display the game's result along with stats, top scorers or a summary of key moments. This graphic offers viewers a conclusive snapshot of the game and is often accompanied by closing commentary.

8. **League/Playoff Brackets**

Brackets graphics illustrate the structure of a tournament, showing matchups and progression through each round. As the playoffs advance, these graphics are updated to reflect which teams have progressed, helping viewers track the tournament journey and anticipate upcoming games.

Each of these informational graphics serves to enhance the broadcast by providing relevant, in-depth information that keeps viewers informed and engaged, adding depth to the viewing experience without detracting from the live game action.

Game recap and score infographic.

- **Implementation Tips:**
  - **Prep:** Gather roster information, player stats and key facts before the game. Design templates with placeholders for this data to streamline updates during the broadcast.
  - **Flexibility:** Use templates that allow quick edits, so you can adjust player names or stats on the fly as needed.
  - **Tip:** Lower thirds are a great way to acknowledge the commentators who are speaking over the broadcast.

Team Rosters & Lineups (Medium Priority)

Roster graphics show the starting lineups or full team rosters. These graphics often appear before the game starts or during player changes. Viewers, especially fans, want to know who is on the field or court at any given time. Displaying this information early in the broadcast helps set the stage for the game.

- **Implementation Tips:**
  - **Prep:** Ensure you have access to accurate rosters well before game day. Double-check for any last-minute changes to avoid outdated information.
  - **Automated Feeds:** If possible, use XML or CSV files from official league or team sources to feed data directly into your graphics software for easy updates. You can also create a standard Google Form or Google Sheet and ask teams to enter the data before the game. This way you can

pull the data in a standard format that is ready for your graphics template.

Replay Graphics & Overlays (Medium Priority)

Replay graphics are used to indicate that the viewer is watching a replay. These graphics are often branded and provide a quick reminder that the action is being shown again. Replays are an essential part of sports broadcasts, allowing viewers to rewatch key moments; a clear indicator lets them know they're watching a replay and not live action.

- **Implementation Tips:**
  - **Prep:** Design replay graphics that align with the team or event branding. These can be reused throughout the season but should be updated if the branding changes. Stinger transitions are often used to signal to viewers that an instant replay is coming up next.
  - **Timing:** Make sure your team triggers the replay graphic quickly when replay content starts to avoid confusion.

Stinger Transitions (Lower Priority)

Stinger transitions are short animations used to transition between shots, replays or breaks in the action. They're usually team-branded or event-themed. While not essential for following the game, stinger transitions enhance the production value and professionalism of your broadcast. They provide a smoother viewing experience.

- **Implementation Tips:**
  - **Prep:** Create stinger transitions before the season begins, so they can be reused throughout. Update them only if team logos or sponsors change.
  - **Combine:** Add the replay graphic to the center point in the stinger animation or create a shortcut to trigger the graphic and then the stinger transition.
  - **Reusability:** These can be used across multiple games with little to no modification.

Key Moments Graphics (Lower Priority)

These graphics highlight major game events like goals, fouls or turnovers with short animations or pop-up text. They help emphasize pivotal moments and keep the viewer's attention focused on the game's flow.

- **Implementation Tips:**
  - **Prep:** Pre-design these graphics, ensuring they match the overall theme of your broadcast. You can set up flexible templates that allow for quick updates as the game progresses. A simple video clip can be used for key moments that you can overlay on top of the live video feed.
  - **Tip:** Websites such as Envato Elements and Story Blocks allow you to download stock graphics and videos that you can use for key moments during your broadcast.

Telestrator Graphics (Lower Priority)

Telestrator graphics are transparent overlay channels that allow broadcasters to circle, diagram and highlight specific areas or actions during a game. These graphics are often used to analyze plays, strategies or key moments, providing viewers with a deeper understanding of the game.

- **Implementation Tips:**
  - **Prep:** Ensure you have the telestrator software integrated with your broadcast system. Familiarize your team with the tools to draw and highlight key areas on the screen.
  - **Usage:** Use the telestrator sparingly to emphasize important points, such as player positioning or strategic plays, to avoid overwhelming viewers with too much information.
  - **Pro Tip:** Practice using the telestrator during rehearsals to ensure smooth operation and clear communication during the live broadcast. There are several NDI telestration apps available to use with a touch screen tablet. vMix recently added a telestrator into their software which is very easy to use.

Social Media Graphics (Optional)

Social media graphics show live updates or fan interaction, such as tweets or shout outs during the game. While not necessary, these graphics can increase viewer engagement by making the broadcast interactive and community driven.

- **Implementation Tips:**
  - **Prep:** Set up a system to pull in social media posts ahead of time and design templates that match your broadcast's branding. Filter out inappropriate content for live displays.

- ○ **Pro Tip**: Pro live streaming software such as vMix and Wirecast offer built in social media integration tools. These tools collect all of the comments on your live stream and allow you to choose the comments you would like to display on your live stream.

Popular Sports Graphics Solutions

In live sports streaming, dynamic and engaging graphics are essential for providing a professional and informative viewer experience. From scoreboards to player statistics, sports graphics enhance broadcasts by keeping viewers updated with real-time information. Here's a look at some of the most popular and widely used sports graphics solutions:

Overlays.uno web-based controller.

1. **Uno by Singular Live**

   Uno by Singular Live is a free sports graphic system that you can integrate directly into any live streaming software. The system includes built-in controllers and everything you need for any sport. You can pick from hundreds of options in the overlay library. Click for a quick preview and simply "Add to My Overlays" to add them to your account where you can customize text, colors, logos and more. From there you can paste the output URL into the streaming solution of your choice. It's that easy.

2. **LIGR (Live Graphic Systems)**

LIGR is a robust cloud-based platform that offers fully automated sports graphics, integrating live data to display real-time scores, player stats and match events. It's popular for its ease of use and scalability, serving both amateur and professional sports broadcasts. With pre-designed templates and branding options, LIGR helps sports streamers elevate their productions without needing advanced technical skills.

3. **NewBlueFX Titler Live Sport**

NewBlueFX Titler Live Sport is a premium solution widely used by broadcasters for its advanced sports graphics capabilities. It offers real-time, data-driven scoreboards, statistics and animations. It integrates with platforms like NDI, vMix and Wirecast and is ideal for both professional sports teams and schools looking to enhance their sports streams. Titler Live Sport's professional-grade animations and flexible customization options make it a go-to for high-quality sports productions.

4. **SportZcast**

SportZcast provides automated, real-time scoreboards that pull data directly from game consoles, making it an excellent choice for sports broadcasters looking for automation. The system easily integrates with various production software like OBS, vMix and TriCaster. With SportZcast, broadcasters can focus on the game while the graphics update automatically, offering real-time data and seamless operation.

5. **SportFX**

SportFX is an open-source sports graphics platform that offers customizable scoreboards, timers and overlays. It's particularly useful for smaller productions or teams with limited budgets. The flexibility of SportFX allows users to adapt it to various sports, making it a good choice for those who want to create professional-looking broadcasts on a budget.

6. **Scoreboard+**

Scoreboard+ is a free and simple tool for creating scoreboards and timers, ideal for smaller sports streams that don't require advanced features. Its integration with OBS allows for easy overlay of scoreboards during live events. While limited in features compared to more robust platforms, Scoreboard+ is perfect for community sports or amateur streamers who need a quick and straightforward solution.

These solutions cater to a range of production scales, from small community sports to large professional broadcasts. Whether you're looking for free, open-source tools or advanced, professional-grade graphics, there's a solution to meet your specific sports streaming needs.

Organizing and Inputting Data Efficiently

Now that we've outlined the various types of sports graphics and how to prepare them, it's important to have a system in place for organizing data and efficiently inputting it into your broadcast. This section covers the tools, workflows and tips to make sure your data management is seamless, allowing for quick updates and error-free graphics during the live stream.

Centralized Data Management

Having a single source of truth for all your game-related data is critical. You want to avoid confusion or delays caused by inconsistent or outdated information. A centralized data management system ensures that everyone on the production team is working with the same, up-to-date information.

- **Use Spreadsheets or Databases:**
  - Tools like **Google Sheets**, **Microsoft Excel** or **Airtable** can serve as your primary source for rosters, player stats, team logos and more. These tools allow multiple users to update and access the same information in real-time.
  - **Organize Data by Category:** Set up separate tabs or tables for different types of data (e.g., rosters, scores, key stats, game events) to keep everything organized and easy to access.
- **Automated Data Feeds:**
  - Whenever possible, connect your data management system to a **live feed** of sports data. Many sports leagues and organizations offer API integrations that automatically pull stats and game info, reducing manual input.
  - **Integration with Broadcast Software:** Software like vMix, OBS or Wirecast often supports integration with live data feeds, automating the update process for graphics like scoreboards and player stats. This is ideal for real-time updates and ensures that your graphics are always up to

date during the game.

Organizing for Multiple Games or Seasons

If you're live streaming multiple games throughout a season organizing your data and graphics efficiently across different events will save you a lot of time.

- **Folder Structure for Graphics:**
  - ○ Create a well-organized **folder structure** on your computer or graphics system for each team or game. This way, you can easily find and update the right graphics when switching between events.
- **Seasonal Graphics Preparation:**
  - ○ Pre-design all your reusable graphics, like **stinger transitions, team logos and replay overlays** at the start of the season. This will give you more time to focus on live data and player-specific updates during each game.

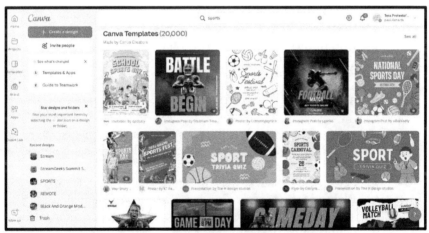
Canva has over 20,000 templates for sports.

Canva is highly recommended

Canva is a versatile, easy-to-use graphic design platform that can be highly effective for creating **sports graphics**. Whether for live streaming, game-day announcements, social media posts or scoreboard graphics, Canva offers a wide range of features that make it accessible for teams, coaches and content creators to design engaging sports-related visuals. Here's how Canva can be used in the sports industry:

1. Templated Content

Canva can be used to create content for any sport and it's particularly useful for pre and post game content. You can easily design templates with team logos and colors to allow your team to quickly output timely posts.

- **Templates**: Start with pre-made scoreboard templates or create custom designs using elements like text, numbers and icons.
- **Customization**: Add team logos, player names and other relevant game data to fit your team's branding.
- **Animation**: Use Canva's animation features to create engaging transitions between scores or display dynamic updates.

2. Game Day Announcements

Canva allows users to create eye-catching game-day graphics that can be shared across social media platforms like Instagram, Twitter and Facebook. These announcements can include:

- **Match details**: Date, time, venue and opposing team.
- **Players to Watch**: Highlight key players or game stats.
- **Countdown Timers**: Design countdown visuals to build anticipation for an upcoming match.

3. Highlight Reels and Post-Game Wrap-Ups

Canva can be used to create graphics for post-game highlights and recaps by importing video clips from your broadcast. These visuals can include:

- **Scorecards**: Final scores, top scorers or key stats from the game.
- **Player of the Match**: Graphics that showcase individual achievements with their picture, stats and notable moments.
- **Game Stats**: Breakdown of shots, assists, possession percentages and other relevant statistics.

4. Social Media Graphics

Sports teams can maintain their online presence using Canva to create:

- **Social Media Posts**: From live updates during the game to post-match reports, Canva allows for real-time, branded content creation.
- **Infographics**: Share team performance, player milestones or

season standings with visually engaging infographics.

- **Animated Posts**: Use Canva's animation features to create dynamic social media content, such as goal celebrations, win announcements or player highlights.

5. Team Branding and Marketing Materials

Canva offers features to design and update **team branding** materials like:

- **Team Logos**: Create professional-quality logos using Canva's design tools or templates.
- **Merchandise Graphics**: Design graphics for jerseys, caps and promotional items.
- **Marketing Flyers and Posters**: Canva can be used to design promotional flyers for upcoming matches, events or sponsorships.

6. Sponsor Integration and Advertisements

Canva makes it easy to incorporate **sponsor logos** and advertisements into sports graphics:

- **In-game ads**: Create banners or graphics featuring sponsor logos for use during live streams or on social media.
- **Sponsorship Decks**: Build professional pitch decks or presentations to showcase sponsorship opportunities using Canva's intuitive tools.

7. Video Thumbnails and Cover Art

For sports-related video content on platforms like YouTube or social media, Canva can be used to design engaging **video thumbnails** and cover art that capture attention:

- **Custom Thumbnails**: Add team logos, player action shots and bold text to draw viewers to your content.
- **Event Promotion**: Use Canva to create graphics that promote sports-related events or highlight specific video content (e.g., game analysis, behind-the-scenes footage).

As we've explored throughout this chapter, graphics play a crucial role in enhancing the viewer experience for sports broadcasts. From essential elements like scoreboards to more specialized graphics such as player stats and social media callouts, each type of graphic serves a specific purpose in keeping the audience informed and engaged.

We've discussed the importance of organizing and efficiently managing data, emphasizing the need for centralized data management systems and flexible templates. These practices ensure that your graphics remain accurate and up to date throughout the broadcast, contributing to a professional and polished production.

The chapter also highlighted various tools and software options available for creating and managing sports graphics, from professional-grade solutions to more accessible options like OBS plugins and Canva. These tools cater to a wide range of budgets and skill levels, making it possible for both amateur and professional broadcasters to elevate their sports coverage.

Remember, the key to successful sports graphics lies in preparation organization and the ability to adapt in real-time. By implementing the strategies and tools discussed in this chapter, you'll be well-equipped to create engaging, informative and professional-looking sports broadcasts that keep your viewers coming back for more.

As you continue to develop your skills in sports broadcasting, don't be afraid to experiment with different graphic styles and techniques. The world of sports graphics is constantly evolving and staying current with new trends and technologies will help you stand out in this competitive field

19 INSTANT REPLAY

Instant replay is a cornerstone of modern sports broadcasting. It offers audiences a second look at critical plays, enhancing the viewing experience and capturing moments that can change the outcome of a game. Whether you're live streaming a local high school game or a professional sports event, understanding how to implement instant replay effectively can set your broadcast apart. In this chapter, we'll explore the tools, techniques and strategies needed to integrate instant replay seamlessly into your live sports streams.

Roland P-20HD Instant Replay System.

When discussing instant replay systems for sports, it's important to recognize the distinction between two types of systems:

1. **Broadcast Integrated Systems**: These systems are designed for live streaming and video production. They are typically integrated directly into the broadcast workflow, providing replays to audiences through software like vMix or Wirecast. These tools are built for high-quality replays during live streams, often with slow-motion capabilities and multiple camera angles, which help enhance the viewing experience.
2. **Coach's Instant Replay Systems**: In contrast, the systems used by coaches, such as SkyCoach, are built for real-time, tactical

analysis. These systems allow coaches to instantly review plays on wireless tablets, like iPads, providing quick access to video feedback for decision-making on the sidelines. They usually support 2-4 camera angles and prioritize simplicity and speed, offering immediate playback and easy control for both coaches and referees.

Most sports organizations choose to keep these two systems separate to ensure redundancy and maintain priority for both operations. However, some cameras can be connected to both systems simultaneously. For instance, a PTZOptics camera can provide an HDMI feed to a coach's replay system while also delivering an NDI signal to production software for instant replays during live broadcasts. This integration ensures that both the production team and the coaching staff can access critical footage without compromising either workflow.

Why Instant Replay Matters

Instant replay adds value to sports broadcasts by:

- **Clarifying close calls**: Audiences want to see critical moments like goals, fouls or pivotal plays from different angles, especially in fast-paced sports.
- **Engaging the audience**: Replays create excitement and provide fans with additional insights into the game.
- **Supporting officiating**: Referees and officials sometimes rely on instant replays to make fair judgments.

Whether you're aiming to impress fans or assist officials, incorporating replay into your sports streams is essential.

Equipment for Instant Replay

To integrate instant replay, you'll need to ensure you have the right tools in place. Here's a list of equipment to get started:

1. **Capture Cards**: Capture cards are vital for grabbing live footage from your cameras into your computer or production system. A reliable, high-quality capture card ensures your replays are as smooth as your live feed.
    1. NDI has emerged as a new IP video standard that essentially eliminates the need for capture cards but requires some networking knowledge. NDI technology does use compression to send video over a standard

network but the quality is optimized and is good enough for even professional broadcasts.

2. PCIe capture cards are generally one to four port HDMI or SDI video capture cards that can be inserted into to tower computers (preferably i7, i9 or better with high-end graphics cards (or high-end Thunderbolt 3 equipped laptops or Macs with an external enclosure). The benefit of capture cards is the video quality which is uncompressed and very reliable.

2. **Video Switcher/Replay System**: A switcher with built-in replay capabilities is critical for instant replay. Software like vMix, OBS with plugins or hardware switchers like the YoloBox, Magewell Director or the Vizrt TriCaster can manage replays seamlessly.

   1. These systems will require a dedicated operator who can start and stop the instant replay system and scrub through the video. A dedicated controller is highly recommended, but you can use a simple keyboard and mouse if you are just getting started.

   2. The YoloBox and Magewell Director Mini are simple touch screens with integrated instant replay. These are a great place to start with instant replay.

Instant replay operator using a Viz 3Play system at the 2025 Lancaster Archery Classic.

3. **Dedicated Instant Replay Systems**: The Roland P20-HD is a standout option for an easy-to-use, HDMI-based instant replay system. It is reasonably priced and includes everything needed for

a single-camera instant replay workflow, featuring HDMI input and output for seamless integration. This system can be added to any video production setup, including software-based systems, with an HDMI-to-USB capture card. Another excellent choice is the **Vizrt 3Play** system, designed for professional-grade productions. It offers advanced instant replay capabilities, supporting multiple cameras and delivering smooth, high-quality slow-motion replays. With its robust feature set and scalability, the Viz 3Play is ideal for high-stakes sports productions requiring precision and versatility.

4. **Multiple Cameras**: Different camera angles will add depth to your replays, so having multiple camera feeds ready for replay is key. Consider PTZ cameras for remote control over multiple angles.

    1. When you start an instant replay, your system can record on multiple cameras. Then during playback, you can switch camera angles at the exact moment of replay you are playing from. This allows you to show different angles and slow down the play for review.

5. **Storage**: Instant replay requires footage storage to pull clips from moments after they happen. Ensure you have fast solid-state drives (SSDs) or other high-speed storage solutions.

6. **Controller/Hotkeys**: For smooth replay operation, using a physical controller (like an X-Keys or Stream Deck) or well-configured hotkeys can help your operator quickly capture, cue and play replays.

7. **Telestrator** - A telestrator will allow you to annotate over the replay video. This is an extra layer of complexity, but it gives your commentators extra depth to their explanations.

Coaching Instant Replay Systems

When it comes to sideline replay systems, SkyCoach stands out as an affordable instant replay system designed for coaches. SkyCoach provides an optimized computer system to run the entire operation, ensuring smooth and reliable performance. The remote camera kit even includes functionality for coding offense or defense while recording, which not only enhances efficiency, saving time later, but also reduces costs compared to other solutions.

SkyCoach is designed to be operated by any touch screen tablet.

A significant advantage of SkyCoach is the elimination of common excuses like "your iPad or computer is causing the issue." SkyCoach takes responsibility for providing a trustworthy, cost-effective system, offering the fastest, most reliable network available. With gigabit wireless network technology, SkyCoach ensures that no opponent will have a faster system, giving your team a competitive edge. Additionally, SkyCoach offers extensive network coverage with more antennas included in its packages, providing flexibility and reliability that other providers lack.

For example, press box coaches using SkyCoach don't need to be in the same room as the camera operators. The sideline antennas can be positioned independently of the end zone antennas, thanks to a dedicated press box antenna. This flexible setup also allows hardwiring devices in congested Wi-Fi areas, addressing potential network challenges during away games.

SkyCoach's replay system offers advanced functionality, such as switching between camera angles at the exact same moment in the video, allowing coaches to analyze multiple perspectives simultaneously. It also provides live reports immediately after the whistle blows, integrating video with stats. This feature is available for more than two angles, unlike competitors who often limit this capability. SkyCoach doesn't rely on having the latest iPads either. lder models work just as well, thanks to SkyCoach's robust system design. This ensures that you aren't stuck upgrading devices unnecessarily and reinforces the reliability of the product.

Using Instant Replays for Highlight Reels

Creating highlight reels from the recorded instant replays is a convenient way to recap the most exciting moments of a game. After the game, these highlight reels can be crafted by stitching together key plays and replays to deliver a dynamic game summary that can engage fans across different platforms. Here's how to put together a polished and engaging highlight reel:

Step 1: Record Replays with Commentary

During the game, ensure that all significant replays or standout moments are recorded with commentary audio if possible. Commentary provides context and excitement, helping viewers understand why each moment is impactful. When the highlight reel features this commentary, it not only enhances the storytelling but also brings viewers closer to the game's atmosphere and emotions. If you do not have commentary, you can add an exciting music clip to your highlight reel instead.

Step 2: Add Graphics for Score, Time and Period

Use graphics that display the score, time and period for each clip is essential for context. These graphics keep viewers oriented within the flow of the game, showing them exactly when each highlight took place. For instance, if a key play occurred in the last few seconds of the game, that time indicator can add drama and emphasize the play's importance.

Step 3: Edit the Reel Using a Video Editor

Import all recorded highlights into a video editor. Begin by selecting clips that represent the best plays or defining moments of the game. Then, arrange these clips in chronological order or group them by theme (e.g., all scoring plays together, defensive highlights together), depending on the story you want to tell.

For longer platforms like YouTube, edit the reel into a 16:9 format. This allows for widescreen viewing, which is ideal for TV or desktop monitors. For short-form platforms like TikTok and Instagram, create a second version in a 9:16 vertical format, focusing on tight shots and avoiding wide views that may lose detail in a smaller frame.

Step 4: Optimize the Reel for Each Platform

For YouTube, a longer, more detailed highlight reel of 3-5 minutes can keep viewers engaged, especially if it covers the game's major turning points or delivers a mini narrative of the game. Add a title slide, end screen and thumbnail to attract viewers. For TikTok, Instagram Reels and other short-form platforms, aim for 30 seconds to 1 minute, keeping the pacing fast with quick cuts to maintain viewer interest.

Step 5: Review and Refine

Before publishing, watch the reel a few times to ensure it flows smoothly and tells a cohesive story. Adjust any graphics for clarity, ensure the commentary audio syncs with the clips and make any necessary tweaks to pacing. For a final polish, consider adding background music or subtle sound effects to amplify the emotional impact of key moments.

By recording replays with commentary, incorporating contextual graphics and tailoring your edit for different platforms, you'll create a highlight reel that effectively captures the game's story, engages fans and reaches audiences across various channels.

Software Solutions for Video Editing Highlight Reels

Adobe Premiere Pro: A powerful, timeline-based editor with advanced tools for quick cuts, transitions and AI-assisted motion tracking, making it ideal for professional sports highlights.

Final Cut Pro (macOS only): Known for its magnetic timeline and multicam editing, it delivers smooth performance on Apple devices, perfect for fast-turnaround sports highlight reels.

DaVinci Resolve: Offers editing, color correction and effects in one platform, with a streamlined Cut Page and advanced tools for creating polished sports highlights, even in its free version.

Software Solutions for Instant Replay

There are many software options available for handling instant replay, each catering to different levels of production:

- **vMix Instant Replay**: Offers robust replay options, including slow-motion capabilities, multi-angle replays and customizable transitions.
- **Wirecast Replay**: Provides a streamlined option for smaller productions while still offering multi-camera replay support.
- **OBS**: A more affordable solution, perfect for smaller sports streams, though it requires more setup and configuration.

241

Step-by-Step Replay Workflow

Here's how to integrate instant replay into your sports live stream:

1. **Set Up Replay Cues**: Designate a replay operator or have automated hotkeys that capture crucial moments. In vMix, for example, use the replay feature to grab video from a set number of seconds before an event.
2. **Select Camera Angles**: If you have multiple camera angles, choose the best one for the replay. This has to be done quickly, so it's nice to have a replay controller with an option for each camera.
3. **Play Replay During Breaks**: Broadcast replays during natural breaks, like timeouts, fouls or player substitutions, so they don't interrupt live game action.
4. **Slow-Motion Effect**: For dramatic moments, slow-motion can add clarity and drama. Use this feature for replays of goals, close calls or crucial plays.

Pro Tip: If you play back a 10 second replay at 50% speed it will take 20 seconds. Depending on the sport you are working with, you need to get a sense of how quickly the gameplay will resume. You may need to do a 5-second instant replay at 50% playback if the team is ready to play in 10-15 seconds.

Best Practices for Sports Replay

1. **Timing is Everything**: Play replays at the right moment without disrupting the live flow of the game. Viewers should see the replay quickly after the action.
2. **Use Replays Sparingly**: Not every moment requires a replay. Focus on significant plays to keep the audience engaged.

Advanced Replay Techniques

As you become more comfortable with instant replay, you can experiment with advanced techniques to add professionalism to your sports stream:

- **Multicam Switching**: Switch between different camera angles in quick succession to build drama.
- **Speed Changes**: You can adjust the speed at which your instant replay plays.
- **Scrubbing**: You can manually scrub through frames of video with a jog-dial to find specific moments during the play.
- **Playlists**: Replay operators will often create a playlist of replays

which are played in sequence. Replay playlists are often used at the end of a segment or during a break in play.

XKeys instant-replay controller designed for vMix.

The Importance of 60fps for Slow-Motion Replays

When it comes to instant replay, especially slow-motion, having cameras that can shoot at **60 frames per second (fps)** is crucial. Here's why:

1. **Smoother Playback**: At 60fps, there are more frames to work with, so when you slow down the footage, the motion remains fluid and natural. In contrast, 30fps footage may look choppy or blurry when slowed down.

2. **Clearer Details**: Fast-paced action, like a soccer ball crossing the goal line or a basketball player making a slam dunk, can be difficult to analyze in real-time. A higher frame rate ensures you capture all the small details, which can be critical for both the audience and officials reviewing the play.

3. **Better for Sports**: Most sports involve rapid movements. Whether it's a fast-moving puck or a quick pass between players, 60fps allows you to freeze-frame these moments without losing clarity.

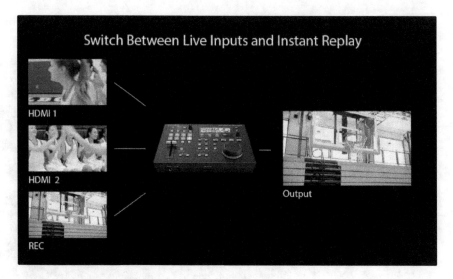

Mastering instant replay can take your sports live streams to the next level. Whether you're covering local sports or professional events, delivering high-quality replays will enhance the viewer experience and increase your production value. Start small, with simple replays from a single angle and gradually build out your system to include multi-camera, slow-motion and advanced graphic integration. As you grow, so will the impact of your sports broadcasts.

20 SPORTS VIDEO ESSENTIALS - LEVEL 4

Ross Carbonite video switcher used for the 2025 Lancaster Archery Classic.

At Level 4, live streaming and video production ascend to professional-grade setups, incorporating advanced technology and workflows used by top-tier sports broadcasters. This level not only introduces high-end video switchers but also expands the production to include multi-screen displays throughout a venue, creating an immersive experience for audiences.

Professional video switchers from brands like Ross Video, Blackmagic Design and Grass Valley are often the backbone of Level 4 productions but are not always a requirement. These powerful systems support many inputs, real-time graphics, advanced transitions and instant replay capabilities. Unlike entry-level and mid-range systems, professional switchers are designed for large-scale productions with dedicated teams. Operators can focus on specific tasks, such as managing cameras, graphics or audio, allowing for seamless collaboration. However, these systems require significant investment and advanced training, making them ideal for venues and organizations that demand the highest production quality. It's important to note that you can take a level 2 NDI system and train a team to operate it, with video quality that rivals TV.

In addition to professional grade switching, Level 4 productions expand the visual experience throughout the venue with multi-screen displays, including video scoreboards, LED walls and projectors. These additional displays can be strategically placed in lobbies, lounges, concourses and other high-traffic areas, ensuring that no one misses the action. A video scoreboard, for example, can be transformed into a dynamic focal point by combining live broadcasts with real-time scores, game statistics and sponsorship graphics. These displays not only enhance audience engagement but also create valuable opportunities for monetization through branded content and advertisements.

Level 3 broadcast systems often integrate with local TV stations and large screen displays in stadiums.

One of the key technologies enabling multi-screen setups is NDI (Network Device Interface). Using NDI to HDMI decoders, production teams can take the NDI output from their production system and convert it to HDMI, allowing video feeds to be distributed across the venue's network infrastructure. This eliminates the need for complex cabling and enables seamless connectivity to additional displays. From LED walls showcasing the game's highlights to auxiliary screens featuring targeted sponsor content, NDI technology makes it easy to scale up and customize the viewing experience for audiences.

The ScoreView solution shown on an LCD.

For venues looking to transform video walls into interactive scoreboards, solutions like Scorebird's ScoreView are invaluable. ScoreView specializes in integrating real-time game data with custom sponsorship content, allowing venues to display scores, animations and branded messages alongside live broadcasts. This level of customization not only enhances the visual appeal of the venue but also opens new revenue streams by maximizing screen time for advertisers.

Level 3 productions represent the pinnacle of live streaming and event broadcasting. They combine professional video switchers with advanced multi-screen strategies to create an immersive and engaging experience for both in-person and remote audiences. By leveraging tools like NDI to HDMI decoders and ScoreView, venues can optimize their workflows, enhance audience interaction and drive revenue growth. Whether it's for sports, live entertainment or corporate events, a Level 3 setup ensures that your production meets the highest standards of professionalism and creativity.

How it looks:

With these systems you should expect your video to look like the pros. If you have the staff and team to maintain a professional video system, you can achieve broadcast-level quality with seamless transitions, advanced effects and precise control over multiple inputs. These systems are designed for complex productions, supporting features like instant replay, multi-camera feeds and sophisticated graphics integration.

While these setups are powerful, the good news is that many features once only available to professionals are now within reach of producers at Level 2. With the right tools and a bit of practice, you can achieve results that used to require an entire broadcast team.

There are a lot of reasons to use a hardware video switcher especially as your video production grows. Hardware is always more reliable than software and a hardware video switcher can be used to take the processing load off your computer. As your skills and production aspirations progress, you'll likely continue to look for reliable hardware that you can incorporate into your productions.

21 REMOTE SPORTS PRODUCTION

The Rise of Remote Sports Production

The landscape of live streaming sports has evolved dramatically in recent years, with the introduction of cloud-based solutions and remote production tools. These advancements allow sports events to be produced and streamed without requiring an on-site production team, significantly reducing costs and increasing flexibility. Remote sports production offers new possibilities for smaller sports organizations, schools and local leagues to produce professional-quality streams, even with limited resources.

In this chapter, we'll dive into the key aspects of remote sports production, including using cloud-based solutions, managing remote teams and addressing network challenges like latency.

Cloud-Based Solutions for Remote Production

Cloud-based production tools have revolutionized the way live sports events are streamed. With cloud platforms, operators can control cameras, switch feeds, manage graphics and mix audio—all from a remote location. This eliminates the need for on-site personnel while still delivering high-quality streams.

PTZOptics Hive used for Tennis.

PTZOptics Hive

One of the leading cloud-based solutions for remote sports production is **PTZOptics Hive**. Hive allows for complete remote control of PTZ cameras, enabling operators to manage everything from camera angles to zoom settings without being physically present. Here's why Hive is ideal for sports production:

- **Remote Camera Control**: Hive enables camera operators to control PTZ cameras over the cloud, allowing them to pan, tilt and zoom in real time to capture the action.
- **Multi-Camera Management**: Hive allows for seamless control of multiple cameras from a single interface, making it easy to switch between different angles and perspectives.
- **Cloud Access**: With cameras linked to Hive, users can log in and access cameras from any location, providing flexibility for remote production teams.
- **Video Switching**: Hive supports video switching and the ability to stream directly from the cloud.

Use Case: PTZOptics Hive is perfect for schools, local sports clubs or small leagues that want to live stream sports without needing a full crew on site.

Other Cloud-Based Platforms

While Hive is a strong solution for camera control, other cloud-based platforms also offer powerful remote production capabilities:

- **vMix Call**: vMix Call allows remote camera operators, commentators or guests to join a live stream from anywhere in the world, all through the cloud. This is ideal for adding remote commentary or integrating guest speakers during the event.
- **LiveU Studio**: LiveU Studio (formerly EasyLive) offers cloud-based remote production tools with strong support for mobile live streaming. It's a great option for field sports or outdoor events where mobility is key.

Advantages of Cloud-Based Production

- **Cost-Effective**: By eliminating the need for on-site production teams, travel expenses and equipment transport, cloud-based production solutions dramatically lower costs.
- **Scalability**: Cloud platforms allow you to scale your production based on the needs of the event. You can manage a simple two-camera setup for a school game or scale up to a multi-camera production for larger events.
- **Access from Anywhere**: Cloud production enables global access, meaning camera operators, directors and technical staff can work

together regardless of location. This makes remote production ideal for organizations with distributed teams.

Managing a Remote Production Team

One of the biggest challenges in remote sports production is coordinating a team that isn't physically together. Effective communication, role assignments and clear workflows are essential for a smooth broadcast. Here's how to manage a remote production team successfully:

Role Assignment

In a remote production setup, each team member plays a crucial role in ensuring the broadcast goes smoothly. Here's a breakdown of common roles and their responsibilities:

- **Director**: The director oversees the entire production, making real-time decisions about camera angles, switching feeds and managing the overall flow of the broadcast.
- **Camera Operators**: Whether using PTZ cameras or remotely operated setups, camera operators are responsible for capturing the action and framing shots. In remote production, operators may manage multiple cameras simultaneously from a single control panel.
- **Technical Director**: This person manages the technical aspects of the production, including streaming software, encoding and network stability.
- **Commentators**: Commentators can join remotely via cloud platforms like vMix Call, offering live commentary and analysis from different locations.

Communication Tools

To keep everyone on the same page during a remote production, communication is key. Here are some tools to help remote teams collaborate effectively:

- **Intercom Systems**: Tools like Unity Intercom or Clear-Com's virtual intercom systems enable real-time communication between camera operators, directors and other team members during remote live production.
- **Collaboration Software**: Platforms like Slack or Microsoft Teams allow for pre-production planning and quick communication

during the event.
- **Video Conferencing**: Zoom or Google Meet can be used for live pre-production meetings, helping to synchronize the team before the event begins.

Workflow Management

A clear workflow is essential for keeping everyone aligned, especially in a remote environment. Create a detailed production rundown that includes:

- Crew assignments and responsibilities
- Key moments in the game (e.g., start of each quarter, halftime, important plays).
- Graphic overlays and replay integration.
- Contingency plans for technical issues or changes during the event.

Tip: Assign a dedicated team member to manage communication during the event, ensuring that all operators and directors are up to date with the latest changes or instructions.

Ensuring Network Stability

- **Test Your Internet Connection**: Before the event, test the upload speed and reliability of your connection. A stable upload speed of at least 5 Mbps is recommended for HD streaming, while 10-20 Mbps is preferable for 4K.
- **Have Backup Solutions**: If you're producing a critical event, consider having backup internet solutions, such as a second broadband line, a bonded router or mobile hotspot, in case the primary network fails.
- **Content Delivery Networks (CDNs)**: Using a CDN, like Akamai or Cloudflare, helps distribute the load across multiple servers, reducing the chance of network bottlenecks or streaming delays, especially for larger audiences.

Advantages of IP Video for Remote Production

Scalability and Flexibility:
IP video significantly simplifies the scaling process in remote production environments. Unlike traditional setups that rely on HDMI or SDI cabling, which can quickly become complex and limited by hardware constraints, IP video allows for a more dynamic addition of sources. A single Ethernet cable can manage multiple

video sources without the need for additional hardware switchers or capture cards, reducing both cost and complexity.

Decentralized Distribution:
Traditional video production often requires all sources to be routed to a central location—typically a hardware switcher. IP video eliminates this necessity by enabling sources to be accessed and distributed anywhere within the network. IP video is also generally bidirectional meaning more than just video can flow back and forth between devices. For example, NDI can send tally light status, PTZ controls, metadata and even KVM (Kernel-based Virtual Machine) controls to remotely control a computer with your keyboard and mouse.

Overcoming Distance Limitations:
While traditional cabling like SDI offers longer reach than HDMI, it still has physical and quality-dependent limitations. Ethernet cabling used in IP video setups not only extends reach but also supports video transmission, device control and even power over a single connection. This capability is essential for remote productions that may span large areas or multiple locations.

Cost-Effectiveness:
IP video reduces the financial barrier to entry for high-quality video production. Traditional setups require expensive hardware such as capture cards to integrate various video sources into a production workflow. While BlackMagic, Roland and other manufacturers have democratized access to professional video equipment, IP video has further-reaching implications for remote production. With technologies like NDI®, video sources can be captured directly through a computer's network interface, circumventing the need for costly hardware and enabling a more accessible approach to remote video production.

IP Video Implementation Considerations

While the benefits are substantial, transitioning to an IP video setup, particularly for remote production, does require consideration of certain challenges:

- **Networking Knowledge**: Those accustomed to conventional video standards may find the networking aspect of IP video daunting. While basic setups can be straightforward, more complex configurations demand a deeper understanding of networking principles. Video professionals often add freelance or staff network engineers to their teams.
- **Infrastructure Requirements**: Implementing IP video for remote production may necessitate upgrades to existing network infrastructure to ensure sufficient bandwidth and reliability, critical for maintaining high-quality video streams across various locations.
- **Training and Support**: Adequate training in IP video and networking is crucial for teams to leverage the full potential of this technology.

Networking Infrastructure for Remote Production

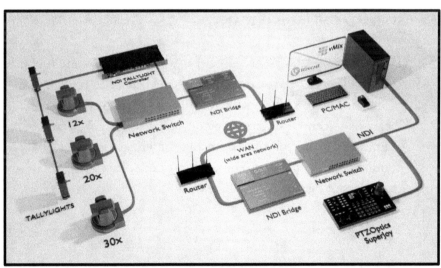

Three camera IP-video system with NDI bridge connecting the cameras to a remote camera operator.

This image above shows two Local Area Networks (LAN) connected together via a Wide Area Network (WAN) such as the Internet, using NDI Bridge software. Each LAN has a Router which is connected to the network. Routers are generally provided by Internet

Service Providers (ISP). Routers can be used to manage the devices on the LAN and your connection to the public internet. In this system, the remote camera operator is using a PTZOptics SuperJoy PTZ camera controller. The camera LAN is shown connected to a network switch on the client side of the NDI Bridge sending video to the far end.

Local Area Networks (LAN)

A Local Area Network (LAN) is crucial in a remote production setting as it connects all the local computing devices, such as computers, servers and production equipment, within a limited area like a studio or production house. LANs are responsible for ensuring high-speed connections and the secure transfer of large video and audio files necessary for production within the local environment.

Wide Area Networks (WAN)

Unlike LANs, Wide Area Networks (WANs), like the internet itself connect devices over broader geographical areas. In remote production, WANs are essential for linking various production locations to central studios or cloud services. They facilitate the seamless transmission of multimedia content across cities or even continents, ensuring that remote teams can collaborate effectively regardless of distance.

Edge Devices

Edge devices play a pivotal role in managing data processing at or near the source of data acquisition. In remote productions, edge devices can process audio and video data before it travels over the network, significantly reducing latency and bandwidth usage. These devices can sit on the "edge" of networks and serve as a simple connection point to the cloud which can generally get around most firewall issues.

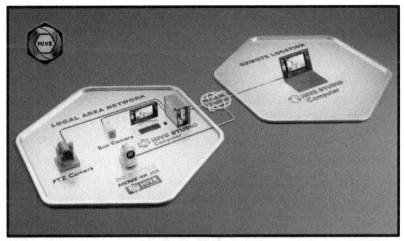

Diagram showing Hive Studio used to remotely control cameras. This diagram shows the difference between IP connected devices and edge devices.

Edge devices operate differently from normal IP-connected devices as shown in the diagram above. While the "PTZ Camera" and "Box Camera" are both connected to the LAN, they do not support a direct connection to the cloud and are therefore not edge devices. These devices require additional software to be connected to the cloud, which in this case is the Hive Studio client running on a computer on the same local area network. The Hive Studio software is able to act as a bridge for these IP connected devices and the cloud.

REMOTE PRODUCTION
PRO TIP

PTZOptics Hive is free to use with one camera. You can learn more about this remote production software here.

The camera at the bottom of the diagram is an edge device. This "Hive-Linked" PTZOptics camera can connect directly to the cloud without the need of a computer in the middle. This is ideal for deployments of multiple devices on a network and remote productions that are looking to streamline their setup. Edge devices are often configured once, on a LAN by the owner of the device. This one time setup involves associating the device with the specific cloud account that it should connect to. For PTZOptics Hive-Linked cameras, this would involve accessing the camera interface and logging into the Hive studio you would like the camera to be connected to.

The web-interface for a PTZOptics Hive-Linked camera. This is how you can link a PTZOptics camera to a specific cloud studio.

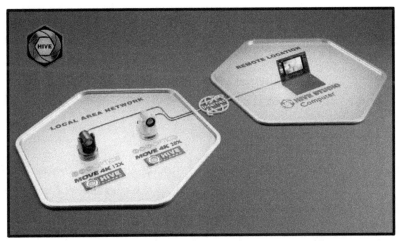

This diagram shows two PTZOptics Hive-Linked cameras connected for remote production.

VPNs and Firewalls

VPNs encrypt data traffic, creating secure connections between remote production sites and central studios over the internet. Firewalls provide an additional layer of security by blocking unauthorized access and monitoring network traffic to prevent and detect malicious activities. Edge devices are often used to get around firewall issues, and they often play a crucial role in simplifying complex setups, allowing remote producers to integrate multiple network segments efficiently. By seamlessly connecting to the cloud, edge devices ensure that broadcasts are not compromised by firewalls in most cases. The strategic use of VPNs, firewalls and edge devices collectively enhances the resilience of remote production workflows against potential cyber threats and technical challenges, ensuring smooth and secure operations across diverse geographic locations.

Static IP Addresses:

Static IP addresses are manually assigned to a device and remain constant unless changed by network administration. In remote production environments, static IPs are beneficial because they ensure that devices such as cameras, streaming servers and production equipment consistently maintain the same address on the network. This predictability simplifies the configuration of networked devices, makes them easier to manage remotely and reduces the potential for IP conflicts.

DHCP Assigned IP Addresses:

DHCP (Dynamic Host Control Protocol) automates the assignment of IP addresses from a defined pool, which means that devices may receive a different IP address each time they connect to the network. This method is useful in dynamic environments where devices frequently join or leave the network, such as in temporary setups or locations with many mobile devices. DHCP simplifies the network management by reducing the administrative burden of manually assigning addresses. However, in a remote production setting, the lack of fixed IP addresses can lead to issues with device discovery and stream reliability, unless additional measures are implemented, such as DHCP reservation or dynamic DNS services to maintain continuity.

In summary, for remote production and IP video, static IP addresses are generally preferred due to their stability and predictability, which are essential for maintaining uninterrupted live video feeds and managing remote devices effectively. DHCP, while convenient for more dynamic or less critical network environments, may require additional configuration to meet the demands of remote production settings effectively.

The Future of Sports Production is Remote

Remote sports production offers a range of benefits, from cost savings and flexibility to increased scalability. With cloud-based tools like PTZOptics Hive and careful coordination of remote teams, it's possible to produce professional-quality sports streams without needing an on-site crew. However, it's essential to manage latency and network stability to ensure a smooth, high-quality viewing experience.

In the next chapter, we'll focus on handling technical challenges during live streaming, including bandwidth issues, equipment failures and stream interruptions.

23 HANDLING TECHNICAL CHALLENGES

Live streaming sports requires more than just great equipment and engaging content—it also demands technical stability. Streaming is highly dependent on reliable internet connections, solid hardware and smooth software performance. But even with the best setup, technical challenges can arise. In this chapter, we'll explore how to ensure stable bandwidth, troubleshoot interruptions and build redundancy into your workflow to keep your stream running smoothly, even when things go wrong.

Bandwidth and Connectivity

One of the most critical components of a successful sports live stream is having sufficient and reliable internet bandwidth. Without proper bandwidth, even the best-produced stream can fall apart due to buffering, lag or dropped connections.

Understanding Bandwidth Requirements

The amount of bandwidth you need for a live stream depends on the video quality you're broadcasting. Here's a basic guideline for common streaming resolutions:

- **720p (HD)**: Requires a minimum upload speed of **3-5 Mbps**.
- **1080p (Full HD)**: Requires **5-10 Mbps**.
- **4K (Ultra HD)**: Requires at least **20 Mbps**.

Remember, these are **upload** speeds, not download speeds. Many internet providers advertise download speeds, but upload speed is what's most important for streaming.

Testing Your Internet Connection

Before every stream, it's critical to test your internet connection to ensure you have enough bandwidth to maintain a stable stream:

- **Speed Tests**: Use tools like **Speedtest.net** or **Fast.com** to check your upload speed. Test the connection multiple times to ensure consistent results.
- **Stability Checks**: Beyond speed, it's also important to verify the stability of the connection. An unstable connection can cause intermittent buffering or dropped frames. Testing over time or

using network monitoring tools can help detect fluctuations.

Wired vs. Wireless Connections

Whenever possible, use a wired Ethernet connection rather than Wi-Fi. Wired connections are more reliable and provide faster, more stable upload speeds, which are essential for uninterrupted live streaming.

Tip: If you must use Wi-Fi, ensure that you are close to the router and that there are no major obstructions or interference sources (like microwaves or Bluetooth devices) that could weaken the signal.

To expand your WiFi reach and ensure a more reliable connection for live streaming, consider using Ubiquiti long-range WiFi extenders. These extenders are designed to enhance WiFi coverage over larger areas, providing a more stable and faster connection that is crucial for uninterrupted streaming. By integrating such devices, you can improve your network's performance and mitigate connectivity issues that might otherwise disrupt your live streams.

Dealing with Streaming Interruptions

Even with solid bandwidth, unexpected issues like dropped frames, buffering or audio/video sync problems can still occur. Let's explore how to troubleshoot and handle these interruptions.

Identifying the Cause

Streaming interruptions can stem from several factors. Here are some common causes and how to address them:

- **Dropped Frames:** If your stream starts dropping frames, it usually indicates that your encoder can't keep up with the settings or your internet connection is too slow. Lowering the video bitrate or resolution can help alleviate the issue.
- **Buffering:** Buffering occurs when there's a lag between the live stream and the viewer's device due to network slowdowns. This can often be resolved by reducing the stream's bitrate or using a content delivery network (CDN) to distribute the load more effectively.
- **Audio/Video Sync Issues:** If the audio falls out of sync with the video, this is usually caused by a delay in either the capture or encoding process. Resyncing the audio in your streaming software can fix this problem.

- ○ Tip: One easy way to fix audio sync issues is to add latency to the audio input. This can be done with almost all streaming software. Start by adding 25 milliseconds and continue adding more as you see the latency reduce to zero.

Lowering Bitrate and Resolution

When faced with unstable internet or hardware issues, lowering your stream's bitrate or resolution is often the easiest way to keep the stream running smoothly. Most live streaming software (such as vMix, OBS or Wirecast) allows you to adjust the bitrate and resolution mid-stream if needed.

- **Bitrate:** Lowering the bitrate reduces the amount of data being uploaded, which can help if your internet connection isn't fast or stable enough to handle higher bitrates.
- **Resolution:** If your stream is stuttering, reducing the resolution (e.g., from 1080p to 720p) can also ease the load on both your internet and hardware.

Backups and Redundancy

No matter how well-prepared you are, technical failures can still happen. That's why having backup systems in place is critical for keeping your stream live even if something goes wrong.

Backup Internet Solutions

If your primary internet connection goes down, having a secondary option is essential to avoid losing the stream entirely:

- **Mobile Hotspots:** As a backup to your primary internet, a 4G or 5G mobile hotspot can be used as a fail-safe. While not ideal for long streams, it can keep you online long enough to resolve issues with your primary connection.
- **Bonded Internet Solutions:** Tools like **LiveU, MR·NET** or **Teradek** offer bonded internet solutions that combine multiple connections (e.g., wired, Wi-Fi and cellular) to create a more stable, redundant internet source.

Tip: Test your backup connection before going live to ensure it's reliable and can handle the stream if needed.

Redundant Hardware Setup

To minimize the risk of hardware failures, you should also have redundant equipment in place:

- **Backup Encoders**: If your main encoder (hardware or software) fails, having a secondary encoder ready to take over can keep your stream going. Some streaming platforms allow you to switch encoders mid-stream without viewers noticing - primarily through use of a backup streaming URL (see "failover streaming" below).
- **Spare Cables and Power Supplies**: Cables are a common failure point, especially in mobile or outdoor environments. Always have extra HDMI/SDI cables, power supplies and adapters on hand.

Use Case: If you're streaming a high-profile or critical sports event (e.g., a championship game), having redundant equipment wired-in and ready (on "hot standby") ensures that no technical failure will result in a complete loss of the stream.

Recording a Local Backup

In case the live stream is interrupted or you lose internet access entirely, recording a local copy of the show can be a lifesaver. Most live streaming software allows you to record the broadcast to a local hard drive, which you can upload later if the live stream is disrupted.

- **vMix**: Offers the ability to record the stream locally while streaming live. If something goes wrong, you'll have a full recording to upload later.
- **OBS**: Similarly, OBS allows for simultaneous streaming and local recording, ensuring that no content is lost even if the stream itself fails.

Failover Streaming

Some platforms offer a feature called **failover streaming**, where if your main stream goes down, a backup stream can automatically take over. This can be as simple as having two encoders set up on different internet connections. If one fails, the platform will switch to the other stream seamlessly.

You can create your own failover solution using **LiveU Studio's Fail-safe Stream Backup (Fallback)** which can insert a still, video or other input into your stream when it detects a loss of incoming content and go back to the original stream when it detects that it's stable.

Keeping the Stream Running Smoothly

Handling technical challenges is part of the reality of live streaming, but with careful preparation and the right strategies in place, you can minimize disruptions and keep your audience engaged. Ensuring strong internet connectivity, troubleshooting interruptions quickly and building redundancy into your workflow are key components to a successful sports live stream.

In the next chapter, we'll explore strategies for engaging your audience, from live chat and social media integration to interactive tools that make your stream more immersive and enjoyable for viewers.

24 ENGAGING YOUR AUDIENCE

In sports live streaming, keeping viewers engaged is essential for maintaining interest and growing your audience. Engagement goes beyond simply broadcasting the game—it involves creating an interactive and immersive experience that keeps viewers involved before, during and after the event. In this chapter, we'll cover key strategies for audience engagement, including live chat tools, interactive features, effective commentary and monetization options to ensure your stream is both engaging and profitable.

Live Chat and Viewer Interaction

Live streaming is unique in that it allows for real-time interaction between viewers and the broadcaster. One of the most powerful tools for engagement is the **live chat** feature which allows viewers to share their thoughts, ask questions and participate in the conversation as the game unfolds.

Benefits of Live Chat

- **Real-Time Engagement**: Live chat gives viewers an opportunity to connect with each other and the production team in real time, making them feel like part of the event.
- **Immediate Feedback**: Broadcasters can gauge audience reactions and adjust the stream or commentary based on viewer input.
- **Community Building**: Live chat fosters a sense of community among viewers, which can turn casual viewers into dedicated fans.

vMix Social is a tool for integrating social media comments into your broadcast.

Tools for Live Chat and Interaction

- **YouTube Live Chat**: YouTube provides built-in live chat features that allow viewers to comment and interact during the stream. Moderators can monitor chat for inappropriate content and engage with viewers directly.
- **Facebook Live Comments**: Facebook's real-time comment system allows viewers to participate and interact with each other, with reactions like "likes" and "hearts" further boosting engagement.
- **Twitch Chat**: Twitch is known for its interactive chat system, where viewers can communicate in real time and even use custom emotes (emojis) that reflect inside jokes or community culture.
- **Interactive Polls and Q&A**: Platforms like vMix or Restream allow you to integrate polls, quizzes or question-and-answer sessions directly into the live stream. You can ask viewers to predict game outcomes, answer trivia questions or vote on players of the game.

Tip: Encourage viewers to use live chat by prompting them with questions or creating conversation topics, such as asking for predictions or reactions to key moments in the game.

Commentary and Narration

A great commentator can elevate a sports live stream from average to engaging. Commentary provides context for viewers, explains what's happening in the game and brings excitement to key moments. This section will explore the role of the commentator and how to tailor narration for different audiences.

The Role of a Commentator

The commentator serves multiple purposes in a live stream:

- **Play-by-Play**: Describes the action as it unfolds, ensuring that viewers, especially those unfamiliar with the sport, can follow along. This is crucial for sports with fast-paced or complex rules, like basketball or rugby.
- **Color Commentary**: Provides insights, background information and analysis of the game, players and strategies. This helps keep the stream engaging during slower moments.
- **Emotional Connection**: The commentator adds excitement to the game, especially during pivotal moments, by building up

266

anticipation and reacting to plays in real time.

Tailoring Commentary for Different Audiences

- **For Casual Viewers**: If your audience includes viewers who are unfamiliar with the sport, the commentary should be educational without being overly technical. Break down the rules, explain key plays and provide context for major events.
- **For Dedicated Fans**: If your audience consists of seasoned sports fans, focus more on strategy, player statistics and in-depth analysis. Viewers in this category appreciate insights into tactics, player matchups and game history.
- **Incorporating Humor**: Depending on the tone of your stream, adding light-hearted or humorous commentary can make the stream more entertaining. Just be careful to strike a balance between humor and professionalism.

Adding Guest Commentators

Guest commentators, especially those with expertise in the sport, can add variety and depth to your stream. Inviting coaches, former players or sports analysts to provide commentary or post-game analysis can engage viewers who want deeper insights into the game.

Maximizing Audience Engagement After the Stream

Engagement doesn't end when the game is over. Post-game content can help keep viewers connected to your stream, encouraging them to return for future events. Here are some strategies for maintaining engagement after the stream:

Highlight Reels

After the game, create and share highlight reels featuring key moments like goals, touchdowns or game-winning plays. Posting these on social media or YouTube can attract more viewers and keep the conversation going.

Post-Game Interviews

Conduct interviews with players, coaches or commentators after the game and share them with your audience. This behind-the-scenes content adds depth to your stream and gives viewers additional insights into the event.

Viewer Polls and Feedback

Send out viewer polls asking for feedback on the stream, their favorite moments or suggestions for future events. This not only engages the audience but also helps you improve future broadcasts.

Building an Engaged Community

Engaging the audience is about creating an experience that goes beyond simply broadcasting a game. By incorporating live chat, polls, expert commentary and interactive features, you can keep viewers involved throughout the stream. Additionally, monetization strategies like sponsorships, ads and subscriptions help you generate revenue while delivering value to your audience. The goal is to build a community of dedicated viewers who return to watch future streams and support your content.

Tip: In addition to using live chat, consider creating a Facebook group dedicated to your live stream audience. This can serve as a space for viewers to discuss games, share insights and connect with other fans outside of live events, further building community and engagement.

25 LIVE STREAMING PLATFORMS AND DISTRIBUTION

Choosing a Platform

When it comes to live streaming sports, selecting the right platform is a crucial decision that can impact your stream's reach, audience engagement and overall success. There are various platforms available, each with its strengths and unique features. In this section, we'll explore the most popular platforms—**YouTube, Facebook Live, Twitch** and more—so you can make an informed decision based on your goals, audience and technical needs.

YouTube Live

YouTube Live is one of the most widely used platforms for live streaming, with several key advantages:

- **Broad Audience Reach**: YouTube's massive user base means your stream has the potential to reach a wide audience, both during the live event and after it's archived.
- **SEO Benefits**: YouTube is owned by Google, so live streams hosted here can perform well in search engine results, especially if you optimize your title, description and tags.
- **Monetization Options**: YouTube offers multiple ways to monetize your live streams, including ads, Super Chats and channel memberships. For sports organizations looking to generate revenue, these options can be a major draw.

Use Case: Ideal for larger audiences, sports events that need wide visibility or organizations looking to generate ad revenue or audience engagement through interactive features like live chat.

Facebook Live

Facebook Live is another popular platform, especially for engaging with local or community-based audiences:

- **Social Sharing**: One of Facebook's strengths is its social sharing capabilities. Viewers can easily share your live stream, helping it reach a broader audience through their personal networks.
- **Engagement Tools**: Facebook's comment system allows for real-

time interaction, while features like polls and reactions can help increase viewer engagement.

- **Targeted Distribution**: Facebook's advertising platform allows you to target specific audiences, such as parents of school athletes, fans of specific teams or local community members.

Use Case: Facebook Live is perfect for community sports events, school sports and local leagues that want to engage with a specific audience and benefit from Facebook's social sharing features.

Twitch

Originally built for gamers, Twitch has expanded its reach into other categories, including sports streaming. Here's why Twitch is worth considering:

- **Niche Communities**: Twitch is known for fostering dedicated, niche communities, so if you're streaming esports or a lesser-known sport, this platform could help you connect with a passionate audience.
- **Monetization**: Like YouTube, Twitch offers several monetization options, including ads, subscriptions and Bits (virtual tips). These options make it easy for sports streamers to generate income directly from their audience.
- **Low Latency**: Twitch's infrastructure is optimized for real-time interaction, which means lower latency and smoother viewer experiences, especially in fast-paced sports.

Use Case: Best suited for esports, niche sports or events where audience interaction and engagement are a priority.

Other Platforms

- **Vimeo**: Vimeo is a premium option, ideal for organizations that need more control over their streams. It offers high-quality video hosting, privacy options and advanced analytics, making it a good choice for schools or professional sports organizations that need a more polished, branded experience.
- **Twitter Live**: Useful for events that need instant updates and rapid dissemination. Twitter Live allows for short, real-time streams, making it a great complement to longer broadcasts on platforms like YouTube or Facebook.

Private Streaming Solutions

For some organizations, particularly schools, amateur leagues and private clubs, public platforms like YouTube or Facebook may not be the best fit. Privacy concerns, the need for exclusive access or the desire to monetize through subscriptions or pay-per-view may make private streaming solutions a better option.

Subscription-Based Streaming

A subscription-based model allows you to create a private streaming experience where viewers pay a recurring fee to access live sports events. This is especially useful for schools or clubs that want to generate consistent revenue while offering exclusive access to parents, fans and community members.

- **How It Works:** Subscribers pay a monthly or annual fee for access to live streams and archived events. Platforms like Vimeo OTT, IBM Cloud Video or Uscreen offer robust tools for managing subscriptions and hosting high-quality streams.
- **Revenue Model:** The subscription model ensures predictable revenue and creates a sense of exclusivity, which can be a selling point for parents or dedicated fans who want to support their team.

Use Case: Schools, local sports clubs and organizations looking for a steady revenue stream from dedicated viewers.

Pay-Per-View (PPV) Streaming

With a pay-per-view model, viewers pay a one-time fee to access specific events. This is a great option for special matches, tournaments or championship games where you expect higher interest or want to generate revenue from a broader audience.

- **How It Works:** Platforms like Cleeng or Vimeo OTT allow you to host pay-per-view events, where viewers must pay to unlock the live stream. You can set different price points depending on the event, making it flexible for different audience sizes or types of events.
- **Revenue Model:** Pay-per-view allows you to monetize specific high-interest events and incentivize viewers to pay for premium access.

Use Case: Ideal for one-off events, like championship games, tournaments or fundraising events, where viewers are willing to pay for exclusive access.

Branded Platforms

For organizations that want full control over branding and user experience, creating a custom streaming platform is an option. You can use services like JW Player or Brightcove to build a branded sports streaming platform where you control the design, features and viewer experience.

- **Benefits**: Full control over your branding, advanced analytics and the ability to offer custom features like personalized user experiences, premium memberships or merchandise integration.
- **Use Case**: Professional sports organizations, leagues or schools with a strong brand and a dedicated fanbase.

Simulcasting: Expanding Your Reach

Simulcasting refers to broadcasting your live stream on multiple platforms simultaneously. This is an effective strategy for maximizing your audience and reaching viewers on different platforms without the need to produce multiple streams.

How Simulcasting Works

With the help of simulcasting tools like **Restream**, **Switchboard Live** or **vMix**, you can send your stream to multiple platforms (e.g., YouTube, Facebook Live and Twitch) at the same time. This ensures that no matter where your viewers are watching, they can access your stream on their preferred platform.

Benefits of Simulcasting

- **Maximize Audience Reach**: By simulcasting, you ensure that your stream is accessible to the widest possible audience, whether they prefer YouTube, Facebook, Twitch or another platform.
- **Tailored Viewer Experience**: Different platforms offer different features, such as live chat on YouTube or reactions on Facebook. By simulcasting, you can engage viewers across platforms and use each platform's unique features to enhance their experience.
- **Backup and Redundancy**: If one platform experiences technical difficulties, your stream can continue on other platforms. This provides peace of mind and ensures that you don't lose your

audience due to platform-specific issues.

Simulcasting Tools

- **Restream**: One of the most popular simulcasting platforms, Restream allows you to broadcast to multiple destinations simultaneously. It supports over 30 platforms, including YouTube, Facebook, Twitch and LinkedIn.
- **Switchboard Live**: Switchboard Live offers a user-friendly interface for simulcasting to multiple platforms and is designed for organizations that want to extend their live streaming reach.
- **vMix**: For those using vMix as their live streaming software, it includes built-in support for simulcasting, allowing you to stream to multiple platforms at once without additional software.

Use Case: Simulcasting is ideal for organizations that want to maximize their reach across different platforms, ensuring they don't miss any segment of their audience.

Summary: Finding the Right Distribution Strategy

Choosing the right platform or combination of platforms is critical for the success of your sports live stream. Whether you opt for public platforms like YouTube or Facebook, private subscription-based solutions or simulcasting to multiple platforms, your decision should align with your goals, audience and budget.

In the next chapter, we'll explore how to create engaging pre-game, post-game, and watch-along live streams to enhance the sports viewing experience. These supplementary streams go beyond the main event, offering opportunities to build excitement, deliver in-depth analysis, and foster a sense of community among fans. By leveraging these formats effectively, you can elevate your broadcast, deepen audience engagement, and unlock additional branding and sponsorship potential.

26 PRE, POST AND WATCH-ALONG LIVE STREAMS

In the world of sports live streaming, the main event is only one part of a larger viewing experience. Pre-game, post-game and watch-along streams play an essential role in delivering a full, engaging journey for fans. These supplementary streams have unique functions—building excitement, providing in-depth analysis and creating a communal viewing atmosphere that enhances the primary broadcast. When executed effectively, they not only elevate the main event but also increase audience retention, drive fan engagement and offer additional branding and sponsorship opportunities.

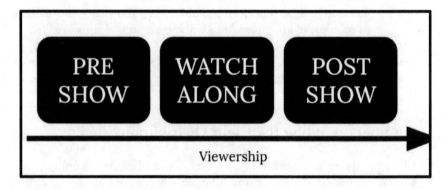

Pre-game streams set the stage, helping fans get familiar with key players, understand important storylines and join in the anticipation. This phase is an opportunity to establish tone and excitement, whether it's through expert commentary, team histories or head-to-head player matchups. For viewers, the pre-game broadcast often transforms a standard viewing experience into one of excitement and deeper emotional investment.

Watch-along streams, on the other hand, provide a unique viewing experience, often independent of the main broadcast. They act as a companion to the primary feed, giving fans an alternative space to enjoy expert commentary, hear unique insights and interact with other fans in real time. In this environment, fans become part of a virtual stadium, creating a shared experience that deepens their connection to the event and, by extension, your stream.

Finally, post-game streams serve to recap the event, highlight key moments and discuss implications for future games or tournaments. With interviews, play breakdowns and open Q&A, post-game streams give fans closure and often prompt them to stay tuned for future streams. This recap phase not only strengthens audience retention but also provides valuable insights, leaving viewers with a sense of completeness after the game.

The Palmetto Tigers hosting a post show talk show.

Producing pre-game, post-game and watch-along streams demands thoughtful planning and dedicated assets—unique graphics, specialized overlays and tailored commentary—that enhance the main event while maintaining a cohesive narrative. This chapter will explore the elements needed to create these supplementary streams, guiding you through content planning, technical setup and audience engagement strategies. With the right production approach, you can transform your sports streams into immersive experiences that keep viewers returning for more.

Pre-Game Production

The pre-game stream is the perfect time to set the stage for the main event. This segment is all about building anticipation, presenting insights and engaging viewers before the game begins. A well-structured pre-game production not only introduces the audience to the upcoming match but also creates an emotional investment that keeps them glued to the screen.

Defining Objectives

Pre-game content should aim to:

- **Build Hype and Excitement**: This is the moment to get viewers energized. Using dynamic graphics, sound effects and engaging visuals, you can amplify excitement as game time approaches.
- **Inform and Prepare the Audience**: Provide context on teams, players and recent performances. This gives viewers a deeper understanding of what's at stake and makes them feel informed.

- **Engage with Fans Early**: Through live chats, viewer polls and other interactive features, you can begin creating a sense of community before the game even starts. This engagement can drive up retention, as viewers are more likely to stay connected throughout the main event.

Setting Up the Look and Feel

The pre-game stream should have a distinct visual identity that aligns with the main event's theme while feeling fresh and engaging. Here are some elements to consider:

- **Custom Graphics and Branding**: Introduce graphics that reflect team colors, logos and thematic elements relevant to the event. Make use of lower-thirds, full-screen overlays and transitions that are visually consistent but unique to the pre-game segment.
- **Countdown Timers and Teasers**: A countdown timer leading up to the main event builds excitement and provides a clear signal of when the game will begin. Consider teaser graphics that hint at key matchups, interesting player stats or game-day conditions.
- **Sponsor Integrations**: Pre-game streams offer a prime opportunity for sponsorship placements. Logos, video ads and branded graphics can all be woven in during this time without distracting from the primary content.

Planning Content

Creating a rich, informative pre-game show requires strategic content planning. Here's an outline for a compelling pre-game lineup:

1. **Team and Player Analysis**: Begin with a look at the teams, including season highlights, recent form and key players to watch.
2. **Game Predictions and Commentary**: Provide analysis from commentators or guest experts on potential outcomes, strategies and player performance.
3. **Viewer Polls and Live Comments**: Boost engagement by inviting viewers to participate in predictions and share their opinions in live chat. You can use interactive polls and real-time chat overlays to showcase these responses on screen.

Technical Setup

Producing a polished pre-game stream requires attention to technical details.

Here's a quick setup checklist:

- **Camera and Lighting**: Ensure that the pre-game studio or virtual environment is well-lit, with high-quality cameras that provide a clear view of the hosts or commentators.
- **Audio Setup**: Use high-quality microphones and sound mixing equipment to ensure that commentators' voices are clear and engaging.
- **Graphics and Media Management**: Load pre-designed graphics, stats overlays and videos into your live production software (such as OBS, vMix or Wirecast) for easy access during the stream. Make sure they're organized and labeled for quick transitions and smooth integration.

With the right planning and setup, your pre-game stream will not only set the stage for the main event but will also leave viewers excited and ready for the action ahead. This careful preparation makes for a seamless transition into the main broadcast, keeping viewers engaged from start to finish.

TENNIS TALK with Cam Williams is a popular watch along channel.

Watch-Along Production

The watch-along stream has emerged as a popular way for viewers to enjoy a game in a social, interactive environment. While the main broadcast focuses on the game itself, a watch-along provides fans with commentary, live reactions and the sense of community they'd experience in a stadium. These streams cater to viewers who want a more personalized or interactive experience, often featuring experts, fans or influencers as hosts who bring unique perspectives and insights to the game.

Objective and Audience

Watch-along streams create a shared viewing space, offering:

- **Live Reactions and Commentary**: Hosts can comment on the game in real-time, sharing their excitement, analyzing plays and reacting to pivotal moments, which creates an immersive experience for viewers.
- **Fan Engagement**: Fans can connect with each other and the hosts via live chat, polls and Q&As. This is especially valuable for viewers who might be watching alone but want to feel part of a larger community.
- **Alternative Insights**: Unlike official broadcasts, watch-alongs can explore topics beyond gameplay, such as discussing team backgrounds, sharing historical insights and reacting to fan comments, providing a richer, more varied experience.

Production Setup

A watch-along stream requires a specific technical setup to ensure a high-quality, seamless viewing experience:

- **Camera and Audio**: The host(s) need to be clearly visible and audible, so invest in quality cameras, lighting and microphones. The production should aim for a clean and professional look to create a comfortable viewing atmosphere.
- **Connecting the Main Feed**: Many watch-alongs overlay or sync their stream with the main game feed. Using software like OBS, vMix or Wirecast, you can bring in the main feed as a background or picture-in-picture element, giving viewers access to both the host commentary and the game itself.
- **Live Production Software**: Use production software that allows for real-time graphics and media management. Being able to switch quickly between commentary, graphics and interactive overlays is essential for a smooth watch-along experience.

By delivering an engaging watch-along experience, you can create a space that enhances the game and builds a community of dedicated viewers. When executed well, watch-alongs foster a loyal following, drawing fans back for each game and keeping them connected to your brand even after the main event concludes.

Post-Game Production

A post-game stream wraps up the event, providing closure and additional insights for fans. This segment offers an opportunity to analyze the game's highlights, address viewer questions and preview upcoming events. A well-produced post-game show deepens viewer engagement, giving fans a satisfying conclusion and a reason to return for future broadcasts.

Focus on Analysis and Recap

Post-game content should aim to:

- **Break Down Key Moments**: Highlight crucial plays, player performances and turning points that influenced the game's outcome.
- **Engage Viewers with Insights**: Provide expert analysis and commentary that add depth to the game, helping fans understand strategies and decisions.
- **Foster Community Interaction**: Address viewer questions and comments to make the stream feel interactive and community-driven.

Gathering Analytics and Insights

Post-game streams benefit from a set of graphics tailored to review and analysis:

- **Final Stats and Highlights**: Create graphic overlays that display team and player stats, such as score breakdowns, possession time and standout performances.
- **Key Plays and Replay Segments**: Use video replays of significant moments with slow-motion or breakdown effects. Adding commentary overlays during these replays can enhance the viewer's understanding of why a play was impactful.
- **Awards and Recognitions**: Highlight the player of the game or any exceptional achievements. Displaying these recognitions with custom graphics adds a celebratory feel and reinforces positive fan engagement.

Planning Content Structure

A post-game stream should follow a structured format to keep viewers engaged. Here's a recommended outline:

1. **Game Recap and Highlights**: Begin with a summary of the game, including key plays, major turning points and any

unexpected outcomes. This can be presented through a highlight reel or quick recap.

2. **Player and Team Analysis**: Discuss individual performances and team dynamics. Comment on standout players, strategic moves and any surprises in the game's flow.

3. **Audience Q&A**: Open the floor for viewer questions and comments. This gives fans a chance to interact with the hosts and feel part of the discussion.

4. **Future Event Previews**: Conclude with a look ahead, discussing upcoming games or events. This encourages viewers to return and stay connected to future broadcasts.

Production Considerations

Post-game streams are often more relaxed than pre-game or live broadcasts, but they still require a professional setup to maintain high quality:

- **Audio and Visuals**: Ensure hosts are well-lit and clearly audible. For smaller post-game setups, a single camera and a simple lighting arrangement may be sufficient, but audio clarity is essential for a professional feel.
- **Graphics and Media Control**: Load final stats, highlight reels and other assets into the production software beforehand. Organizing these elements ensures a smooth flow as hosts move through the post-game content.
- **Viewer Interaction Tools**: Set up live chat or Q&A integration to bring in audience comments. Software like vMix and OBS allows for live chat overlays, enabling real-time interaction with the audience.

Final Tips for Post-Game Success

1. **Encourage Active Engagement**: Prompt viewers to share their thoughts, opinions and questions. Engaging with these comments creates a sense of community and ensures fans feel heard.

2. **Keep it Concise and Relevant**: While some fans may stay for in-depth analysis, many will appreciate a focused and to-the-point wrap-up. Keep the content engaging and avoid overly lengthy segments.

3. **Finish with a Call to Action**: Conclude with a call to action, such as inviting viewers to follow for future streams, visit social media pages or tune in to the next game. This is a key opportunity to build loyalty and keep your audience engaged beyond the game.

With a well-structured post-game show, you can provide a rewarding experience for fans, leaving them satisfied and eager to return. Post-game content not only serves as a closing chapter for the main event but also strengthens the connection between viewers and your brand, building anticipation for the next big game.

Summary

Pre-game, watch-along and post-game streams have become essential components in sports live streaming, turning each broadcast into a complete and engaging experience. By planning and producing these supplementary segments, you not only extend the excitement beyond the main event but also build a dedicated community around your content. Each phase offers unique opportunities: pre-game streams set the tone and draw viewers in; watch-alongs create a shared, interactive experience during the game; and post-game streams provide valuable analysis and closure, leaving fans eager for future events.

Producing these streams requires thoughtful preparation and attention to detail, from developing engaging graphics and overlays to setting up technical elements that ensure smooth transitions and high-quality production. Leveraging audience interaction tools across each phase keeps viewers engaged and enhances their sense of involvement, ultimately strengthening their loyalty to your broadcasts.

When done well, these pre, during and post-game productions can transform a single event into a memorable journey, fostering a sense of community and encouraging fans to return game after game. By embracing these elements, you'll be able to deliver a professional, immersive experience that resonates with viewers, elevating your sports live streaming to a truly professional level.

27 CASE STUDIES AND EXAMPLES

Learning from real-world examples can be one of the most powerful ways to understand the benefits and challenges of live streaming sports. In this chapter, we'll explore several success stories of sports organizations, schools and local leagues that have successfully implemented live streaming. We'll also look at key lessons learned from their experiences, providing valuable insights into overcoming common challenges and achieving successful broadcasts

PTZOptics cameras set up for sports production.

Student-Run Sports Broadcasting System

Overview of Salesianum School's Broadcasting Initiative

Salesianum School in Wilmington, Delaware, has enhanced its sports broadcasting capabilities through a student-operated video production system. This advanced setup includes a comprehensive array of tools, including multiple cameras, live streaming software and a cloud-based production platform, enabling the students to deliver professional-quality live broadcasts.

A Game-Changing Setup for Student-Run Broadcasting

Salesianum's sports program, known for its commitment to excellence, now has a production system that reflects this standard. The setup includes six cameras strategically placed around the football field, providing clear, reliable video feeds that capture every moment from various angles. These wireless connections ensure uninterrupted streaming while empowering students to produce dynamic, multi-angle broadcasts.

Under the guidance of their broadcast team, students are learning real-world production skills beyond simply pressing "record." They use vMix software to live stream games and NewBlueFX Captivate adds instant replay capabilities, bringing fans and coaches an immersive viewing experience.

Reviewing the vMix system and SuperJoy controller before Friday night football.

Plans for Expansion in 2025

Currently focused on football, Salesianum School is planning to expand broadcast coverage to include baseball, soccer and swimming in 2025. With the ability to scale their production setup, they aim to deliver the same high-quality broadcasts across multiple sports, maintaining a consistent experience for viewers and enabling students to refine their production skills across various settings.

Cloud-Based Management for Efficiency

The school is also testing a cloud-based platform for remote production management. This tool provides a centralized interface for controlling and managing cameras, simplifying the production of complex, multi-camera broadcasts with fewer resources. For a school balancing multiple sports and events, the remote management capabilities allow their student team to operate effectively without requiring on-site presence for every broadcast.

Professional Tools in the Hands of Students

A key part of the setup is a dedicated controller that allows students to manage all six cameras with ease. Linked to an HDMI monitor, it offers a real-time view of all angles, enabling the production team to switch seamlessly between shots during live broadcasts. With this technology, students are not just learning basic camera operation—they are gaining hands-on experience with industry-standard tools, preparing them for potential careers in broadcast production and sports media.

Conclusion

Salesianum School's sports broadcasting system serves as a benchmark for high school sports production. Their combination of student talent and professional-grade technology has created a system that engages audiences, supports coaches and, most importantly, equips students with skills for the future. With plans to expand coverage and explore deeper integration with remote management platforms, Salesianum is setting an inspiring example for other schools looking to advance their broadcasting capabilities.

vMix is used for sports production connected to auto-tracking Move 4K cameras.

Case Study: Enhancing Coaching with Video

Overview of the Project

In an exciting initiative, the Julian Krinsky School of Tennis implemented a cloud-based live streaming solution for a tennis match, leveraging remote camera control, high-quality video streaming and cloud integration. This setup allowed coaches to monitor, analyze and enhance player performance remotely, transforming how coaching is conducted.

Enhancing Coaching Through Web-Based Camera Control

This case study highlights how remote camera control and cloud integration can revolutionize coaching techniques. With web-based access, coaches could view live footage, zoom in to analyze specific player techniques or zoom out to observe court strategies, all from any location. This approach provided coaches with unmatched flexibility and efficiency, helping improve both coaching and player performance analysis.

Hive connects the video from your cameras to the cloud so that you can share access with coaches and video team members.

Cloud-Based Camera Management

The system used PTZOptics Hive for connecting and managing cameras, enabling coaches to remotely access live footage and select which camera angles to view. This setup allowed for in-depth analysis, as coaches could zoom in for technique-focused views or zoom out to monitor strategic gameplay. The remote control capabilities ensured that coaches could adjust views to suit their needs, even from a distance.

Live Streaming and Video Recording Software

For live streaming and recording, a vMix was used. It supports high-quality, low-latency video streams, essential for professional sports broadcasts. The software's ability to handle multiple video sources and its recording features made it a suitable choice for delivering seamless video feeds.

All-IP Video Solution for Seamless Connectivity

One of the project's highlights was its all-IP video solution, with cameras and computers connected to a shared network. This setup simplified the workflow, ensuring consistent video quality across the system. Remote users could access the cameras on Hive through the internet, enabling a cohesive and professional live streaming experience.

Enhanced Court Management and Operational Efficiency

The cloud-based dashboard provided an overview of multiple tennis courts, allowing coaches and administrators to control multiple camera views from a single interface. This centralized approach improved court management and allowed for real-time session review, making it easier for coaches to collaborate and communicate efficiently with athletes.

Conclusion

The live streaming setup for the Julian Krinsky School of Tennis demonstrated the power of advanced technology in sports coaching and broadcasting. Through remote camera control, high-quality streaming and cloud connectivity, this project delivered a flexible and professional solution that enhanced the coaching experience, setting a standard for integrating technology in sports environments.

Cloud-based video solutions and remote camera control are transforming sports broadcasting and coaching, as illustrated by case studies from Salesianum School and the Julian Krinsky School of Tennis. By integrating high-quality streaming software, network-connected cameras and user-friendly, web-based control platforms, these institutions are equipping students and coaches alike with professional tools that enhance real-time analysis, audience engagement and operational efficiency. These innovative setups not only elevate the viewing experience for fans but also provide invaluable hands-on learning for students and powerful remote coaching tools that redefine how sports performance is taught and evaluated.

28 FUTURE TRENDS IN SPORTS VIDEO

The world of sports video production is experiencing a transformative era, fueled by groundbreaking technologies that are reshaping how games are experienced, shared and celebrated. From live-streaming innovations to cutting-edge production tools, the sports industry is evolving rapidly, creating dynamic new ways for fans to engage with their favorite teams and athletes.

Emerging technologies like artificial intelligence, augmented and virtual reality and 5G connectivity are revolutionizing the sports video landscape. AI-powered automation simplifies production workflows, making high-quality broadcasts possible even for smaller organizations. Augmented and virtual reality are enhancing fan experiences by creating immersive environments, while 5G is enabling real-time mobile streaming from virtually anywhere. These advancements are redefining how sports stories are told, blending creativity with technical prowess to captivate global audiences.

As connectivity continues to expand, sports video production is becoming more accessible than ever before. Social media platforms, dedicated streaming services and custom-built fan engagement apps have turned sports into a 24/7 experience. Fans can follow every play, engage with teams and connect with fellow enthusiasts across the globe in real time. This constant interaction is fostering deeper connections and fueling an insatiable demand for fresh, immersive and interactive content.

A Ross Carbonate video switcher is connected to Mac computer running

OBS for live streaming to YouTube at the 2025 Lancaster Archery Classic.

Perhaps the most exciting aspect of this revolution is the opportunity it presents for creators at every level. Professional leagues and major broadcasters are leveraging state-of-the-art technology to deliver premium content, while community organizers, entrepreneurs and even high school broadcast clubs are stepping into the spotlight. With multi-camera setups, instant replay systems and cloud-based production tools becoming increasingly accessible, anyone with a passion for sports and storytelling can produce professional-grade content.

These grassroots efforts are cultivating the next generation of sports media professionals. Students are gaining hands-on experience with live broadcasts, learning technical skills that will prepare them for future careers. This democratization of sports video production is fostering innovation and ensuring that even local events can reach global audiences.

As we conclude this journey through the ever-expanding world of sports video production, the future has never been brighter. Whether you're a seasoned professional, a dedicated enthusiast or just beginning your adventure in sports media, the potential is limitless. Every broadcast, every creative idea and every push toward greater connectivity helps shape the future of sports storytelling.

Embrace the technology. Stay curious. Push boundaries. The impact you make today will resonate far beyond the game, creating unforgettable experiences that connect people across the world. The future of sports video production is here—and you're already a part of it.

ABOUT THE AUTHOR

Paul Richards is a father, author and business executive leading his company in the field of digital video communications. Richards is the author of multiple top-selling books including, "The Unofficial Guide to NDI," "PTZ Camera Operators Handbook," "The Unofficial Guide to OBS," and "Remote Production".

Richards' books draw on his hands-on experience in the multimedia technology industry. As the Chief Brand and Identify Officer for HuddleCamHD and PTZOptics, Richards is the host of multiple online shows that feature his work on YouTube, Facebook, LinkedIn and Twitch.

Richards is also the Chief Streaming Officer at StreamGeeks and teaches Udemy courses online to over 100,000 students. Course topics include live video production, online communications and social media connectivity.

GLOSSARY OF TERMS

3.5mm Audio Cable: Often a male-to-male stereo cable, common in standard audio uses.

4K: A high-definition resolution option (3840 x 2160 pixels or 4096 x 2160 pixels)

Application Program Interface (API): an (often) web-based interface between one or more software applications (including browsers) and another that allows commands to be sent that provide external (remote) control.

Bandwidth - The range of frequencies within a given band that are used for transmitting a signal.

Broadcasting - The distribution of audio or video content to a dispersed audience via any electronic mass communications medium.

Broadcast Frame Rates - Used to describe how many frames per second are captured in broadcasting. Common frame rates in broadcast video include: **29.97fps and 59.94 fps.**

Capture Card - A device with inputs (and often outputs) that allows cameras and other video sources (and destinations) to connect to a computer.

Chroma Key - A video effect that replaces a color in the scene (usually a background color like blue or green) with other video content
Cloud-Based Streaming - Streaming and video production interaction that occurs within the cloud and is therefore accessible beyond a single user's computer device.

Color Matching - The process of managing color and luminance settings on multiple cameras to match their appearance.

Community Strategy - The strategy of building one's brand and product recognition by building meaningful relationships with an audience, partner and client base.

Content Delivery Network (CDN) - A network of servers that delivers web-based content to an end user.

CPU (Central Processing Unit) - The electronic component within a computer that carries out the instructions of a computer program by performing the basic arithmetic, logical, control and input/output (I/O) operations specified by the instructions.

DAW - Digital Audio Workstation.

DB9 Cable - A common cable connection for camera joystick serial control.

Dynamic Host Configuration Protocol (DHCP) Router - A router with a network management protocol that dynamically sets IP addresses so the server can communicate with its sources.

Encoder - A device or software that converts a piece of code or info to then distribute it.

H.264 & H.265 - Common formats of video recording, compression and delivery.

High Definition Multimedia Interface (HDMI) - A cable commonly used for transmitting audio/video.

Internet Protocol (IP) Camera/Video - A camera or video source that can send and receive information via a network & internet.

IP Control - The ability to control/connect a camera or device via a network or internet.

Latency - The time it takes between sending a signal and the recipient receiving it; usually measured in milliseconds (ms)

Live Streaming - The process of sending and receiving audio and or video over the internet.

Local Area Network (LAN) - A network of computers linked together in one location.

Multicorder - A feature of Vmix and some other streaming software that allows the user to record raw footage or multiple camera feeds to separate files from the stream output.

Network Device Interface (NDI®) - A software standard developed by NewTek to enable video-compatible products to communicate, deliver and receive broadcast quality video in a high quality, low latency manner that is frame-accurate and suitable for switching in a live production environment.

NDI® Camera - A camera that allows you to send and receive video over your LAN.

NDI® | HX - NDI® High Efficiency, optimizes NDI® for limited bandwidth environments.

Network - A digital telecommunications infrastructure which allows nodes to share resources. In computer networks, computing devices exchange data with each other using connections between nodes.

NTSC - Video standard used in North and South America, Japan and the Caribbean. It's also used in some other countries,

OTT Streaming (Over-The-Top) - When a content creator or media service bypasses typical cable media outlets (often called "walled gardens") and goes "over-the-top" (or the wall) to distribute content through other means (ie. Facebook, YouTube, Twitch)

PAL - Analog video format widely used outside of North America.

PCIe Card - Connects to a computer's motherboard or external enclosure to enable high bandwidth communication between an internal or external device (i.e. a graphics or video capture card) and the computer

PoE (also PoE+ and PoE++) - Power over ethernet (and higher wattage versions)

PTZ - Pan, tilt, zoom.

RS-232 - Serial camera control transmission.

Real Time Messaging Protocol (RTMP) - RTMP is a standard protocol for sending and receiving video to a server. RTMP is used to deliver video streams over the public internet to CDNs such as Facebook or YouTube.

Real Time Streaming Protocol (RTSP) - Network control protocol for streaming from point to point.

www.ingramcontent.com/pod-product-compliance
Lightning Source LLC
LaVergne TN
LVHW051433050326
832903LV00030BD/3068